No Goodbyes

No Goodbyes

✦

A Father-Daughter Memoir
of
Love, War and Resurrection

Naava Piatka

iUniverse, Inc.
New York Bloomington

No Goodbyes
A Father-Daughter Memoir of Love, War and Resurrection

iUniverse books may be ordered through booksellers or by contacting:

iUniverse
1663 Liberty Drive
Bloomington, IN 47403
www.iuniverse.com
1-800-Authors (1-800-288-4677)

ISBN: 978-0-595-49815-4 (pbk)
ISBN: 978-0-595-49603-7 (cloth)
ISBN: 978-0-595-61259-8 (ebk)

Printed in the United States of America

iUniverse rev. date: 06/29/2009

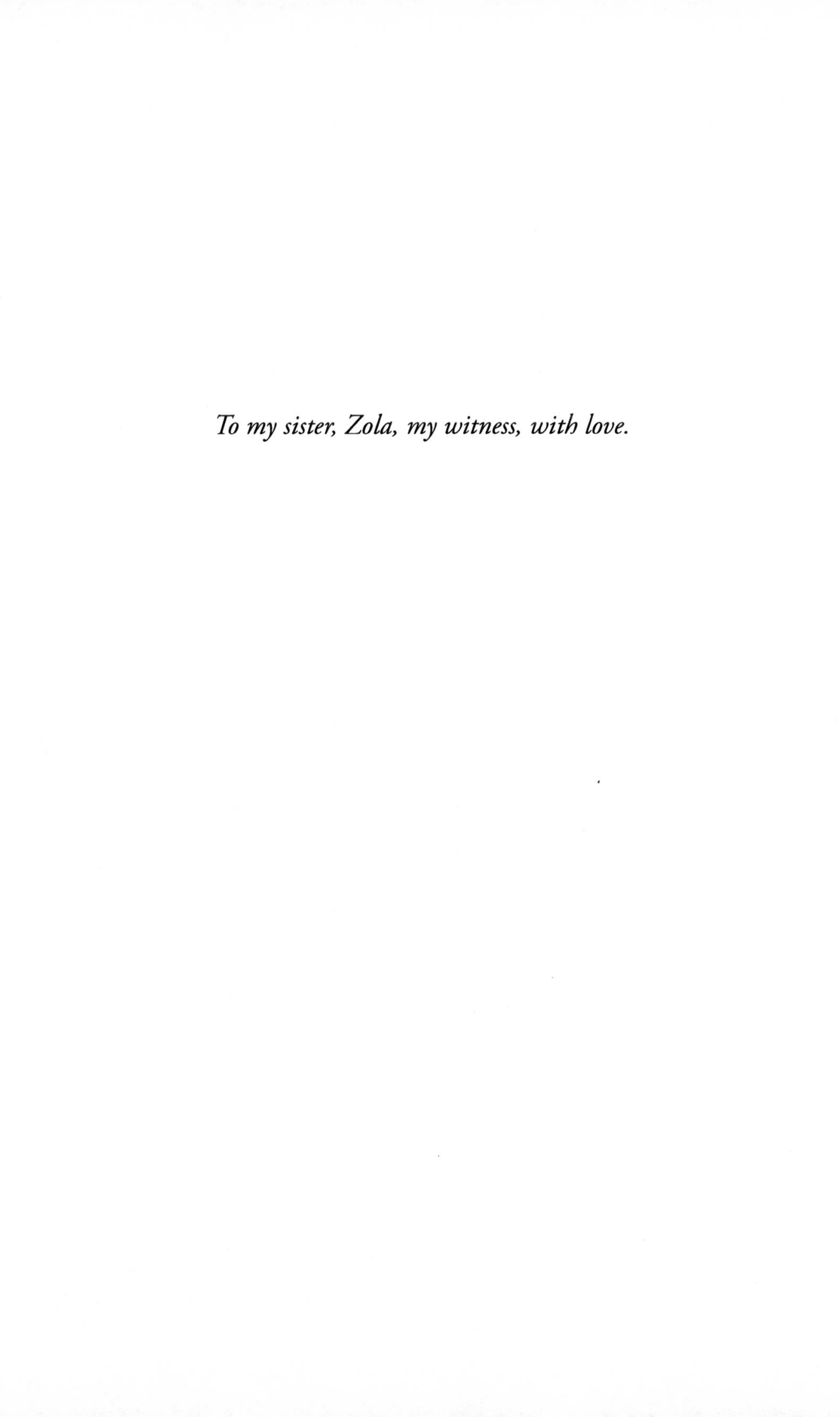

To my sister, Zola, my witness, with love.

Preface

The Mystery Man
London, 2005 and 2007

We become the stories we tell.

When the ones who mean the most to you are gone, what remains behind are the stories. Stories they told you. Stories you told yourself. Some you asked for, others you never saw coming. Some you try hard to remember, others you cannot forget. Stories from family you never knew you had, and stories from strangers that lead you home.

Stories had long ago filled my lonely childhood with fantasy worlds of fairy-tale characters; cackling witches casting magic spells, gallant princes kissing sleeping princesses, grotesque giants terrorizing villages, ugly ogres lusting for blood, and lost, frightened waifs wandering in the woods. Those stories taught me early on that children entering the forest invariably had encounters with some kind of evil, and, when they finally emerged, they were changed forever. Apparently, the forest was the way to grandma's house, but for me, a child with no grandparents, living far away from forests by the seashore tip of sunny South Africa, a trip to grandma's house was in itself a fantasy.

The little girl who had eagerly lost herself in stories of fictional kingdoms grew into an idealistic young woman, yearning to find herself in real life family. When someone resembling a handsome young prince arrived on the scene, I promptly married him, traveled to distant shores, and naively cast myself in my own happily-ever-after story of wife and mother, exchanging the old world of Grimm's folktales for the more modern, less grim world of a suburban American housewife. With the passing of years, I discovered, to my amazement, that raising a family required much more than three wishes, no elves arrived magically overnight to clean a messy kitchen, the emperor was blatantly all too naked, and there was still that persistent pile of ashes that could not be so easily swept away. Secrets once hidden from an innocent young girl now began to tantalize the fragmented woman I had become, mired as I was in the mundane, struggling to maintain my shifting identity, distracted by wanderlust and yearning for liberation.

Untold stories of missing characters, vanished towns, hidden crimes, and forgotten children began to haunt me. Questions, muted for too long, began popping up like wildflowers. Somewhere amid midlife, empty nest, and looking at my aging reflection in the mirror on the wall, I realized that the stories I had not been told—about my parents and their past in a faraway land—were the very ones I needed to hear. Perhaps if I followed that trail of ashes, I might find what seemed to be missing from my life. It was time to enter the proverbial bewitched forest, empty basket in hand, to visit my phantom grandma's house in the vanished Vilna of long ago Lithuania.

Who better to lead me into the deep, dark woods where those stories lay buried, than the marked man of many moods, who could turn himself instantly from kindly king to wise wizard or angry, cruel giant? He was the one who first introduced me to the enchanting realms of fables and fairytales, reading them to me at night, tucking me into bed, kissing my forehead, and switching off the light. The tender-hearted, charismatic, handsome, cosmopolitan man who flirted in French, cursed in Russian, pontificated in Latin, argued in Polish, translated in German, joked in

Yiddish, wrote philatelic articles in Afrikaans, and gave frequent orders and speeches in heavily accented English was also the domineering patriarch who had ruled over my childhood with an iron will, firm fist and thunderous voice. The Jewish man who gave himself the Catholic name Xavier, pronouncing it to sound like "savior," who signed his name with a large, definitive "X," who was nicknamed Ksuvver by my mother, who servants deferred to as Master, and many in my hometown of Cape Town, South Africa, knew as Mr. Piat, was the god I called Daddy.

Whoever my father had conjured himself to be—changing names, assuming roles, switching locations, resurrecting and reinventing himself—one thing was certain: Mr. Piat, my original storyteller, was now the only one left alive to tell me the true stories of our legacy of real-life monsters and unhappy endings. This time, his stories would not help me fall asleep, but help me awaken.

Daddy, what big eyes you have! All the better to see what some people would rather forget and some people dare to deny. Daddy, what big ears you have! All the better to hear ghosts talking. My, what a big mouth you have, Daddy! All the better to speak of my life, and of those who came before, so you may understand the unfulfilled dreams, unfinished songs, unspoken agreements, and unrequited love, contained in our tears, in our touch, in our memory. So you may record and remember, and set yourself, and all of us, free.

So began the spiritual journey with my father to break the silence of the past and resurrect the stories for the future. Spending a series of summers together, I sat by his side with a tape recorder, capturing his recollections of his life in war-torn Europe. Sometimes I asked questions, but most often I simply listened as he spoke of the times and people who had affected his life. Those summoned ghosts of the departed, the ones with no graves or tombstones, who had hovered in the shadows of my childhood waiting to be seen, needing to be heard, longing to be remembered, now walked freely in the light of day. When I emerged from the not-so-enchanted forests, like those storybook children from once upon a time foreign lands, I too came out changed.

Like an ocean's ebb and flow, my father's revealing life stories drew us closer, then pulled us apart. His stirring recollections of the significant roles my deceased mother and her murdered brother had played in the cultural resistance of the Holocaust,—she, as actress-singer, and he, as lyricist-playwright—sparked my imagination and ignited my creativity. Much to my father's chagrin, I abruptly shelved the book about his life I had promised to write and began merrily skipping along to the tempting tunes of my new muses, my mother and uncle, who, I was convinced, had come to entice me back to the exciting world of theatre. After a couple of years, I had written a full-length musical about my mother's inspirational life as a singing star in the Vilna Ghetto. That soon turned into *Better Don't Talk!* my one-woman show, which I began performing locally in the United States and around the world, traveling to Australia, Canada and Germany and even back in South Africa, as I devoted myself to the telling of *her* remarkable story, rather than his. My father's memoir was left to languish, ignored, even long after his death.

But the power of stories is such that they persist. Undaunted, they linger, ever patient, waiting for right timing and new expression. Through different voices, they return to find us, to remind us that one person's memories belong to us all, for we are all connected, one to another, in ways we cannot fully understand. My father's stories, without my knowing, had already begun to cast their spell in another part of the world.

Timing, as they say in comedy, is everything. So too in life.

In November of 2005, I was scheduled to perform my show in London. In late September of that year, I received a surprising e-mail from someone in Oxford, England, claiming to be a relative from my father's side. Introducing herself, Lizzie explained her serendipitous quest that had led her to me. Just as I had sought to find meaning and identity in my midlife, she and her cousin Caroline had suddenly felt compelled to trace their forgotten Jewish heritage, lost in a maze of assimilation and intermarriage. They vaguely recalled a story, passed down to them in their childhood, about a Jewish relative of their Lithuanian born great-grandfather. The mystery man, one of the last remaining Utins left in Vilna, had come out of Europe and, stopping over in London en route to South Africa, had shared his gripping wartime accounts with the specially gathered Utin family in London. Though no one alive could remember his name, the cousins' determination to track down the mystery man resulted in discovering and meeting another Utin descendent, a spry ninety-three-year-old lady living in London. Among the many old photographs she showed them was an old black-and-white photograph of a group of people at a London train station. On the back of the photograph, written in blue fountain pen ink, was the inscription: *Please don't forget us! Chayela and Xavier Piatka*. Lizzie's speedy Internet search of the names brought her right to my Web site, with its description of my one-woman show, and my mother, Chayela Rosenthal, star of the Vilna Ghetto Theatre.

"When I saw on your Web site that your father was originally called Israel Jutan," Lizzie wrote, "I must confess I was rather '*farklempt*.'"

I too became choked up. I never dreamed that the addition of one small detail of my father's original name in a summary of my mother's remarkable life on my Web site would produce such an outcome—a family I never knew I had! "On the back of the photo I mentioned," Lizzie continued, "your parents had asked us not to forget them. I'm ashamed to say that, eventually, people did. I would love for our family to start remembering again."

Her words hit home. What was once lost, I realized, can and will be found again. Old from new, new from old, the stories keep unfolding in spiraling, concentric circles, evolving and revolving, repeating the eternal universal promise of resurrection, reminding us who we are and where we came from. I knew, without a shadow of doubt, that it was the spirit of the legendary Mr. Piat, pulling whatever strings necessary, up on high, to guide young Lizzie into my life to steer me back to my path of remembrance. My formidable, commanding father had returned, once again.

T'shuvah. Return, response, repentance. Sounding like a sneeze, this one Hebrew word, with its many meanings, is used to denote the period of renewal preceding the Jewish New Year, Rosh Hashanah, and Yom Kippur, the Day of Atonement. Tradition dictates that we spend this time on self-reflection and contemplation of our spiritual connection to the source of all things. Maimonides, the revered twelfth century Egyptian Rabbi and physician, defined *T'shuvah* as having four distinct steps. First, we acknowledge where we have gone off the path. Second, we feel regret and atone for errors along the way. Third, we offer an apology to others, or the Creator, and ourselves. And lastly, we make a commitment to actively reform ourselves in the future.

The arrival of Lizzie's e-mail right before Rosh Hashanah was no mere coincidence. No more could I escape my Job-like duty and the commandment of honoring my father. Admitting my regret about the neglected memoir, I apologized to Lizzie over in Oxford, and my father up in heaven, hauled out the unfinished manuscript stuffed at the back of a desk drawer, and vowed to fulfill on my past promise to finish the book and get it published.

That November, in a hotel outside London, I met Lizzie and her family and other descendents of the people whose names my father had long ago neatly written on scraps of paper in his many efforts to reconstruct the Jutan family tree. What to tell my new British relatives about the man with the made-up name of Xavier Piat? Where to even start? Blurting out the story of his unusual death, I watched former strangers, now my cousins, weep for a man they didn't even know. Their faces told me that there had been other lonely souls, besides my father, longing for lost family, wishing to enter the forest of remembrance too. Shuffling through old sepia photos of cousins who married cousins, and mothers and brothers who died too young, we ate our sandwiches and sipped our tea, hungry and thirsty for more stories that affirmed our connection.

When I returned to London two years later for a reunion in honor of Mr. Piat's original postwar visit, I met many more previously unknown relatives of all ages, most of whom were disconnected from their partial

Jewish roots and more familiar with churches than synagogues. How to portray my father this time? Ah, yes, the famous Passover sneeze story! Passover, I explained to my newfound relatives, is the Jewish holiday celebrating the hasty Exodus of Moses and the Israelites from ancient Egypt, where they were slaves under the cruel tyranny of the pharaoh. Occurring in the springtime, coincidentally around Easter, it symbolizes a chance for new beginnings, marking our liberation from slavery and triumph over those enemies wishing to harm us. Passover is when Jews and invited guests, especially strangers, come together for the traditional *seder,* the ritual-laden, drawn-out, seven or eight course feast, and observe the mandate of eating lots of matzah, drinking and spilling even more kosher wine, asking the famous four questions (beginning with "Why is this night different from all the rest?") and repeatedly reciting a seemingly endless litany of historic events. It's a holiday, I joked, that you would either enjoy or endure, depending on your family. In Sea Point, Cape Town, my father, mother, sister and I would spend our Passovers at the home of the generous family who had befriended my immigrant parents when they first arrived in South Africa. So why was this night different from the rest? Because each year, at the completion of the *seder*, my father would sneeze. Not an ordinary sneeze, mind you. Oh, no, nothing ordinary about Mr. Piat, who made a big production out of his much-anticipated, dramatic sneeze. First came the anticipatory build-up of suspense—the drawn out hah ... hah ... hah ... hah, sniffs, snorts and snuffles, interspersed with dramatic pauses, headshakes, and more breathy intakes. Everyone, including our hosts' children and grandchildren and their related families, would sit glued to the table, watching my father, waiting for the grand finale, that last release of the sonorous, crescendoing ahhhh-chooooooo, accompanied by more shudders and my father's signature trumpet-like nose blowing into his large, ever-handy white handkerchief. When he was done, everyone would burst into applause. "*Uffin Emmes*!" my laughing mother would say, adding her Yiddish dose of superstitious wisdom: "Sneezing on the truth!" It was decided by all who gathered around that large, bountiful table that our *seder* wasn't truly over until my father performed his signature sneeze. Mr. Piat, the Holocaust survivor, had started a new Passover tradition.

But there was far more to my father than his dramatic sneeze, I told them. The full dimensions of the man who had lived through extraordinary times to tell the tale could not be conveyed in a few anecdotal reminiscences. It might take a whole book, I hinted.

And yet, now that the book is done, I recognize that the whole picture of a person's life can never be fully drawn. Even in this memoir, in which I tried as faithfully and objectively as I could to get a deeper understanding of who and what had shaped my father's life and therefore mine too, I see that questions were left unasked and the portraits are drawn only in part. This collage of his recollections mingled with mine is but a compilation of select impressions—sketches smudged by our respective personal perspectives of pains and pleasures, somewhat tinted with stains of sentiment, bias or nostalgia—the delicate nature of memory, after all.

Perhaps it's best that you meet my father first through the words of a stranger, someone with a more objective vantage point.

"Xavier Piat: Font of warmth and wit after journey to hell and back," read the headline of a 1997 article written about him in the leading Cape Town newspaper. What made his subject so interesting, the interviewer wrote, was "how throughout some hellish times, he has endured and survived through his natural acumen and wit. Here is a person who, after spending four nightmarish years in incarceration, is today without rancor. On the contrary, he preaches universal tolerance. Instead of a lugubrious old man (Xavier is now 77) I found myself in the company of a consummate raconteur, resigned with a quiet equanimity to the absurdity of the human condition."

In a little village outside of Cape Town, an Afrikaner woman named Christina Van Der Westhuizen read the article and was instantly spurred to find out more about the person whose stories had so moved her. Finding the unique surname in the phone book, Christina called him and after just one conversation became a fast friend and fan. Reading the news of his sudden death several months later, she was heartbroken. Obtaining my phone number, she specially made the rather expensive, long-distance call to the U.S. to tell me just how much Mr. Piat—with his friendship, advice, and fatherly caring—had meant to her.

Christina's words in her subsequent letter to me confirmed my belief that my father's stories, like all those of the Holocaust, belong not only to one tribe or one religion, but to all of humanity. Linked by the same oceans, breathing from the same air, spinning on the same planet, we all share the same deep longing to belong—beyond language, beyond religion, race, boundaries, continents, gender or species. Beyond even time. So I share her words with you, keeping her original spelling mistakes and grammatical errors intact. English is Christina's second language. Like my father, her first language is that of the heart:

> *I see only one Piat in the phone book so I phoned your father, still trembling. I was very nervous. Shaking. I did not know how your father would respond to me, especially as a Christian. Your father answered the phone. He was so nice. I immediately feel on ease, and I tell him my whole story. He was so kind, helpful, and understanding. He invited me to come and see him. I arrange for meeting him the next Sunday. He then already had made for me a fotostat of a map of Poland and Germany. He showed me where he was born and grown up. He tell me of his family. Then he marked on the map his route of his four year incarceration. He tell me how he did not even know that his father was also in the cattle train, and that he never saw him again, and that he also never knew what happened to his mother, and that he never saw her again. But, Naava, you must remember, he was so big in spirit that he never give the feeling of "oh, the poor man." I wish I had his way with words to put on paper what I really feel in my heart.*
>
> *I was afraid at first that he must think I was interested in the horror and sorrow the Jewish people went through, and that I want to pry into their lives only to hear of the horror. But after meeting him I knew out of my heart that he did not see it as that. I asked him, then, but why did*

the Christian people do that to the Jews? He said that we Christians say that the Jews killed our Christ. I don't want to overstay my welcome that first time, so when I leave he asked me to come and visit him again. I occasionally phone him to talk and ask him how he was. I tell him that I talked to my friends about him and also the fact that some of them did not even know what the Holocaust is. I make it then my point to tell them what happened and that we, as Christians, must do all in our willpower to never let it happen again. He was very pleased with that. He showed me the photograph of his family and that only he survived. You know in moments like that I want to put my arms around him and be of comfort to him. He don't have to be a strong man in body. But I see he is a survivor because of what he has inside. I once asked him if he carry a hate or something like that deep in his heart for the German people. He said no, and told me that he once had a German girlfriend after your mother died. You see, Naava, that was Xavier Piat. You see, he told you something and every time you learn from him. He talked a lot about your mother, who he loved very much. So when you come to Cape Town with your show, "Better Don't Talk," he arrange tickets for me. So you see, after the show, it was for me if I know your mother all my life and especially I know how much your father loved her. Your father, I always know he was there if I want some advice. Can you understand now, Naava, that I also missed your father very much even if I did not see him so much. During April 1995 on Remembrance Day, he invited me to the service at the Jewish Cemetery in Pinelands. I did go and it was a very moving experience for me, so I hold it dear that he invite me. He also show me your mother's grave that day. In future, when it is possible, I will go there and put flowers on her grave for her and him. Naava, your father moved in high circles, he knows important people and still he always made me feel special to him although I am only a Christian, coming from the country and speaking Afrikaans—that I will never forget. I used to talk to him and feel better. I will never forget your father, never. I learned from your father that the human spirit can still triumph, however brutal life can be. I, as a Christian, salute a great Jew: Xavier Piat.

PART I

✦

Love

The Daughter: A New Start

✦

Newton, Massachusetts, U.S.A. 1991

To move forward in life, sometimes we need to slip back into the past.

1991. A palindrome year. Same forward and backward. All things being equal.

The first number and the last begin the decimal system.

One: a beginning.

Nine, nine: the two middle numbers. If you say them out loud, it sounds like "No! No!" in German. Add them together and you get the number eighteen, the numeric value of the two Hebrew letters that make up the word *chai*, symbolizing life.

Two Ones on the outside squeezing forth life from the declamatory German "No's."

1991. The year the first One, born in the year 1919, will tell the One who follows about the life in between.

It's the year I begin the journey with my father to remember what some people choose to forget and others want to deny. The year I decide to reclaim the Ones I never knew, now on the outside, to make sense of the life I still don't know, on the inside.

1991. Ten and ten. Two perfect scores. Is this a test? What once seemed like pat answers now become nagging questions. Things aren't adding up the way I thought they would. People I counted on have let me down, while those I miscalculated or maybe discounted have lifted me up. If I went back into the dark, will I be able to shed some more light? Will hindsight become insight? How ironic that with the passing of years, my eyesight has faded, but my vision has become clearer. Even my hearing has improved. Sounds from within are becoming louder than those from without. The phrase, "There's more, there's more," keeps gnawing at my restless mind, urging me to go exploring, to be curious about what lurks behind closed doors. As a child, I creatively used the art of camouflage and gifts of pretending to mask feelings of being different. Now, as an adult, my growing sense of alienation demands that I shed my protective cloak of obedient silence and dare to venture on a quest for nothing less than the truth.

When was it that I suspected there was something dark and sinister around the two Ones who raised me? How old was I when I first sensed the shadow hovering over my family, setting us apart from the other Ones in my hometown at the tip of the African continent where two oceans merge? A child of five or six years old perhaps? Younger? Young enough to keenly feel the unspoken taboo—that heavy, sad presence of the unknown and the unnamed, that palpable void of those who were missing. Young enough to imagine ghosts drifting in dreams at night or remembered by whispered foreign names into flames of specially lit candles. Young enough to comply with the undeclared covenant of silence.

Growing up in the 1950s, in the English colony of South Africa, I found refuge immersing myself in fanciful fairy tales contained in the secondhand books my father bought for me at the flea market. While I savored the exquisite artistic renditions of beautiful princesses drawn in their opulent medieval gowns, those other scratchy black pen and ink illustrations of bodies impaled on iron stakes and talking horse heads protruding from stone walls would become the stuff of my nightmares, sending me running, crying and scurrying into my parents' bed. The warmth of their live bodies holding me close would soothe me, keeping my mind off the dreadful things that interrupted my sleep. But during my waking hours, there was something that scared me more: my own adored father's terrifying ability to transform himself instantaneously into a raging monster or a howling, threatening big bad wolf. At those times, I felt even more desperately alone than ever. There was no one to rescue me, not even my own mother who watched quietly, tears slipping from her wide, brown eyes. I consoled myself with my own make-believe story: My father had been cast under an evil spell by wicked ogres whose names evoked such fear that they dare not be mentioned.

Silence back then was the order of the day: The big, bad, and ugly were not to be discussed. It was the way people shielded themselves and their loved ones from a world deemed too ignorant, too insensitive, too indifferent, and too ill equipped to openly address the subject of man's inhumanity to his fellow man, woman and child. My young brain might have heard the hard, hollow-sounding word it couldn't understand, interpreting from strangers' hushed voices and pity-filled eyes that whatever horrific thing it was, it was much too grotesque, too monstrous to be described. But my young heart had its own intelligence. Its arrhythmic beat echoed the muffled message of the enormous pain of my parents' past and their unexplained suffering that slipped and slithered in and out of my father's angry outbursts and my mother's sighs into my very pores. To me, my parents' secret, unintelligible mutterings sounded like conspiracies. Mine was no ordinary family. The absence of grandparents and the presence of short, specter-like people, who sometimes gathered in our living room, conversing in a cacophony of strange accents and sporadic outbursts of hysterical, high-pitched voices, confirmed my childhood conviction.

This summer of repeated numbers, I decide to break the silence and tackle the mystery of my father, Mr. Piat. Now, I'm eager to start putting together puzzles I was once happy to leave lying in their boxes, trusting that the day would come when I'd have the presence of mind to recreate the big picture, even if many of the pieces appeared to be missing. It's one of those challenging, giant 5,000-piece puzzles, I bet. Not until recently have I had the time, interest, or patience to sit and work on it, piece by piece, one by one, first fitting together the outer edges to construct a frame and then slowly working toward the middle. How do all the different roles of son, father, husband, immigrant, journalist, philatelist, PR man, and entrepreneur fit together to make the man who was stamped with the one defining label: Holocaust survivor? What was his life like before the war? What helped him endure the worst and still hold on to what's best? How could he continue to advocate forgiveness when all is not said and so much is undone? In piecing together the story of Mr. Piat, perhaps I might discover what constitutes my own puzzle.

Like a Jewish Dorothy in *The Wizard of Oz*, I'll walk down my yellow star road to pull back the curtain to reveal the wizard to find my way home. I'll need a heart to listen without judgment, a brain to formulate the right questions, and courage to lift up the suffocating heavy rock of suffering. Isn't it the secret desire of every child of an abused parent to be the rescuer, the superhero, freeing the beloved one from their oppression? I was five years old, sitting on my own in the back of a darkened movie house, when I saw my first magnificent hero, the tanned, muscled Moses in the epic film *The Ten Commandments*. My little heart leapt in my chest and my eyes filled with tears as I watched my tall, handsome hero lift the heavy stone that threatened to crush and kill his fellow kinsman. Unable to contain my mounting emotions, I jumped out of my seat, waving my arms and yelling victoriously at the top of my voice, "Yaaaaay!" My unbridled enthusiasm was quickly suppressed by the stony stares of several annoyed adult audience members, who turned around to hush me up. Ashamed and confused, I slumped back down in my seat, still secretly reveling in Moses' triumph. Was I truly that different? Didn't everyone want to jump and shout with joy at the rescuing of a life, at the bold rebellion against abuse? Didn't everybody else but the kid in the back row want the Jews to be saved?

More than anything, I longed to be normal, like the other children at my school and the rest of the English-speaking people in my sunny seaside neighborhood. But that seemed impossible. How could I be the same as them, when the numbers were stacked against me? I could count the ways in which my little family was different.

One: My immigrant parents were ignorant of and unaccustomed to the "propah" civilized customs of their adopted Anglicized South Africa. Walking on my own and showing up bright and early one morning at Kings Road Primary School, I was greeted by screams from the Christian girls, already gathered on the playground, behind the fence. "Go home! Go home!" they cried. "You're not supposed to be here!" they yelled at me. "It's a Jewish Holiday!" Mortified, I turned around and stared down at my secondhand, brown button-up shoes. The tight elastic hatband from the school uniform white panama hat we had to wear cut even further into my neck. Fighting back my tears, I headed back up the hill, taking the slow walk of shame back down the long indifferent road to our rented apartment on Main Road in Sea Point. My parents explained later, that back in the old country, Hanukkah was not regarded as a major Jewish holiday, and certainly never celebrated as a commercial occasion for gift giving. Besides, how would my officially "alien" parents have known that Jewish holidays were observed in a public school? Even our food was different. While our elegant neighbors dined on crumpets and scones with jam and clotted cream, my Polish parents devoured dishes designed to clot one's arteries, with deviant names such as *perogen* (meat pastries), *p'tchah* (a wobbly mass of jellied calves' hooves combined with other unmentionables), pumpernickel, (chocolate colored bread that tasted like cardboard) *tchollent* (stewed brisket, prunes, and carrots; the more burnt, the better), and my mother's favorite, *gribbenish* and giblets in *shmalz*, (a chicken's innards and who knows what else fried in a thick yellow emulsion of chicken fat). When other kids' school lunches consisted of tame white-bread-and-cheese sandwiches cut into perfect triangles, my lunchbox was crammed with love-packed, garlic-smothered salami and pickles that clearly labeled me as strange, if not smelly. Kosher we were not. Untraditional we were. Distinguishing himself in a class of his own, my father did not deign to do the ordinary, mundane things commonly practiced by other fathers I knew. He didn't smoke cigarettes or drink hard liquor. No wine, gin, whiskey, or beer. He didn't play sports like golf, bowling, or tennis, like my school friends' energetic dads, nor did he take his family on road trips for vacations, like they did. My father, the resident do-it-yourself dentist, tied my wobbly baby teeth to the doorknob with a string, slammed the door shut, and proudly extracted my teeth the old-fashioned way. Luckily, someone must have told them about the tooth fairy, because I was compensated for my pain with a few pennies under my pillow. In a colonized culture of reserved refinement and false politeness, where most people were trained to stand patiently in line and to converse in a discreet and genteel manner, my parents' jarring, street-smart Eastern European manners exposed me to an entirely different marketplace approach: "Etiquette, shmetiquette! Why stand in a queue? Just shout at the manager—he'll get it for you."

Two: The weird accents of my two Polish parents, who spoke in foreign tongues to each other and in broken English to me, their communication flavored with Yiddish, Polish, Russian, and a few dollops of French. I grew up surrounded by guttural noises and superstitious spitting, their banter banning me from their hidden world of harsh life sentences. Soon enough though, like all gifted children, I was able to interpret their secrets exchanged in Yiddish, the language associated more with the grandparents of my Jewish peers than with their parents.

Three: The missing grandparents and lack of extended family. There was no safety net of ready-to-rescue relatives, aunts, or uncles for when the dangerous high-wire balancing triangle act of mother, father, and child became too precarious. I envied the other kids at my school whose resplendent families came with an assortment of doting grandparents, aunts, uncles, and cousins who had grown up in the same place and still lived in the same neighborhood. At holiday time, my lucky schoolmates and neighbors would be transported away on fun-filled vacations, escorted by their various grannies and "oupas," traveling to meet up with cousins and friends and returning to school with their show-and-brag rewards of trinkets and lavish gifts. Bereft of the benefit of those kinds of stories or material proofs of love, I comforted myself by biting my nails, creating paper-doll families, and reading my fable-filled storybooks. Permitting myself only brief indulgences of private moments of sweet self-pity, outwardly I would sing, dance, and laugh with gusto, putting my best smiling face forward. Deprived of a big family, I reluctantly learned to appreciate the gift of solitude. In the void of grandparents, aunts, uncles, cousins, and even a sibling for eight years, I happily turned strangers into friends and friends into family. That way I would not feel so alone in the world. Strangers were just relatives I hadn't been introduced to, I told my young self.

Four: My marvelous mother, Chayela Rosenthal, whose physical size was just short of five feet tall but whose presence was enormous. Unlike the other "regular" working or stay-at-home moms in the neighborhood, my mother was a professional comedienne, cabaret singer, and actress who performed in theatres and nightclubs, singing her foreign songs and telling her translated jokes in her funny Polish-Yiddish accent. Nobody else's mom I knew was in show business or kept her maiden name along with her married name or left home for months at a time to perform overseas—or starred in Yiddish theatre on Broadway. My diminutive, energetic, and comedic mother poked fun at herself and others in her accented English, easily making people laugh with her ready wit, comedic, exaggerated facial expressions, vocal inflection, impeccable timing, and rapid-fire delivery of rehearsed jokes, told with delightful, typically Jewish self-deprecating humor. I remember sitting in the audience as a young teenager, watching her perform one of her skits in her variety shows, feeling that odd combination of embarrassment and awe when she unabashedly appeared, her buxom body squeezed into a tight-fitting black leotard, and proceeded to do a headstand in the middle of the stage. I had no inkling of how ahead of her times she was, as a woman and an artist, creating and performing her own stand-up comedy routine in the early 1950s in remote South Africa. But Chayela was also a demanding stage mom. She had no qualms putting her "tullented" young first-born child on the stage with her, drilling me to perfection for my performances in the recitals and local talent competitions that invariably garnered me awards and notices in the newspapers. For a woman denied the chance to complete high school, her standards of excellence were exceedingly high. My boasting that I got 9 out of 10 on a test at school was not good enough. "What happened to the other point?" she'd ask in a tone that implied I had been negligent in letting it slip away. In her critical and creative mind, everything and everyone could be improved upon. For those of us she loved, her aspirations were clear: nothing but the best or nothing at all. My mother was a hard act to live up to, and even harder to follow.

Five: My peculiar, strange-sounding last name, which I found out later was entirely concocted by my imaginative father, the maven of invention. He once told me the origins of Piatka: "*Pointka* in Polish means five—the best score in school. I wanted to be the best." As an imaginative, young student journalist in search of the perfect pen name, he had adopted the name of Piatka, which he later abbreviated to Piat to make it more convenient for business, and easier for the keep-it-simple English speakers who dominated our colonial culture. The immigrant's daughter, however, was left with a name few people could pronounce, let alone spell.

Six: All those weird superstitions from the old country, ridiculous rituals repeated by the important Ones in my family, the Ones in control, the Ones telling me what to do. Top of the list was the spitting over the left shoulder three times—*ptu, ptu, ptu*—against the Evil Eye, *Kayn'n horah, ptu, ptu, ptu*! (Who was that malevolent

Cyclops we needed to fear?) Then there was the sitting down before departing anywhere, and the stepping out on the right foot, and the not turning back once you started walking, and the no knitting or sewing in the theatre, and the magic potion *goggle moggle* raw-egg drink and hot-milk-and-honey cough remedy meant to soothe the sore throat that just made me gag and vomit and feel even sicker than before, and the no wearing green because it's bad luck, God forbid, *Ptu, ptu, ptu*! *Kayn'n horah*! *Ptu, ptu, ptu*! and the slapping across the face to celebrate your first menstruation: "Now you're a woman—*mazal tov*!" Slap, slap! Clap! Clap! (What kind of crazy celebration has you get hit in the face and applauded for something you didn't even do?) To me, it seemed like we were the only family with those bizarre practices meant to protect the innocent from the ever-present evil that leads to events ending with the tragic number six, as in million. Even though, as a child, I faithfully followed the stepping and spitting routines of my mother, I secretly doubted that amulets, charms, or deflective gestures could prevent tragedy or erase its scars hidden behind the smiles and nods dispensed so quickly to the outside world by my caretaker Ones.

Seven: The unusual array of my parents' friends. In a country teeming with hale and hearty, tall and tanned, tennis- and bowls-playing folk, my odd parents attracted a host of eccentric artistic types and a slew of tiny, taciturn, tortured-looking friends, some with deathly white skin and blue numbers tattooed on their parchment-like arms. They would take me to visit Henyek, the short, stern-faced man from Germany with his sullen, woeful wife who could not have babies because of what happened in the war (better don't ask!) in a house that came alive with the sounds and movement of his wall-to-wall collection of ticking antique grandfather and chirping cuckoo clocks. They would drive me to the poultry farm of the bird-like Cleto, the bald, bony former Italian prisoner-of-war, who later founded the first holistic spa and retreat center near the wine region outside Cape Town. Thankfully, my mother's cast of theatre characters brought moments of welcome comic relief into our modest home. I remember the two Maxes: Max Adler, the heavyset, friendly giant who accompanied my mother on accordion and piano (imagine the heavy set, six-foot-four Max and the agile, four-foot-ten Chayela together on stage) and Max Perlman, the Yiddish star from Argentina who wore his shiny, slick black wig, heavy brown pancake stage makeup, and eyebrow-pencil moustache day and night, on and off stage. With the procession of motley misfits of idiosyncratic, emotional foreigners, cigarette-smoking bridge players, gay interior designers and visiting dramatic show-business types parading through our doors, life was hardly dull or boring in the Piatka household.

Eight: The vertical sign of infinity, a symbol for the interconnecting loop of loss that was my parents' history and my heritage. Born into their void of gaping holes woven one into the other, I was always searching, grasping for something that might have been. With the sense that my parents and I had been robbed of something valuable, something so precious it could not be articulated, only keenly felt as some kind of psychic violation, I knew that what was missing was irreplaceable. And yet, strangely so, the intangible made itself palpable. Whatever that nameless ache was, I had sucked it in with my mother's milk. I had breathed it in from the air still singed from my father's smoldering rage. The toxic aftershocks of evil and cruelty that reverberated across the oceans, along the continents down through the generations—that insidious legacy of war—infiltrated my father's constant barrage of controlling rules and orders: *Finish your food! Clean your plate! Say "thank you!" Be home by half past five for dinner—no later or else! Sit quietly! Don't talk back! Go to your room! Face to the wall! Down on your knees! Kiss the hand that smacked you! Say you're sorry! Again, I didn't hear you! Louder!* They festered in his stinging smacks across my face and hits on my bare bottom, and the degradation I felt, forced to bend over his knees and submit to punishment. Vestiges of deprivation and devastating loss seeped out in my mother's sighs and longing stares as she twisted my hair into braids or played her silent games of solitaire by her bedroom window. They were there in the eagerness with which she ate her food and licked her fingers and stacked her purse with leftover pastries from dinner parties and laughed too loud and plastered my face with avalanches of hungry kisses. And they were there when she gazed teary-eyed at the tiny gray photo of her older brother, whom I was never to know, which she kept tucked under the glass top of her dressing table.

Nine: *Nein*! No! No talking about the negative, about the horrors of what came before, in another country, from another time. *Shhh! Shah! Shweig! Keep quiet!* In the prevailing tight-lipped 1950s and early '60s culture of my youth, where the adults were superbly efficient at blanking and blotting out any of the prevalent daily injustices, the subject of the Holocaust was something to avoid. In those ignorance-is-bliss days, just preceding our information and Internet age, most people were not ready for talk about genocide or racism, or man's intentional, institutionalized torturous treatment of fellow human beings. As to the evil perpetrated upon my parents, the simplified version handed down to me was that once upon a time, far away in a land called Germany, there came to power a villainous dictator, you shouldn't mention his name—*ptu, ptu, ptu*—whose murderous soldiers killed my grandparents and uncle and countless others for no other reason than that they were born Jewish. One shouldn't know of such things, *ptu, ptu, ptu!* As if spitting over one's left shoulder was the cure or the prevention for systemized brutality, oppression and deprivation, which also happened to be going on daily, right under our lily-white noses in apartheid South Africa. I remember being curious about those carved ornamental statues, placed over entrances to buildings, depicting three little monkeys sitting in a row, their tiny hands cupped either over their eyes, ears, or mouth. Someone told me what they meant: "See no evil, hear no evil and speak no evil!" Only later did I realize those adorable monkeys I thought were so cute ironically represented the social and political mandate of preferential blindness, deafness and dumbness to the racial discrimination policy of the South African government. Apparently, stone monkeys do not hear the pained outcry of "Never again!" *Nein! Nein!*

In the land of bright sunshine, I wasn't about to go looking in the dark, asking about things which might lead to more punishment or an even greater ache than what I'd already vicariously absorbed from my parents.

Ten: One left with zero, the nothing, the vanished, the open, mute scream. The one little freckle-faced girl next to the encompassing quiet of the void, the empty hollow circle, the gaping hole that is her parents' past.

Eleven: Father and daughter, One and One on the outside. Between us, the Yiddish nein, nein, no, no of my mother, who postponed telling me her stories and took them with her to the grave. We are the Ones left standing, on either side of her eighteen, chai. Chayela. A little life, larger than life, leaving a large hole. Together, my father and I, we'll fill the empty spaces, not only of his life but of that of my mother's, and who knows, maybe of mine too. "Go home!" my schoolmates had shouted at me once upon a time. But what was home? South Africa was my country of birth, not my home. I was still trying to find home. Perhaps my all-knowing father, the one whose die was cast, could cast his spell and spell it out for me.

Twelve: Me, the One with my two parents. The Tribes of Israel, signs of the zodiac, months in a year, hours of a day, Apostles retelling stories told to them, the age of a girl becoming *bat mitzvah*, daughter of the commandment, keeper of the faith.

In the palindrome year of ones and nines, nine years before the new millennium, before the days of natural disasters of famine and floods, of tsunamis and towering infernos of 9/11s yet to come, I will begin to record the voice of one of the few Ones remaining. When I tell my father that I'd like to capture his life stories for a potential book, he is more than delighted and eager to begin. "It's about time," I'm sure he's thinking. Everyone wishes for remembrance. My father lives for it.

The God

✦

Cape Town, South Africa, 1955–60

In the refracted light of the water, things seem larger than they really are.

On a warm July day, in the summer of 1991, I wait at Logan airport for my god to descend from the hazy sky. "How is life in the *dacha*?" my widowed father asks when I pick him up for his annual visit to my home west of Boston. When I ask him to explain the word, his face tenses up, his mouth purses with impatience, and he replies curtly, "I already told you!" The air between us prickles with static. I am used to my father's undercurrents of anger, splattering in sporadic discharges, leaving me in no-man's-land, in the midst of a war I never began. Trapped in my own love-hate relationship with the man I was taught to obey, too tired to even wave the white flag of surrender he once told me about, I sit behind the wheel of the car, mute, holding back tears. "*Dacha*—it's just a word," I tell myself. To interrogate a god about such trivia is too formidable a task for a suburban stay-at-home mom whose engine runs filled up with regular guilt. Much easier to stew in silent, simmering frustration. I will find out later that *dacha* means a "house in the country" in Russian.

It is to my *dacha* that my father comes to stay every summer, for several months at a time. Leaving his flat by the beach in Sea Point, Cape Town, sitting on an airplane for practically a whole day, Mr. Piat, the sun worshiper, flies to the northern hemisphere for a perpetual summer, granting his body a great tan, and his two beloved daughters, who fortunately live within five minutes of each other, a long visit. My father enjoys staying at my *dacha*, a comfortable, beautiful home nestled halfway up a dead-end street in the desirable suburb of Newton, "The Garden City." He spends most of his time out in the backyard, lying by the inground swimming pool, reading. I had made sure, in the planning of the newly built pool, to position it where it could receive the most sunshine for the longest amount of time. A problem arose during the construction. Apparently, the surrounding soft clay soil was not firm enough to withstand the heavy weight of the pool water. When I was told we had to dump more rocks, stones, and gravel into the soil, at an extra expense of course, my mother's frequently used Yiddish expression about wasted money popped into my mind: "*Oy! In d'rerd mine gelt*"— Money gone into the soil, literally. The ready humor of my mother could soften any blow. The seriousness of my father, on the other hand, could deal a blow on any humor. The subject of finances was no laughing matter to Mr. Piat. Every hard-earned penny was to be saved and invested wisely. I rationalized that the dollars spent on extra rocks buried in my backyard were a good investment. After all, the swimming pool was a popular summer gathering place for my family of husband, three kids, my sister and her husband, my husband's visiting family and our growing list of invited friends. And my father, of course, who especially enjoyed that pool on his annual visits.

Before his visit, I had decided that I could not let this be yet another season of small talk and large disappointments. *Nein!* There is more to life than petty squabbles or unresolved expectations between god and mortal, master and servant, father and daughter. Why did I still expect warm, friendly affectionate hugs that do not come naturally from my rather formal father? Why did he is still expect his married daughter to immediately cater to his particular demands? I resolved to do my best to extricate myself from the emotional knot of a father-daughter relationship tangled in too much wanting, too little giving, and not enough forgiveness. I would have to let little conflicts that grew like storms in a teacup pass by me by like drifting clouds. Easier said than done for the daughter who liked to have the last word. Combatants in a battle neither of us can win, my father and I have spent our summers together, jabbing and jousting at the delicate dialogue of mutual understanding. In our efforts to recreate that blissful love that once existed between parent and child, before words were even necessary, we try to sort out differences and acknowledge painful similarities. Detached comments on current events would be our truce between sporadic sniper shots. Having too much at stake, we remain, at best, polite enemies, at worst skirmishing rebel factions, reluctant to lay down our protective shields and handy verbal spears. The older my father gets, the more I begin to recognize and resent the entitled deity in him; the older I get, the wearier I am of nurturing anyone other than my own three children and, sometimes, even my own husband—and, yes, the golden retriever I rescued from the pound, who turned out to have epilepsy. When does parenting end, and when do we release ourselves from slipping automatically into childish roles? Can't we ever be friends or even old acquaintances, independent, like those number ones in this palindrome year, single pillars, bookends firmly holding the stories of our lives in place?

This summer, I am determined to finally lay down the sword of alienation and pick up, instead, the pen of reconciliation to record my family heritage. That is the way to appease my god. Words shall now become our little embraces. Words shall roll the heavy rock from off the former slave turned master. Words on paper. Paper over rock. We always had words between us, my god and I. Not all of them kind, not all of them gentle. But our mutual love for words, written, read, and spoken, was a bond that could not be cut. Carefully snipped newspaper or magazine articles, casually presented to me, were his tokens of affection. I was left to find the hidden messages that might convey to me what he couldn't state out loud. "Something for you to read!" was my father's way of saying he loved me. Stories were our hugs, our words of endearment, ever since I was a child.

The fortunate passage of time has brought us to this perfect meeting point of coincidental yearnings; my wish to gather my father's stories and his desire to pass them on to me. I imagine it must be an old man's dream to recount his stories to a willing, enthusiastic listener.

He now lies stretched out like a lazy lion on his towel spread on the chaise longue, soaking in the sun in my backyard. Suitcases unpacked, lunch served, son-in-law and grandchildren hugged, he is back in his favorite summertime place, the patio by the swimming pool. Having the gift of rapt attention of his dutiful daughter at his side, a clear, warm summer's day and the refreshing cool waters of a turquoise swimming pool in which to dip his aging body at his leisure, must surely feel like paradise for Mr. Piat.

Today we are sitting poolside, a chilled glass of water waiting patiently by the ready tape recorder on the little plastic table between us. Gazing at the man I revered, feared, and obeyed with such devotion for so long, I wonder what will emerge from his childhood that was so vastly different to mine. At his request, I have already rubbed the suntan oil on his shoulders, the smearing of suntan lotion our well-established father-daughter summertime ritual from as far back as I can remember. Whatever sunscreen company he was advertising for work would be brought home in sample tubes, forcibly squeezed out till the last drop and brusquely rubbed all over my little freckling body to ensure his fair-skinned daughter was well protected against sunburn. After smearing me with cream from front to back, he would announce: "Now my turn!" and I would have to rub the lotion onto his back. I knew that back well—from the contours of his broad shoulders to the fleshy moles on his mottled skin to those wayward, stray hairs that grew randomly on his neck down to his waist.

Summers with my father were synonymous with sitting by pools of water. Right next to the ocean, a short walk from where we first lived in Sea Point, was the Pavilion, the expansive, elegant municipal swimming pool, with its beautifully landscaped lawns and different size pools. It was where I spent much of my formative years with my father. At the large, shallow wading pool area for toddlers, babies in their bonnets and little else would crawl along the mosaic-tiled floor of clear, aquamarine colored water. There, you would find us, my father patiently holding my tiny hand, guiding me along the steps of the dividing fountain, watching my every move, and sitting with me on the staircase under the streaming waterfall, my creamy face turned to the sun, my back splashed by the cool water cascading from one tier to the other. It was my personal baby-blue heaven.

For reasons unknown, my mother avoided the beach, preferring to stay indoors, making me my father's constant beach companion at his favorite haunt, a beach named Broken Baths, right next to the Pavilion. While he sat on his beach chair reading his pile of newspapers and magazines, I would clamber over the jagged, black rocks jutting into the sea and explore the tidal pools at the water's edge, collecting shells, and constructing sandcastles. Once, I ran up to my father, proudly displaying my treasured find of a large conch shell. He took it from my hand, placed it next to my ear, and said: "Listen! If you listen carefully, you can hear the ocean. What is it saying?" My spontaneous, imaginative answer made him smile. That alone was reward enough. Good girl. A royal nod and half-crooked smile meant I'd made my king happy.

The Pavilion was where my father first taught me how to swim. Placing me on his back, he'd entwine my hands firmly across his broad shoulders and around his neck. Then off we'd go, my face nestling snugly against his nape as he swam his leisurely breaststroke through the sunlit water. "Splashy, splashy!" he'd call out, urging me to kick. Swishing my floppy feet as hard as I could, I believed it was all up to me to keep us floating forward. Teaching me to swim, he showed me how to love the water. Clinging to my father's back, I was fearless. My father, the only man in my little life, was my Poseidon. Sink or swim. Just hold on tight. In the eyes of a child, the one who takes you out into the big world on his back, appears to be the god of all things.

To me, his firstborn daughter, there was no question he was almighty, all-knowing, and all-ruling. It was the consensus of all who knew him, including some intimidated ex-boyfriends of mine, that the memorable Mr. Piat, with his commanding presence, left an indelible impression on everyone he met. He could turn strangers into fans and loyal servants in a few minutes, after a couple of conversations. He could silence a room with a spontaneous speech of such conviction that you could forget to breathe. He could order people around, and they would be happy to grant him his requests. To my childish vision, Mr. Piat was the authority of all matters that mattered.

My god was to be obeyed. Dictating with his resonant bass voice and pointed finger, he spoke and you listened—or else. I knew what that "else" meant: a good hiding. A loud yelling. A stern lecture. The leather belt from off his pants and onto my behind. Straight to bed with no dinner. The merciless tugging of my delicate ears. My face pressed to the corner of the wall. To me, the tacit threat of punishment hung on every pronounced consonant of every booming word. Taught by society to be a good girl with good manners, trained by my master to listen and be obedient, I knelt at the altar of my sometimes wrathful, always vigilant deity whose accented voice could be both whip and whisper, and I dutifully did his bidding.

Now, four decades later, in a different hemisphere, I am a grown woman with children and even a mosaic tiled swimming pool of my own, and yet, somehow, I still remain daddy's little girl, his devoted summertime companion, sitting by another pool of water, ready to serve him—to write down his life story. This time, swimming upon my father's back into deeper waters, I shall listen more carefully to hear what I could not before.

The Jew

✦

Vilna, Poland, 1919

What are the ties that bind, and the binds that sever the ties?

"God, you see, had done most of the work to mark me as a Jew, even before I was born," my father begins. "At my birth, my father, Zacharias Jutan, pronounced that I was one in a million in our faith. One in a million! I didn't know until much later why he kept telling me I was one of the chosen of the chosen, or why Mother would laugh, predicting I would be lucky in love. I thought at first, it's because I am a Cohen."

Who are they, these grandparents I never knew, the ones who raised the man who raised me, the missing pieces of the large, unfinished puzzle? My father's mother is a vaguely remembered image from an old photo, her Modigliani-like face peering out from under a hat pulled down low over her forehead. My father seemed to resemble that woman with the longish face and prominent nose, whose eyes I could barely see and whose mouth didn't seem to want to smile. My grandfather, Zacharias Jutan, is a short, stocky, serious-looking man, posing in his winter overcoat and fedora in a gold-framed sepia photograph that my father kept in a drawer.

At a young age, I remember my father telling me I belonged to the prestigious Cohen Tribe. "We are descendents of the high priests from ancient Israel," he had pronounced, exuding pride about something I couldn't even understand. The revelation of my ancestry just made my father seem even more special in my eyes. However, to me, that feeling of belonging, that visceral sense of being linked to ancestors, real, live people who came before my parents and even before them, remained elusive. I was missing something I never had from the start. A Cohen, my father informed me, was forbidden from walking inside a cemetery. "Good!" I thought to my young self. I don't ever have to go where dead people are buried. Too spooky. I would find out much later, in turn, that even ghosts without a burial place could come and find you wherever you went, if they so desired.

Demonstrating the special Cohen hand sign, he made me practice it with him. Raising our hands in tandem, spreading and dividing our four fingers apart, two by two, to form a V shape, my father explained to me that this was how we Cohens cast a blessing. When I thought no one was looking, I proudly walked around practicing my secret Cohen sign, blessing stray dogs and drunken derelicts lying in the streets, anything or anyone that looked as if they could use a quick zap of good luck. Even Hamat, our favorite Malaysian Moslem street hawker, who sold my mother fresh fruit and vegetables from a wooden cart at the corner of the street, was blessed by my secret sign that I also waved over his long suffering work horse, standing strapped to the heavy, produce-laden cart, leather blinders at the corners of its eyes, its scraggly tail swatting the swarming flies. It was exciting to think my hands contained magic powers.

"What made me so unique," my father announces, "was my birth."

At eight o'clock in the morning on July 8, 1919, Israel Jutan was born in Vilna, in his mother's bed in the family home, ushered into the world by his Aunt Asya, a midwife. When his father Zacharias, a doctor, examined his firstborn son, he noticed something unexpected and rather remarkable. Checking his baby's genitalia, he gasped. "Oy! He is already a Jew!" His baby boy had been born already circumcised.

As soon as he noticed this remarkable evidence of natural-born Jewishness, Zacharias rushed off with the news to his own father, Reuven, who immediately hurried off to consult with several rabbis in Vilna. How would they conduct the *brith milah,* the ritual sacrifice of the foreskin, when the foreskin wasn't there to begin with? A common medical procedure today, circumcision was at that time practiced solely by Jews, distinguishing Jewish males as different from others, in accordance with the ancient covenant between Abraham and his Hebrew God.

The rabbis convened and, as I imagine it, with a great amount of head scratching, shoulder shrugging, and beard tugging, came to a decision about what to do with an already circumcised penis. On the morning of the *bris,* occurring on the baby's eighth day, according to Jewish custom, the Jutan family gathered to celebrate little Israel's joining the brotherhood of Jews. The *mohel*, deprived of his usual job, simply recited the prayer and blessing over my father, his parents and the whole Jewish nation, and then, according to the rabbis' decision, made a tiny cut to release a little bit of blood. Because it was a very auspicious sign for a Jewish boy to be born already a Jew, a special prayer was said at the nearby Orthodox synagogue. The rabbi thanked God and blessed the uniquely sculpted baby, the firstborn son, destined to be the only child of Zacharias Jutan, doctor, prominent city councilor, *gabbeh*, president of that synagogue's congregation, and member of the elite Cohen tribe. My father adds that his mother, Vava, a sophisticated, modern woman from an intellectual, upper-class, non-religious Russian family, apparently never set foot in that synagogue.

My father's *bris* or *brith milah* marked the only occasion that his very religious grandfather, Reuven Jutan, came to visit their house.

"He was the grand dictator of our family, a strict Orthodox Jew, and a domineering patriarch who ruled over his wife and family of five children with a firm hand. Grandfather Reuven was one of twelve brothers, and he owned three inns on the outskirts of Vilna and a twelve-room hotel in Vilna, in Biskupia Street, in the city center, facing the square and the opulent Napoleon Palace, right near Vilna University. Outside that hotel, in a cobblestoned square, stood a broken marble pedestal that once held the monumental statue of Mouraviev, the governor of Russian Vilna. When Poland gained its independence from imperial rule, that statue was torn down and replaced by a giant bust of Lenin to mark the Russians' triumphant return in 1939. Of course when the Germans came, Lenin got knocked off, too," my father says, amused by the fickleness of men and their false idols.

Like the twelve tribes of Israel, Reuven and his eleven brothers had varying last names. Reuven's father had struck a deal with the police chief to register his sons under different surnames, taking advantage of the law stating that if a family had only one son, he would not be eligible for military conscription. Thus, he saved his boys from the certain cruel fate of being a tormented Jew in the Tsar's rigorous army. Most of Reuven's younger brothers immigrated to different parts of the world, taking their surnames of Jutan, Utin, Utan, Cohan, Kaufman, and Katzeff with them. At the time my father imparted this information to me, I had no clue that a decade later, some of the descendants of Reuven's brother, Sam Utin, would become my newfound extended family.

Most of my father's early memories of his *zeyda* or grandfather are of his visits to the men's municipal bathhouse, where Grandfather Reuven would deposit his three-year-old grandson under the supervision of a Russian helper and disappear upstairs to the sauna. The young boy was left to stare in terror at the alarming sights of naked, sweating men soaking themselves in large iron tubs of steaming water, shouting to one another in Yiddish, a language he did not hear at home, while other half-toweled men got their backs pummeled with bundles of twigs by burly masseurs. Once Grandfather Reuven was done, he gruffly handed his grandson back to Zacharias, who waited for him in the foyer with a piece of chocolate or a cookie to accompany their trip home.

My father remembers his grandmother Ethel with fondness. "She was an angel," he says. "Small and kind, was always smiling, running around attending to her home, her family, and food, and never interfering in her husband's affairs or other people's business. She was the one who hugged and kissed me on my occasional visits to their home. But when my father took me to the small synagogue on Mostova Street, where Grandfather Reuven, with his long white beard, was the president, it was a different story. My *zeyda* would put his hand on my head, mutter something I could not understand and then push me back to my father. Why he seemed so angry with me I didn't understand. Only later on did I realize it was because of Mother."

Grandfather Reuven had not approved of his oldest son's marriage to Vava, the "foreigner." During the First World War, Zacharias had been a paramedic in the Russian army. As a young medical officer, he was well known in his regiment for his distinctive footwear, particularly his bright yellow boots. When a German bomb fell on the Red Cross tent in which he was working, he was thrown up into the air, landing headfirst, face down in the earth. Spotting his yellow boots sticking up out of the sand, rescuers quickly plucked him out by the feet, working hard to bring him back to life. He was taken to the St. Petersburg hospital, suffering from chest and stomach injuries, which would later be the cause of several nagging health problems. While recuperating there, he met several young Jewish ladies, volunteers from various Jewish organizations, who tended to the wounded.

One of the more charming and striking volunteer nurses assigned to him was Basya Goldman, affectionately referred to as Vava. When she told her parents about the wounded young Jewish medical student from Vilna, they recognized the family name, determining that they were third or fourth cousins with the Eitans or Jutans, all of whom originally came from a small village by a derivation of that name in the Vilna province. In the hospital, Vava told Zacharias all about their shared ancestry and her family. Her father was the owner of an orthopedic shoe salon on Nevski Prospekt, one of her two brothers was a doctor like him, and her three sisters were all blessed with musical talents. It seemed only natural that the romantic Vava would bring her distant relative to her family home, where she would nurse him back to life and love. In 1918, the distant cousins were married in St. Petersburg, Vava's hometown. When the Russian Revolution broke out, bringing chaos to the region, the newlywed couple decided it was best to leave for the safety of Zacharias's birthplace, Vilna.

When Grandfather Reuven discovered that his oldest son had gotten married without his knowledge and prior approval, he was shocked and outraged. It didn't matter to him that mail service was poor during the war and the Bolshevik Revolution. Marriages in those times were customarily arranged by the family and celebrated in community. He had been denied that traditional honor. Worse still was the girl from Russia who had married his son without his consent, who did not keep kosher and who walked about with an air of confidence and sexuality decidedly offensive to an observant Orthodox Jew like Reuven. They did not even share a common language. Vava spoke no Yiddish or Polish; Reuven spoke no Russian or French. For him, this modern Jezebel deserved no place in his life nor in his respectable son's life, even if she had just produced for him a distinctive grandson, who was the talk of the town.

On the eighth day of my father's newborn life, Grandfather Reuven made the special trip to Arsenalska Street, where his son lived, the only Jewish family out of twelve in the elegant, three-story apartment block in an affluent area near the river and the park, a distance from the old Jewish section. Witnessing the mock *brith milah* of his pre-circumcised grandson, he ate the *lekach*, the honey cake that his wife, Ethel, had made, tasted the sweet cakes and confectioneries set out so attractively near the gleaming *samovar* on the lace tablecloth, drank a little kosher wine to celebrate the birth of another Jutan offspring, complimented the *mohel* on a job well done, shook hands with all who congratulated him, took a peek at the baby lying in the cradle, put on his black hat, said a formal good-bye to his son and the guests, and walked out the door without so much as a polite glance at the mother of his special grandson.

"That was the first and last time he entered our house. Grandfather Reuven never accepted his Russian daughter-in-law. Grandmother Ethel, as always, meekly followed her husband," my father says.

As a solitary child playing with my cardboard cutout paper dolls, I used to fantasize about the large, loving family I might have had if not for the war. I filled in the blanks with blurry, idealized pictures of kind and doting elders who bought me gifts and hugged me close and took me away from my lonely house to play with a group of lively cousins. Now the fleshed out memories of my father are flushing out any myths I might have had. It bothers me that my own so-called religious great-grandfather scorned his daughter-in-law with such disdain. My idea of a religious, observant Jew is someone who would practice what the revered high priest of the Second Temple, Simon the Righteous, proposed was a cornerstone of Judaism: *chessed*, the act of loving kindness. Isn't the point of all spiritual pursuit and religious practice to bring us to that very understanding, that realization that we are all one, made in the image of the all-seeing eye of *Adonai*, the Holy One? Wasn't that after all, the final prayer that pious Jews, shoved into the crematoria along with all kinds of Jews from all kinds of nationalities, speaking all different languages, repeated in Hebrew with undying faith on their dying lips: "*Shmah!* Hear, oh Israel! The Lord our God, the Lord is One?"

How religious or observant a Jew was, or where he or she came from did not matter at all to the mass murdering Nazis, who had no problem seeing all Jews as one—a nation to be destroyed. And how ironic it is that their plans to annihilate the already divided Jews only helped to bring a fragmented people closer together as one, united by memory and a burning desire and commitment to rebuild a nation.

The Boy From Vilna

✦

Vilna, Poland, 1920s
Vilnius, Lithuania, 2003

The same rivers may flow, but the waters will always be different.

"Once upon a time," my father tells me, as if remembering the golden age of a Jewish Camelot, "Vilna was a place where Jews and other people of all kinds of faith lived as one, in harmony with one another. Writers and composers would make songs in Yiddish about our beloved home. So beautiful was our Vilna, that people fell in love with it, and we all wanted to sing its praises. Our town was a haven of enlightenment, learning, and culture. The famous Vilna Gaon, the esteemed spiritual leader made his home in the town Jews from all around Europe referred to as 'The Jerusalem of Lithuania.' For us, Vilna, our home, was a place of great pride." Eager to share its background, he tells me that the town formerly named Wilno, now known as Vilnius, which the Jews called Vilna, was once an important city on the trading route between East and West, governed by wise men who understood that the safe integration of different ethnic and religious groups was the foundation of a flourishing economy. In my father's time, Jews could spend their whole lives in their home of Vilna actively involved in matters of trade, business, education, philanthropy, health, and culture, without ever encountering a non-Jew.

Home. Is it a town, a house, a community? Listening to my father talk about the city of his birth, I wonder why it is that we continue to call the town of our cherished childhood, our innocence—home, long after we have left and settled in new places in foreign lands. It's as if the city, town, or village in which we spent our early years lends us a sense of identity. Like a lover, it demands our allegiance, holding us close or spurning and turning us away, forever claiming a part of us. Vilna was such a place.

My father tells me how important it is that we know the history of our origins. It gives us a sense of belonging, a sense of continuity. We can better understand how and why things come to pass and what we have to lose if we don't pay close attention. He rattles off the dates he considers significant: In 1497, Prince Casimir IV, King of Poland, unites neighboring Lithuania with Poland. In 1519, Wilno becomes a center of Polish and Jewish culture, boasting a modern printing press. In 1795, Russia annexes the territory when it partitions Poland, renaming the capital Wilna. In 1920, the Polish troops recapture the city after the Bolsheviks hand it to the Lithuanians. In 1939, the Soviets occupy it again, and Vilna is transferred back to the Lithuanian Socialist Republic on October 10. During all those transitions of foreign power, he explains, Vilna remained a hub of Jewish cultural and spiritual life, "the town of great learning," sprouting many rabbinical schools. The famed Yiddish institute of YIVO, now in Manhattan, was founded in Vilna. The Great Synagogue, built in the seventeenth century, housed the famous Strashun Library. Each little suburb had its own small House of Prayer (a *Kloyz* or *Shul*) named after the founders or traders or businessmen who made substantial contributions in some way. The Choral Synagogue in Zawalna Street, with its famous green roof, was the concert venue for internationally known cantors. In the early 1920s of my father's youth, Jewish life in Vilna was flourishing, rich, and vibrant. To the more than 60,000 Jews proud to call it home, Vilna was a city of prosperity and beauty, a veritable Eden.

In 1941, the invasion of the Nazis changed everything. Four years later, at the end of the Second World War, the Soviets resumed their Communist rule, giving the capital of Lithuania, Vilnius, a city now devoid of most of its former Jewish population, to the socialistic Poles to govern. Those Jewish sons and daughters of Vilna who had miraculously escaped the intended genocide and who had scattered themselves to all corners of the earth to create renewed lives with replaced families, still clung dearly to their memories of their previous Vilna. Only a handful of former Vilna Jews would choose to return to live in a town of ghosts they once called home.

"Yah," my father sighs. "I left my childhood there in Vilna, far away. But I tell you, with my eyes wide open, I can still walk back down Dominikanska Street on my way to high school and see Napoleon's Palace, the grand white stone building. You know, the French emperor stayed there in 1812 on his way home after his army's crushing defeat in Russia. What a history!"

My father asks for a pen and pad of paper. I rush inside the house and bring back a yellow-lined foolscap pad and pen and watch as he draws a rudimentary map with cartoon-like pictures of little houses and churches and roads, carefully labeling everything. Here is the watchtower of the old fourteenth-century castle on top of Gediminas Hill that he climbed as a schoolboy. There is Cieletnik, the beautiful botanical park and gardens just below Gediminas Hill, named after the prince who founded Vilna, where he walked as a child with his governess. And here is the bell tower in the square, where a trumpet call would signal noontime, their signal to return home from their walk.

"How I loved that big park," he says. "Just imagine a little four-year-old boy with long, curly black hair, dressed in a sailor's outfit—

white shirt with blue stripes, matching blue shorts, knee-high navy socks, and fancy black shiny shoes. That's me. Mother would spit on those shoes and rub them with her handkerchief to make them shine. On my head, she put a sailor's cap to keep down the curls she refused to cut," he says.

As I try to imagine my father as a little boy in a park in a country I have never seen, memories of my own favorite seaside park pop up. There, alongside the Atlantic ocean, an exuberant, skinny, ponytailed girl can be seen scampering around from the spinning merry-go-round to the top of the metal jungle gym, climbing up and down the monkey bars, flying high on swings carved out of halved rubber car tires, and gliding down shiny, silver metal slides glinting in the hot southern sun. The gray photos with the scalloped white borders that my father took and carefully placed in an album serve as documentation of my carefree Sea Point childhood. No photos exist from my father's childhood to prove a little sailor boy once played under trees in a park in Vilna.

"Vilna, of course, was famous for its collection of cathedrals, over forty of them," my father says. "My religious Catholic governess took me with her to quite a few. At the old town gate, known as the Ostra Brama, it was customary for citizens walking by to uncover their heads in homage to the sacred picture of Mary, Mother of Jesus. Of course, the pious Vilna Jews would deliberately avoid those streets, seeking out other routes to reach the outer city rather than acknowledge the picture of Mary."

My father pauses for a moment. Thirsty, he asks me to bring him another glass of water. I stop the tape recorder and head indoors to the kitchen. Walking toward the house, around the pool and up the stairs, I think about those religious Jews in their black garb harking back to a previous era, taking the long way home to avoid the painted image of Mary. Was my great-grandfather Reuven one of them? What a testament to the power of art, that a single picture could cause a whole rerouting of traffic. No wonder so many Catholics are inflicted with guilt, I muse to myself. Their religion's matriarch is a Jewish mother. *Oy, Vey!* It still baffles my mind how so many of her most loyal devotees turned into such virulent haters of her tribe. Did they forget that Mary gave birth to a Jewish boy, who was very likely circumcised according to tradition at his *bris*, who Rome's governor of Judea, Pontius Pilate believed to be the king of Jews, and who was depicted in artistic masterpieces, sitting at a *seder*, at the Passover table, at what he knew would be his last Passover? What a pity, that in focusing on the small picture, we tend to lose sight of the bigger one. In the forgetting of the origins of the storyteller lies distortion, discrimination, destruction. In the forgetting of the morals of the story, murder becomes easy. What would have happened to Jesus and his family, I wonder, had he, like my father, been living in Vilna during Nazi times. Wouldn't the son of Mary and Joseph have been hunted down and murdered for the very sin of coming from a Jewish lineage? What manner of torture might the rebel rabbi, the epitome of sacrifice and suffering, have had to endure then?

"Forgive, but don't forget!" was my father's message to me when I was old enough to know what the word Holocaust meant and that he had survived its horrors. Ultimately, he had come to understand that one is far better off letting go of the suffering, hate, and desire for vengeance, for we hurt *ourselves* more if we hold onto past grievances. He had seen and experienced that revenge was merely the seed of more violence and the cause of more agony. Coming from compassion and profound awareness, forgiveness paved the way to true freedom. "Make no mistake! People must still be held accountable for their wrongdoings," he would say. "I will never condone the evil that was done to me and to others. No! What I am saying is if we can, if we are able, we must forgive, for our own sake. Better to put the pain of the past away, than bring more suffering into the present or the future."

When many diaspora Jews were vehemently boycotting German products to make a new generation pay for the sins of their fathers, Mr. Piat, the Holocaust survivor Jew from the Jerusalem of Lithuania was unknowingly echoing the Yom Kippur philosophy of an ancient Jewish mystic from the Jerusalem of Judea.

"You know the Vilna I described to you?" he asks. "It does not exist any more. Only in my mind." Dipping his fingers into the glass of water I have brought back to him from the kitchen, he sprinkles some drops onto his forehead. For my father, talking about his hometown, the Jerusalem of Lithuania, is a sacred pilgrimage.

"I see pictures today in magazines of the rebuilt Vilnius after the war—the new suburbs and institutions of learning and sports. I read about the Cathedral, which was a museum during the Soviet Communist occupation, then opened again for the faithful Catholic worshipers and I wonder, in years to come, will anyone remember that we Jews were such a vital part of that city's history? Do the young generations today even know what happened on those streets less than sixty years ago?"

At the time my father tells me the tale of one city with two rivers and many names, I cannot give him an answer to his question. Five years after his death, I can.

In September 2003, I went to Vilnius to perform my one-woman show as a specially invited guest for the national commemoration of the sixtieth anniversary of the liquidation of the Vilna Ghetto. While walking one morning in a park near the hotel at which I was staying, I came across a group of lively high school students and asked them where they were from and why they weren't in school. They had skipped school that day to celebrate a friend's birthday, they said, pointing her out to me. I then posed my father's question to the casual truants. Shaking their heads, they admitted that they didn't know much about the Holocaust. "Would you like to come with me to a museum that's close by?" I asked. To my surprise, some of the students, including the birthday girl, accepted my invitation, following me up the hill to the little wooden Holocaust museum of somber memories, The Green House, run by a few dedicated Vilna Holocaust survivors.

Once inside, the young students' exuberance turned to hushed reverence. Walking around slowly, they stared at the exhibits of black-and-white photos, artwork, official testimonials, and authentic documents chronicling the imprisonment and extermination of the Jews who had lived alongside their grandparents in their beloved hometown. Telling them why I was there, filling them in about what had happened to my Vilna-born father and mother, I showed them a different view of the city they had been so quick to tell me they adored—a piece of their history still not taught at their schools. When they left, visibly moved, they each shook my hand and thanked me. Hugging the birthday girl, I did what my father would have done. I told her to tell others what she had seen and to never forget.

When the teenagers originally asked me if I liked their beautiful town, I had withheld my true feelings. "It's certainly beautiful," I replied, remembering how much my father had loved the city of his youth. For me, though, something was amiss. Modern Vilnius felt shabby, sad. It seemed as if the soul of the city had been gouged out, leaving a beautiful but bare shell. Listening carefully, I could hear an ocean of mournful sighs.

In the summer of 1997, my father had wanted to take me to Vilnius, hoping, I think, that the visit might motivate me to finish the book I had abandoned in pursuit of performing my mother's play. The timing was bad, I told him. My marriage was breaking up and the increasingly stressful financial crisis in my husband's business had necessitated my reentering the workforce. My pre-scheduled sales job prohibited taking a week off in the summer. Next year, I promised him. Next year in Jerusalem of Lithuania.

The next year, my father was dead. For a while, I regretted my decision not to honor his request. It had been the first time my father expressed any interest in going back "home," to his birthplace, which he had not seen after the war. His wish had been to travel there for a few days, just with me, his summertime companion, the two of us, another special father-daughter excursion. I had let him down.

When I went to Vilnius eight years later, in 2003, alone, I took along the yellow foolscap piece of paper on which my father had sketched his crude map of the important landmarks of his childhood.

Everywhere I went, I would speak to him, as if he were there, walking by my side. I found the apartment block where he and his mother had lived and strolled in the park of his youth under the hill with the tower that he had climbed. I even sat inside the grand Napoleon's palace for an official ceremony honoring those righteous Vilna gentiles who had saved Jews during the Nazi occupation. "Look Daddy! Look where I am!" I silently called out to him as I sat behind the president of Israel and other international political and religious dignitaries who had come to mark the sixtieth year of the expulsion and execution of the Jews at the end of the Vilna Ghetto. "Aren't you proud?" I whispered, after boldly introducing myself to the young president of Lithuania and suggesting he do a better job of teaching the Holocaust to the new generation. "Can you believe this?" I added, sitting in the Lithuanian Parliament, listening to the translations of ministers giving their seemingly sincere speeches of atonement, admitting the need for their country to face and admit their criminal past treatment of the Jews.

But in the old city of Vilna, only a few remnant markings of Jewish life could be seen: some faded color shop signs in Yiddish gracing doorways on the street where the illustrious Strashun Library once stood, a few commemorative plaques and a carved imprint of a Star of David high on an exposed brick wall of a large bare building. There were other signs that I did not expect to see. Passing an alleyway, I noticed a black spray-painted swastika on a low wall. There it was, a reminder that history is ever present and hate is only a symbol away. On another side of town, near what used to be the old Jewish section, I came across some other graffiti. Apparently there were some liberal-minded and openhearted urban artists with more positive messages for tourists coming to Vilnius. Spray-painted in blue paint on white stucco walls were slogans in English. *YOUR LIFE BECOMES MORE AND MORE OF ADVENTURE* prophesized one wall; another proclaimed: *THE IMPORTANT THING IS TO EXRESS YOURSELF.* The missing P was inserted above the X and R of "express" to correct the misspelling. I brought back the photos of that graffiti with me. The image of the swastika, I left behind on its dirty, dilapidated, broken wall in an alleyway of modern-day Vilnius. I imagine the pedantic Mr. Piat would have come up with the appropriate Latin saying for "A city ignorant of its history cannot see the writing on the wall."

The important thing is to express yourself, declared the English graffiti in modern-day Vilnius. For expressing my views and ideas will I be nailed, stoned, stonewalled, misinterpreted, criticized, or condemned? "Nu vi den," I hear my mother say in Yiddish. Of course! It's only human and rather commonplace to judge and condemn others with whom we don't agree. I'll take my chances and express away anyhow. Being a writer is not for the faint of heart. Neither is being a woman. Or a questioning Jew. God help me—I'm all three!

After that visit to Vilnius, I felt that my decision not to go with my father in 1997 might have actually worked out for the best. Vilnius is nothing like what my sentimental father's mind had held so dear for all those years. History, the impartial observer, had intervened, bringing changes along with the passing of time. No doubt he would have wept to see what was no longer there. His nostalgic version of his childhood Vilna, the city resplendent with the vitality of Jewish culture and learning, was far removed from the stark reality of a recovering post-Communist city, trying to catch up with Western society and still hugely ignorant of its loss. For my father, I believe it would have been like stepping into a graveyard. And that, as I recall, is forbidden to a Cohen, even under the guise of the Catholic-sounding Xavier Piat.

◆ ◆ ◆

Vision

Scene: A wide stretch of desert, similar to the one in Dali's painting, *The Persistence of Memory*. A troop of skeletons drop from the sky like marionettes. "The words of one become the weapons of many!" they shout, their unhinged jaws clamping up and down. The skeletons juggle their own bare bones, flinging them up into the air, spelling out the word EXPRESS across the sky like smoke signals. I try to read the bones like signs. At the beginning, XP—my father's initials. The last letters spell SS, the German death squad. At the end, *Ess, Ess!* Yiddish for "Eat, eat!"—my mother's refrain. God forbid you should starve and end up like skeletons. PRESS, my father's love of the printed word. PR, my father's professional field. The chorus line of skeletons throw their skulls back in laughter as they dance the macabre, parting in the middle to reveal a parade of midget Munchkins from the *Wizard of Oz*. Spielberg's E.T. appears, followed by George Lucas's Yoda with Woody Allen's Greek chorus bringing up the rear. Mel Brooks' Yiddish Indians from *Blazing Saddles* come galloping in on their horses, stirring up a trail of dust. "No stone unturned," warbles Yoda. "Ideas tossed about turn to rocks thrown around," mutters a Munchkin. "Those who challenge their beliefs will get rocks in the head," whispers a sallow-faced woman with coals for eyes. I remember her. Wrapped in a black shawl, she's the shunned woman from *Zorba the Greek*, only now she is wearing Vava's face. "Ideas become ideology, ideology a movement, a movement change, and change brings conflict!" declares a blind bald man draped in white robes. Is he Greek or Roman? I can't tell the difference. "No difference!" shouts Woody's chorus. "Ancient history, modern times!" Hanging upside down from Dali's branch, Yoda mumbles: "Different Wars. Same thing. Wars of Words, World Wars. Too close it is." E.T. sticks his long finger in his own ear. He wants to leave this planet. A man painted blue with shaggy hair and a kilt howls: "Defend! To the death! Defend!" Rocks fall like hail. There are bones upon bones piled in ditches, dumped in pits, stuck between wooden logs, floating in rivers. Suddenly, as fast as they appeared, the cast of extras evaporates. A lone figure remains behind. One solitary Orthodox Jew dressed in black, scurries through an archway, running away from a picture of Jesus' mother, Mary, painted by an unknown artist who mixed a bit of oil and pigment to create a fabricated image of a Jewish woman he never knew.

Are we doomed to forever live in a world of us versus them?

The Son

✦

Vilna, Poland, 1923–26

Gender has its own agenda.

"If I talk about my childhood," my father says sitting up straight in his chaise by the pool, "I must speak of course, about my mother, Vava, who was not at all like the other housewives in Vilna." Coming from St. Petersburg, from a cultured family in which Yiddish was not spoken, his mother regarded herself as more sophisticated and cosmopolitan than the women of Jewish Vilna she considered rather provincial. "Mother liked everything to be done her special way," he says. "She insisted on discipline and accuracy in my upbringing, which, of course, served me very well later in life in my organizational skills."

On many occasions she had told him, "Your father wanted to have a girl as his firstborn, not a son." Refusing to let her son's hair be cut, Vava let it grow long and curly around his head, so that by the time he was four years old, my father's hair was almost down to his shoulders. One day, she came into her young son's room and told him, "Papa is coming back from his travels today, and we are going to do something very special for him. You and me. We're going to play a game called 'Let's surprise Daddy!'" She then showed him a brand new dress she'd made—it was pink and lacy with long ribbons—and said, "Isn't it the most beautiful dress you have ever seen? Today, you are going to wear this dress, especially for your father." She put the dress on him, kissed his forehead, brushed his long, curly black hair, placed a large pink bow on the top of his head, told him to stay in his room and to "act like a girl" when his father came home, and invited the little girl from downstairs to bring along her dolls and play with her son in his room. "My neighbor was full of giggles—hee, hee, hee, hee—all the time staring at me dressed in a girl's clothing," my father continues.

"When I heard the front door open and my father's voice in the hallway, my heart started beating faster. I listened to his footsteps coming closer across the wooden floor toward my room. I was very excited. I knew I must play my part well—the part of the daughter he wanted. When my father stepped inside my room, what did he see? Two girls sitting on the floor, playing dolls. Turning around, he called out my name. I quickly jumped up of course. 'Here I am, Papa! Here I am!' I shouted. He stood for a moment, confused, staring at me in disbelief. 'But—but—what is this? You are not a girl!' he stammered. I repeated what Mother had instructed me to say: 'Yes, but you wanted me to be a girl, didn't you, Papa? Didn't you?'"

Suddenly, Zacharias swooped down and embraced his child, adorned in pink bows and frills, and hugged him tight against his smooth woolen overcoat, kissing him over and over. "He began to laugh and started to say, in a joke, you understand, 'Oh, my sweet little girl—ha! ha!—give Papa a hug, what a pretty girl in a beautiful dress,' all the time holding me in his arms, squeezing me close to his body, and kissing my face, which he had never done before. Ah! All those kisses I always wanted from him. That was the first and only time he did that," my father says. "Hugged and kissed me. When I was a girl."

Zacharias Jutan was a highly regarded city councilor and well respected in the community for his involvement with civic affairs. "In his buttonhole," my father says, "he wore the miniature replica of the gold medal awarded him for outstanding community service." In addition to his official roles with the World Association of Jewish War Invalids, Widows and Orphans and as Honorary President of the Volunteer Firemen of Vilna, Zacharias worked as a sales representative for a medical supply company. His active professional life and volunteer positions kept him busy with fundraising and travel, and meant he was often away on business.

"I wished my father would spend more time with me and less time thinking about strangers, getting clothes and money for the poor. I was his son, and I needed him. Upon his returns from his travels, he would give me the most beautiful presents. But I was not grateful. I ignored them. That is how I was," he admits, "an only son, missing his father."

He pauses as he recalls his former petulant feelings of resentment and loneliness. "But I see now that I was wrong to have such bitterness against him," he adds reflectively. As an older man, he realizes, he can understand his own father better, having more appreciation for Zacharias's commitment to philanthropy, civic duties and improving the conditions of the impoverished, values that he himself shares today. Hindsight allows him to see how noble it was that his responsible father took it upon himself to take care of the small Jutan tribe after Reuven's death, settling debts left by his father and providing for his two single sisters as well as a couple of Russian orphan girls left parentless and penniless at the death of their father, a porter at one of Reuven's hotels. Zacharias applied the Jewish commandment of *tzedakah,* of doing good deeds and charity work, in his every day actions.

"But as a boy I was always jealous," my father admits, "especially of those girls he paid attention to. I always wanted to hear him say to me that he loved me. But I never heard those precious words—'I love you'—from him."

I stare at the man who had often and quite unabashedly told me, when I was quite young, that he had wished I had been a boy. My father had wished his firstborn to be a son, he told me—to perpetuate the name of his revered father, Zacharias, in upholding the Jewish tradition of naming babies after dead relatives. When I turned out to be a girl, I was given a combination name, in memory of his mother, Vava and my mother's father, Nochum. The precious initial Z was saved for the anticipated male offspring. When eight years passed by and another girl was born, my father surrendered to the inevitable. My baby sister Zola received the honor of the precious letter Z.

I tried my best to make up for disappointing my father. Desperately wanting to be one of the boys, I climbed trees and joined the neighborhood gang in their back alley games of throwing mud pies and playing cricket. Secretly, I berated myself for being emotional, thin-skinned, and softhearted, so susceptible to swells of feelings that spilled too easily into tears. When I came home from first grade one day, in tears, complaining that a boy had called me names and teased me, my father gave me his best consolatory advice: "Next time, kick him! That will teach him a lesson." Kick him? But I'm a girl, I thought. Girls aren't supposed to kick, are they? My father's message was clear: You must be tough in this world. You must be prepared to fight back. Crying was a sign of weakness and God forbid you should show any weakness. But bursting into tears seemed to be my automatic response to the helplessness I felt in the face of injustice, violence, and pain I witnessed everywhere around me. If boys weren't supposed to cry, this tough-acting, tree-climbing tomboy didn't quite make the grade. One dismissive remark or sneer from the teachers at school or the boys next door or the father at home sent my girlish heart into flood mode, branding me with the secret shame of being a "sissy." Pity I didn't know then what I know now—that the release of toxins in tears is actually good for one's health.

My father's own first strict lesson about the difference between boys and girls and having a good cry came at the age of five. "My first education in sex," he grins.

Below the apartment where my father lived with his flamboyant mother and absent father, lived the family of the janitor of the building, Wicenty, in the basement of the building. *Vinchenti*, as my father pronounces his name, "was a gigantic red-faced peasant of a man with a big moustache, Polish style, curling up at the ends, who cleaned the courtyard, took care of the garbage outside the apartment house, yelled at his six children, and regularly gave them and his wife a good round of beatings when he was drunk, which was quite often." Wicenty had a son the same age as my father, and daughters younger and older. "We used to play all kinds of games together: cowboys and Indians, pirates and robbers, hiding games and, of course, "Doctor, Doctor." Because my father was a physician, I felt a special connection to this last game and thought I deserved to play the main role. We children were very creative in finding instruments to make the game as real as possible. A shoe-polish tin, with a hole punched in, then a long string pulled through the hole, was our telephone. If you adjusted the string, the telephone could become a stethoscope to measure the heartbeat or whatever else we thought a doctor might listen to, including the mysterious parts below, which the janitor's children told me all about with great enthusiasm. Yah. They told me all about making babies, but I couldn't understand how you could make babies with the same thing you used to make pee-pee. Of course I was very curious to find out! One day, while playing "Doctor, Doctor" downstairs, Wicenty's young daughter lay down on the floor and picked up her skirt over her head. To my surprise, I saw she had no underwear. 'You must put it in!' she told me. Eager to play the game, of course, I tried to do what I thought she wanted. All of a sudden, she began to scream at the top of her voice. I was very impressed with her acting. I thought it's all part of the play." Wicenty's wife ran in to save her wailing daughter, telling her surprised five-year-old neighbor he needed to go back home, upstairs, immediately. My father was playing quietly with his toys in his room when he heard his mother return and the front door slam shut. The next thing he knew, Vava burst into his room like a tornado.

"She kept screaming and waving her hands in the air," my father recalls. "'You brute, you pig,' she shouted at me with a torrent of Russian words I didn't understand. Then she sat on my bed, pulled down my pants, threw me over her knees and gave me a hiding on my bottom like I never had before. After she was done with the torrent of hitting, she stood up, walked out and slammed the door behind her. I remember crying in my room. I was not allowed any food for the rest of the day and had to go to sleep hungry, the sounds of Mother's curses still ringing in my ears. I didn't know what I had done to deserve such a beating, but I had a feeling it was something to do with the game I played with the janitor's daughter. The next day, she sat me down and told me I must not put 'it' anywhere near a girl. Mother was so strict that, in the cinema, she used to cover my eyes when adults were kissing on the big screen," he says. "Funny to think of it now. Times are so different."

Vava was firm in her dealings with her maids, too. My father would accompany his mother on her various expeditions around town, especially to the house of an old Lithuanian or Russian woman known as the "employment auntie," where a semicircle of peasant women would sit, waiting to get hired. "Mother used to go right up to the women, glare into their faces and say: 'Show me your hands!' and then inspect their hands closely. Some secret philosophy of hers before she hired anyone, I suppose," he recalls. "Mother would speak in her broken Polish—a mixture of Lithuanian and Russian, and a bit of Baltic. But those peasant girls always understood her better than the upper-class people did. On our shopping trips, when the shop clerks had trouble understanding her questions, she would get so angry, she would simply turn around, walk out, and curse the shopkeeper in Russian. But there, at the employment place, the maids holding out their hands never had a problem understanding what the Russian lady wanted."

"And then I will never forget the *kantletti* episode," my father grins. "Mother taught the new maid how to make her favorite dish—ground beef or chicken cutlets made with egg and flour." Animatedly, he claps his hands, patting the invisible *kantletti* from hand to hand to show me how it's done. "You pat it into a patty, then you put it on a plate, then in the oven, or on top of the oven; I'm not sure. I remember a big fireplace with coal, to make the oven hot. Anyhow, whatever it was, the maid had made the *kantletti* somehow. When Mother came back in the evening and entered the kitchen to check if everything was as it should be, that is when the *kantletti* episode occurred."

My father sets the scene: he's standing in the doorway, the maid is next to the stove, and his mother is beside the kitchen table. The unsuspecting *kantletti* lie next to the potatoes on the big china plate, waiting to be served. "Mother took out a fork and stuck it into the cutlets, but the fork would not go into them. The *kantletti* were hard as stone." My father begins to chuckle. "In a second, Mother took them in her bare hands and, one at a time, began throwing them across the kitchen at the maid, along with her native Russian curses. 'You idiot! *Balvanske kop!*' she kept shouting." Now my father is laughing. "The cutlets went flying like hand grenades through the air, and the poor maid," he says in between laughs, "she was ducking and dodging, this way and that, trying to escape the attack of the flying *kantletti* speeding one after the other across the room toward her. And with every throw of the cutlet—oy, oy—Mother hurled another Russian insult on top. And, because they were so hard, these *kantletti*, they were bouncing all over, from the floor —boom!—to the oven—boom!—to the wall—boom!—back to the oven. It was something to see, the flying *kantletti*."

My father wipes the tears of laughter from his eyes. Rarely have I heard my usually serious father laugh so loud and long. If he ever found anything amusing, he would simply curl his mouth and nod his head, slowly, as if in agreement—a reserved, formal acknowledgement of a joke in distinct contrast to the hearty enjoyment of my mother, the queen of laughter. The professional joke teller, she delighted not only in being funny herself but in anything amusing or humorous that could provoke a giggle. Not so my intellectual father, who would stifle his amusement and reluctantly, it seemed, give his token smile and royal nod, even when my mother skillfully told some of her own hilarious jokes that made others howl or weep with laughter. To see and hear my dad laugh like this was truly a special occasion. He was a young boy again in his mother's home.

"And when I saw all this, I couldn't help it—I started to laugh. I couldn't stop either. Mother, in her angry rage, now directed her shouting at me: 'What are you laughing at, you imbecile?' Then she turned on me, hitting me, over and over, until, of course, I ran back to my room crying."

Suddenly I understood the origin of that perverse warning my father would often repeat to me when I was a child. "Be careful. You laughing now? Soon you will be crying!" he'd say grimly. I'd be happily giggling with friends, talking on the phone, when he'd walk right up to me, with that menacing look of his and utter that phrase, pronouncing my future like a dour, doomsday prophet. His pointed finger, stern voice, and gloomy prediction would erase in a heartbeat whatever lighthearted moment of joy I might have had.

My father's boyish laughter subsides and his brief levity vanishes. He is no longer the little boy bursting into laughter in his mother's kitchen, or crying into his pillow in his bedroom in Vilna. He is the old man, sitting in the backyard of his daughter's home, solemn again. "That is how it was with my mother. A very strong character. Yah!"

I was a teenager when my father began to call me "Vavka's dugh," especially after I'd answer him back, dare to give my opinion, or, worse yet, challenge him. When I asked what that phrase meant, he enigmatically translated it as "Vava's spirit." I was left to infer from his smirk and sarcastic tone that the comparison to a woman I knew next to nothing about was not exactly a compliment. Still, it was never made clear to me why he likened me to his mother and I never asked for further explanation.

My father pauses for a moment. Reverence. Remembrance. "But also a heart of gold," he adds.

"I will tell you another story so you know what I mean when I say 'heart of gold.' Down below, in the courtyard, people would wander in and out, hawkers and merchants peddling their wares and services, shouting up to windows of the three floors of the building that faced the courtyard," he says, imitating their various melodic calls. '*Shmattes, shmattes*—give me your old clothes!'; 'Glass repairs, glass repairs!'; 'I sharpen knives, scissors—best sharpening.' When all these artisans would come around to our buildings, the maids were sent down to buy this and that for fifty *groschen* or so. From time to time, some kind of duo or trio would arrive to do a circus stunt, like a man who would put a flame on his tongue or swallow a sword, or a fellow who could juggle fruit or flaming torches. Mother always gave me five *groschen* to fold in a piece of paper and throw down to the minstrels from our window. But when it was October or November, because the windows were now closed tight for the winter, she wrapped a warm scarf around my neck and sent me downstairs to the street level, to hand the money to the street performers myself. She wouldn't let anybody, the performers or the poor beggars, leave without getting something. She never said 'I don't have.' And she told me that in her home, back in Russia, that is how it was, too."

There was one man in particular to whom his mother was especially kind. He was a gypsy minstrel who wore a colorful fringed shawl, a big, round black Spanish-style hat and unusually bright red boots. His specialty was Russian ballads, which he played on his guitar, his nimble fingers dancing out from the frayed edges of his cutoff gloves. When he sang his plaintive songs, windows would open and money would rain down to the ground, landing at his red boots in the open courtyard. "He never picked up the money until after he was finished with the song. I admired that," my father says, struggling to hold back the tears that come so easily to an old man whose dam of nostalgia seems always close to overflowing. "He used to come to our place with a guitar, this gypsy, and gently strum it, singing his Russian songs of love, desire and romance. He knew very well the melodies and lyrics of a famous

Russian composer and singer, called Wertinsky. Vehrrrr-tinskeee! I remember one song by him, 'An Evening in Shanghai,' about a girl and a man and their last night together. He is leaving. She must remain behind. All kinds of heartache … ahhh!" My father breathes hard and chokes up. It's too much. The dam has burst. He begins to weep, his voice cracking as he tries to finish his story, tears streaming down his cheeks. "Mother, gazing out the window, hearing him sing … she used to cry … and I, I stood at the window, and I cried with her. Such beautiful stories the gypsy was singing. Even though it was Russian, pure Russian singing, I understood them all … and Mother, she used to pour out everything she had in her purse, all the small change. 'Go! Give it to him! Give it to him,' she'd say to me. And I would run down the steps as fast as I could, into the courtyard, to give the coins to the gypsy whose singing made us both weep. When the gypsy was finished with his song, he would take off his large hat and with a grand sweeping motion take a deep bow first to this side of the building, then to the other side, to all the ladies and their maids peering out of their windows, listening and crying and looking down on the courtyard in which he stood singing his songs of love. Then, only then, would he bend down and pick up the money from the ground."

Leaving the courtyard of his childhood, my father leans forward on the chaise and grabs the corner of the beach towel to wipe the tears from his face. Perhaps it is true then, what my father had warned me about. Tears do follow laughter.

I wait in silence, part of me still standing by an imagined Vilna window next to the grandmother I never knew. I imagine those Russian songs must have transported her back to the home she left behind in 1918 during the Bolshevik Revolution, the home to which she was forbidden to return. My father remembers that she kept in contact with her siblings for a few years, even sending parcels to her sisters in Leningrad. In 1925, all outside contacts were prohibited and she was instructed by her family not to write to them anymore because the Soviets were persecuting anyone suspected of having ties to the

West. "I remember Mother talking about it for many months, always in anger," my father says. "Sometimes I would hear her crying, too, in her room, alone. She only learned about her parents' death after the revolution. That was to be her fate. Yah. A woman alone, far from home, separated from family."

My father pauses. "After the war," he continues, "I tried to find out through the Red Cross what happened to Mother, but they did not have any information. When I went to live in Paris in 1949, I met one of my mother's friends who worked with her in the fashion trade. She told me that Mother kept my photos all over the apartment and in her purse, too, always saying how much she missed me. She even saw her crying while reading my letters. All those years as a child, I longed to know that my mother loved me. You see how it is? No matter how old we are, we still want to hear how much we are loved by our mothers."

And our fathers, I think to myself as I gaze at the man who, as I recall, never uttered out loud to me those same words of love and affection I too longed to hear.

The Father

✦

Cape Town, South Africa, 1950–1960
Newton, Massachusetts, 1992

Waging a war within, we become our own worst enemies.

Whether it was due to an innocent, coerced game of playing with dolls, or seeing his father take such good care of his aunts and those poor, destitute orphan girls, my father turned out to be a devoted, nurturing parent, and for many years my primary caretaker. While my actress-mother was off performing in plays and concerts overseas, it was my father who looked after me. He was the one who dramatically read me bedtime stories from the children's books he bought at the flea market opposite city hall. From those used books, treasuries of poems, fiction and fables, whose first pages were inscribed with the crayon scribbled names of other people's children, I would learn my many lessons about life, character and identity. With their magnificent illustrations, those books became my magic carpets, flying me instantly to courtyards of dancing princesses, talking cats and orphaned girls who managed, through their actions and kind words, and many times with the aid of animated spirit creatures, to transform beasts into pets and toads into handsome, charming princes. In those mystical lands, I discovered that cruel kings and wicked giants invariably come to their deservedly bitter end.

It was my father who diligently taught me how to take good care of myself, demonstrating how to shampoo without blinking and to towel dry my hair, and with the firm grip of my hand trained me in the art of deftly crossing the street while maneuvering through traffic on a busy road. With infinite patience, he taught me how to button my pajamas, buckle my shoes, and tie my shoelaces. He even concocted creative costumes for me to wear for fancy dress (costume) parties, and those annual, festive Purim celebrations at the Jewish nursery school I attended. It was he who arranged my memorable birthday parties, with fancy printed invitations, hand-drawn signs to direct my schoolmates to the right apartment, and fun games like innovative treasure hunts. It was the caretaking, artistic Mr. Piat who chronicled all my "firsts" in elegantly handwritten entries in my pink baby book, inserting telegrams from well-wishers, photos, and cutout magazine illustrations for added decoration. Even the delicate wisps of brown hair from my first haircut I gave myself at age four can still be found in its labeled envelope. For the nostalgic Mr. Piat, the photographer and custodian of all documents marking any milestone or achievement, everything was for recording and safekeeping.

But there were also those embarrassing "Ugh, Shame!" moments. "Ugh, shame!" was a frequently used South African expression to impart a combination of pity and empathy. On the way to the beach, near the Marine Hotel, was a giant billboard advertising a popular sunscreen lotion. There she was, that oversized copper-toned little girl whose pesky little brown dog had pulled down her bikini bottom, revealing her backside, her pale *tochus,* to show off her tan line. Ugh, shame! I felt so embarrassed for her. I knew how she felt. Exposed for the whole world to see.

One day, my father, the only man sitting with all the mothers and their maids with their children at the beach, took off my wet bathing suit from my three-year-old body and realized he had forgotten to pack a change of dry underwear for me. Standing, waiting in my nakedness, I watched my father ask some nearby mothers for a spare diaper. When it became clear that no one could help us out, he shook out his ever handy large white handkerchief with the blue X.P. initials, folded it into the familiar triangular shape of a lady's scarf and positioned it on me like a diaper, tying the ends into knots at the sides of my tiny hips. Voila, a new bikini bottom! Even at that young age, I had the distinct impression that wearing my father's handkerchief over my private parts wasn't exactly normal. Far too young to appreciate the creative resourcefulness of my genius god, I was not too young to feel the embarrassment of being different.

And then that fateful day of The Haircut. I was twelve. My mother was away performing in the United States on Broadway with Jacob Jacobs, a big name in Yiddish theatre. My father, now the uncontested, unmitigated dictator, decided that my hair was to be cut short. I don't even recall if he chopped my hair off himself with the long silver scissors he used to slit open envelopes, or if he took me to his barber. Probably the latter. No doubt I repressed the offending incident. All I remember is the tight knot in my stomach when I saw my new reflection in the mirror after the dreadful deed was done. The freckle-faced boy staring back at me was not the pretty girl I longed to be. On my head was a helmet of unrecognizable wiry hair that looked like a bad wig. My beautiful long, silky, straight hair I loved to wear in a ponytail, and feel bouncing against the nape of my neck, had disappeared. Instead, I was left with a frizzy mop that my father insisted on smoothing down with globs of his hair gel, called Brylcreem. At the tender age of twelve, when my deepest desire was to feel feminine and look beautiful, I was stuck with an ugly haircut that made me look like a boy. Ugh, shame! There was no recourse, no argument, no going back. Not with this father, who could demolish me with a threatening look if I dared offend him and whose anger could explode into an ambush of fearful shouting and spankings meant to teach me to behave. Buried beneath my devotion to the handsome man I called Daddy lay terror and shame. Father knew best, no matter that I felt the worst. After that haircut, I banished into exile my childish adoration of the father who would be mother. Gone was the close bond we once had. Chop-chop. Scissors over paper.

Like skin molting from a snake, we began our separation. Where once tiny hands clasped around Daddy's firm neck with fierce devotion, now came folded arms and angry, sullen stares to protect my soft heart on the inside from the severity of the hard taskmaster on the outside, whose restrictive curfews and demands to know where I was going and with whom clashed with my lust for freedom. The girl with the short bobbed hair, budding breasts, and sprouting opinions, began honing the art of questioning and the skills of debating. Discussions became arguments. Arguments became accusations. Accusations became poundings of a father's fist on the dinner table, and "I hate you" hissed under a daughter's breath. The gremlin duo of Guilt and Resentment moved in, hanging the invisible "Do Not Disturb" sign on the bedroom door they slammed shut.

My former hero was now doubted, discarded, disdained, and dismissed in words I used as weapons. Recklessly, I turned random, long-haired young men with frayed bellbottom jeans and smooth talk into covert coconspirators in romance. I made it easy for them to steal my heart, heavy with remorse, where a part of me still remained Daddy's little girl.

As soon as I graduated from college, I left home and traveled to Europe, courtesy of my benevolent king. Was it any accident that the place I chose for my pursuit of happiness and exploration of independence happened to be the country that bore his birth name, the place that had symbolized hope and liberation to the once idealistic young man, caught in the snares of anti-Semitic Europe? While my mother stayed at home with my younger sister, my father came to visit me in Jerusalem, reinstating our past ritual of daddy-daughter duo spending summertime together.

A couple years later, when I brought home a tall, dark-haired, handsome young man, my father expressed his pleasure. "I put my eye on him," he divulged years later. "When he walked in the door, I said to myself, '*That* one I like!'" I wouldn't put it past him if my father took the naive and friendly Johannesburg born man secretly aside and made him an attractive offer to marry his still single firstborn. In the days of no more dowry, who knows what gifts—aside from his precious daughter—were promised.

When the much-awaited wedding took place at the opulent Nelson Hotel at the foot of Table Mountain, my mother beamed at her bridge club friends, relieved that she could stop worrying about her oldest daughter remaining an old maid, never to marry. At age 24, *Gott tsu dunken, Tanks Gott in himmel, ptu, ptu, ptu*, I was finally off the dreaded "spinster" shelf. Mr. Piat, the confirmed teetotaler, sipped a glass of champagne in celebration and, drunk with joy, kicked up his heels and danced the *horah* and the *kazutzka* with delirious abandon. I don't think he considered that my marriage meant the loss of his beloved daughter. For him, he was gaining what he'd always wanted—a son.

The marriage, of course, was my gift to my parents to compensate for their lost world. Just as *my* happiness was, no doubt, one of my parents' main goals, *their* happiness was no less a priority in my life. Wasn't that why I was born? To make up for what was taken away? To be their source of renewal and solace? To bring them *naches*, the perfect Jewish blend of joy and pride, and the bright promise of grandchildren?

Mr. Piat had performed his fatherly duties exceedingly well. He had raised his daughter to think like a man, speak her mind, be curious about the world, and marry the son he had chosen for himself.

When I told him I wanted to leave South Africa, he was quick to offer his support. "Do not stay for our sake. Do not do as I did. Go make your own destiny," the farsighted, worldly Mr. Piat said to me. Perhaps he enjoyed the idea of my fulfilling a former dream of his, to emigrate to America. He also understood that the child he had raised could not in full conscience begin a new family in what I considered to be a morally reprehensible, racially divided South Africa. The country that had once opened its splendid harbor to welcome a couple of Jewish war refugees had become, in my time, a police state, ruled by a brutal, totalitarian, fear-inducing minority government. Rock over scissors.

The institutionalized prejudice I witnessed in the streets was unbearable to me. I rationalized how my parents were loath to pull up roots from the beautiful place that had given them comfort and acceptance after their ordeals. But for me, it was crystal clear: As a Jew, a daughter of Holocaust survivors, I no longer wished to live in a country that governed its citizens by prejudice and persecution, where the guilt of oppression weighed heavily on us all. I had expressed my views about wanting to leave South Africa to the man who would become my husband. Anticipating the waves of revolution, most of my school friends and peers who objected, as I did, to the crimes of humanity around us, began making plans to emigrate, looking to start their adult lives overseas, preferably in other English-speaking countries, such as the U.S., Australia, England, and Canada. I knew my destination: America, land of the free—choices, home of the brave—voices.

Gratefully aware that my emigration was being undertaken in vastly different circumstances from those of my father, I came as a newlywed to the U.S. on a one-way ticket and student visa. Two years later, I was seven months' pregnant with my first child, and settling down nicely into our first new home outside Boston. It was upon my return from a Labor Day weekend vacation in Cape Cod with my in-laws that I received a surprise long-distance phone call from my younger sister in Cape Town. Her usually sweet voice sounded strained. "Sorry, I don't know how to tell you this, but Mom's dead." From across the ocean, her words rattled and jangled in my ear.

I was stunned. I didn't even know my mother was sick, let alone dying. I was busy excitedly preparing for her visit to the States, to Boston, to witness the birth of her first grandchild. All I knew from our communications, either through letters or our rather limited, expensive long-distance calls, was that she was starring as Golda in the national theatre's production of *Fiddler on the Roof.* That perfect tailor-made role for my authentic Yiddish mama was to be her swan song. True to form, she kept her cancer a secret, and her pain hidden from her audiences and most of her fellow actors until close to the end. "On with the show!" she went, smiling, singing, and dancing her way through each performance, night after night, to the chorus of "To life, to life, l'chaim!" until the end of the run. When the doctors informed her that her time had come, she specifically told my father and my sister not to tell me. A few weeks after the show ended, she was pronounced dead of ovarian cancer in Groote Schuur hospital on September 1, 1979.

My sister's phone call arrived after the funeral. Apparently my superstitious, protective mother didn't want me to worry. Nothing bad, *ptu*, *ptu*, *ptu*, should happen to me or the baby, God forbid! Against his better judgment, my father had honored his beloved wife's dying wish and kept the bitter pact of secrets. Much later, I would hear from my mother's friends that she had desperately hoped to beat the odds and make it to America for the birth of my child. Mr. Piat, the one who had on so many occasions taken my mother's place in raising me, would be the only one to fly across the Atlantic to Boston to hold his precious first granddaughter in his arms, when she was born a couple months later. This time, when the tears rolled down his cheeks, we both knew it was not a sign of weakness.

Keeping the tradition, I named my first daughter in honor of my mother, choosing the French name Chantal, for its combination of the elements of my mother's first and last name and its reminder of her gift of song.

After my mother's death, my father turned his lonely Cape Town winters into lively father-daughter Boston summers, as he came to visit every year. We steadily grew closer again, helped by our respective maturing. My increasing appreciation of him happily coincided with his decreasing expectations of me. As a married woman, I felt I had gained a new level of respect in my father's eyes. With a husband and children, a dog, a home, a two-car garage, *and* a swimming pool, I had achieved what many refer to as the American dream. What more could this immigrant father want for his immigrant daughter? I too had what I wanted: a devoted and generous grandfather for my American-born children, some adult dignity for myself, and, at last, my father on *my* turf, which I naively imagined would enable me to dictate at last. However, old habits proved hard to change, and I fell into old patterns, instinctively reverting to putting my father's needs first. Besides, who I was kidding? In my world, Holocaust survivor trumps everything.

Then, just like that—a defining moment happens, when the things we take for granted simply change in a blink of an eye. One evening, I came into the den to tell my father, who was watching TV that dinner was about to be served.

◆ ◆ ◆

Vision

Scene: A summer's evening in Newton, Massachusetts: My father in my house, in the den, seated on the salmon-colored sofa. On the TV, the voice of the elegantly coifed blonde anchorwoman recites her usual list of bombings, fires, fatal crashes, and disasters that has become our daily bread.

Flashback: A summer's evening in Sea Point, South Africa. My father in his house, seated at the head of the dining room table. From the compact black portable AM-FM transistor radio, his lifeline to the world beyond the remote, coastal resort we call home, come the voices of all kinds of announcer "aunties" and "uncles," floating into our corner of the world on short-wave radio beams. Because the paranoid, censoring Afrikaner government will not allow TV into the country until the mid-1970s, it's those familiar disembodied voices from Springbok Radio, that accompany my father's activities from morning to night, feeding him his daily diet of information and entertainment. Hey, presto! Waving the magic, thin silver wand of an aerial, he conjures up Kol Israel, the "Voice of Israel," followed by a BBC bulletin, to dish our latest heaping of bad news, called current affairs, to prove the world is a dangerous place. Tuned into a male universe far greater and more significant than his small domestic realm, Mr. Piat expects his family of females to share his voracious appetite for world events. The news must be swallowed along with our tasty dinners of fried sole and steamed squash or grilled lamb chops and baked potatoes, and my favorite guava pudding dessert. With Mr. Piat, the king of the castle presiding, we three women along with Blackie, the mongrel, know our place at the table. No interrupting his trusted advisors reporting their international politics from the black plastic box! We would not want to spark yet another war.

Flash forward: The American voice from the TV in my den has lulled my father into an impromptu nap. Sitting straight-backed against the sofa, my father is fast asleep, his bare feet folded one on top of the other on the rug, his long slender toes gently touching. His head is drooped, his chin resting on his chest, his mouth a thin pencil dash, his slow breath barely audible.

I stand for a moment, looking at him sitting there in such calm repose.

Suddenly, a shadow passes over him. Before my eyes, the thin veil dividing the "here and now" from the "there, and then what?" lifts, and in an instant, a flash, I glimpse his imminent death. With a surge of psychic energy, I feel the powerful spiritual connection between us. I remember who he is.

Mr. Piat was my first true love.

Flashback: I am clinging to his neck in the water. I am listening to his stories at bedtime. I am perched up high on his shoulders, watching the blazing bonfires on the beach and the rainbow fireworks in the indigo night sky. I am feeling his hands wiping away my fever with a damp cloth and pressing my forehead as I vomit my various sicknesses into the toilet. My feet on his, I am dancing in my aquamarine polka-dot summer dress that he bought for me, after repeatedly insisting that he couldn't afford it. I am a little child, innocent and trusting, loving this man with all my heart and soul.

Scene: A desert in ancient Canaan. I am Abraham of old, the wide-eyed, ancient Hebrew worshiping his demanding god Yahweh of many names. When my commanding god with his booming voice and grandiose sneeze calls out my name, I must rise up quickly and offer myself in service, saying: "*Hineini.* Here I am. Present. What is it you want from me?" Sacrifice is required for a daughter dedicated to pleasing and appeasing her larger than life father, who dispenses Justice and Protection, Vengeance and Wisdom, all with the same terrible might and awesome majesty.

Flash forward: Everything becomes illuminated in that one still moment of my father's sleeping and my awakening. I see both past and future with new eyes. The man sleeping on the sofa sitting up is no longer a god to be worshipped and feared. He is a frail, mortal, aging man needing his midday nap, whose time on earth is running out. We are each other's beloveds, caught in the loop of the infinite light of love that sometimes gets switched off due to human error. Now I know why he returns to my home, summer after summer, enduring those exhaustive cross-Atlantic flights, to come stay with me in my *dacha.* Now I know who I am.

I am the granddaughter, "Vavka's dugh," the descendent spirit of his beloved, missed mother. I am the daughter, his precious possession, whom he nurtured and raised and gave away as a bride. I am the mother, the source of his grandchildren. I am the keeper of the flame of his memories. I am the fulfillment of a promise. I am the link in a long spiraling chain that goes both forward and backward. *Heneini.*

◆ ◆ ◆

I tiptoed quietly over to the TV to turn it off. My father awoke with a jolt. "What did you do?" he grumbled, frowning at me. "Why did you do that? Couldn't you see I was listening?" "Sorry, Dad," I murmured. I had made another mistake. It was not the noise of the TV that disturbed him, I realized. It was the silence. I should have known better: Let sleeping gods lie.

The Stepson

✦

Vilna, Poland, 1926–1939

Everything's relative, depending on which relative.

Sitting by the pool, my father continues his story. "But now I must tell you about something that changed our lives . . . about my father's good friend Bernstein who spent time at our house" he says, his tone turning serious. Before Zacharias left on his business travels, he would invite his friend Bernstein to the house to take care of his wife and son. As my father recalls, Bernstein, the owner of the only soda-water factory in Vilna was considered an eligible bachelor. "He was good-looking, always generous with money, a party person, a good dancer, and one who knew how to mix with different people," my father says.

"I am sure my father, who knew how much my mother enjoyed entertainment and going out on the town, told Bernstein, 'Please escort my wife while I am away. Vavushka must not be by herself. You know how she loves to dress up and go out to dances and film shows,'" my father says, imitating his father's voice. In Zacharias's absence, Bernstein did as he was asked. "I presume some kind of romance developed between them," he adds. "Anyhow, people began to talk, because when my father arrived home from one business trip, Grandfather Reuven called him to his home and told Father about the rumors about Mother and this man Bernstein."

My father remembers the charged atmosphere in their home. "It was not good," my father says. "Heavy silences. Sudden shouting. Mother crying. I knew something was wrong even though no one said a word about the situation to me. I suppose my father confronted my mother and demanded to know if there was any truth to the rumors about her and Bernstein. I don't know the details. I just know the ending. Not good. Not good at all. Father may have been a doctor, but he was not clever in love," my father adds. "And as he was not clever, his answer was to get a *get*—a Jewish divorce. The end of the story is that he gave Mother a quick Jewish divorce. How? Remember the Cohen sign I showed you? Well, Father, being a Cohen, spread out his hands in the sign, and said, 'I divorce you, I divorce you, I divorce you,' three times in front of witnesses. And so it was done."

I ask if the divorce was influenced by Grandfather Reuven. "Oh, most definitely so," agrees my father. "And my father's brother, Uncle Samuel and Aunt Sonya also. The whole family didn't accept Mother. She was too foreign for them, I think. Too unconventional. She was the type to wear a gold chain around her ankle. Very avant-garde with her fashion. The family believed Father could have married a rich woman from Vilna, perhaps even one of their friends. When my father divorced Mother, he told her: 'I will provide for you until you remarry, and I will care for my son,' which he did. Yah. He kept his promise well. He took good care of us financially. Oh, one other thing I remember. Something Mother said to me. I was young and couldn't understand what she meant, but I felt the urgency in her command. 'You must never in your life have anything to do with anyone by the name of Bernstein. Never in your life, you hear me? Promise me now!'"

At the tender age of six, my father became something rather uncommon in his day—a child of divorce. Zacharias moved out of their apartment into a large room of his own in his Uncle Simon's hotel, gave up his medical practice to work for a medical supply company, and traveled more frequently than ever. Soon after the divorce, Zacharias met and married a highly educated older woman, Rachel, a pediatrician, who moved in with him. My father's new stepmother, whom he addressed as Aunty Rachel, tried her best to be nice to her husband's young son. "But I never gave her the satisfaction of showing her any real affection," admits my father. "That special honor of my love I reserved only for Mother."

A year after the divorce, he says, Aunt Asya approached his mother with a proposal: "You know, now that Zacharias is getting married, what about you? You shouldn't be alone like this, with a young boy. *Pas nisht*. It's not suitable. You need a man in the house for both of you. Let me introduce you to my brother, Joseph. Maybe you'll like him," Asya, the wife of Zacharias's brother Sam and a well respected midwife who had helped with the birth of my father, kept trying to persuade Vava to marry her brother, who at 20 had left for Germany and France to avoid being called up to the Polish army. Now he was back home, living with his parents.

Vava was all alone in Vilna. The Bolshevik Revolution in Russia had prevented her from communicating with her family in St. Petersburg, and even if she wanted to, she could not return home. Bernstein had left town by now, and she was stranded, alone and vulnerable, stuck in a foreign country.

"I believe in a weak moment Mother must have given in to what seemed like a workable business arrangement. A family within the family. Something familiar. And so they got married, Mother and this Sor character," my father says with resignation, "and she took his last name, instead of Jutan."

When he was seven my father acquired a stepfather—a tall man with bright eyes that, according to him, looked in all directions for how to make a living. Between Vava and Joseph there was never any big love. It was a marriage of convenience—to have a man in the house. Soon, both mother and son realized that the marriage was a huge mistake. His new stepfather was away often, just as his father, Zacharias, had been, begrudgingly working as a traveling salesman in the Sor family framing business.

"Oh, Sor was good at keeping himself busy all the time," my father recalls contemptuously. "That family brought us one problem after another. Lots of *tsorus*—trouble and heartache. First of all, Joseph had an illegitimate son from a Jewish girl. Maybe this was the real reason he left town in the first place. His son, four years older than me, already had a criminal record, spending time in a juvenile correction home. Mother had to take care of Sor's son when he came to our apartment asking for money or food, especially when he knew his father was not at home. She was always kind to him and helped in the little ways that she could. Even though she told me not to report to my stepfather that his son had visited, I would, knowing I'd be in big trouble with Mother for doing so. I didn't care. I hated my stepfather, Joseph Sor, and I liked his mean, delinquent son even less," my father says.

"The happiest moments for my mother at that time were with her three friends, Dora, Anushka, who was also my father's first cousin, and Raya. The women, all single, would spend time together, at our home or on outings to cafes and nightclubs," my father says. "Mother called her trio of good friends 'The Three Mooskateers.' I could hear them from my room, always gossiping or laughing together in the living room," he adds, describing in detail the layout of his mother's apartment. His bedroom adjoined the living room, where his mother would take her nap in the afternoon on the *couchette,* he explained. When I ask him what *couchette* means, he explains that it's a Napoleon-style backless sofa, like a chaise. How odd, I think to myself. I've always fantasized about having one of those. (Many years later, after my own divorce, one of the first things I buy for the apartment in Manhattan is a beige *chaise longue*. Even in my taste for furniture, I seem to have incorporated my grandmother's spirit.)

My father had complained to me when he arrived at the airport that he was concerned about how with his advancing years he kept forgetting things. Yet here he was, retracing the exact details of a home he hadn't seen in six decades with the ease and agility of a young boy, sprinting away from trouble. "One night," he continues, "Mother put me to bed and said, 'You must not get out of the bed!'" Of course, my father did exactly the opposite. From his secret hiding place in the hall, he watched the furtive comings and goings of his mother's friend Raya and a well-dressed man in their apartment. Eventually he heard about the scandal that involved his Aunt Asya, who was being threatened and blackmailed by a young girl from her midwifery practice. Asya had come desperately seeking Vava's help in the matter to see if she could help her avoid going to court. Summoning her *troika* of well-connected friends, Vava shared her sister-in-law's potential lawsuit problem with them. A solution was proposed, and Vava arranged for a clandestine rendezvous between Raya and one of Raya's paramours, a prominent judge, to take place in her home. The scheme worked. "In gratitude, Asya baked Mother a nice *babka*, presenting it to her with a little thank-you card," my father recalls.

This story of Vava helping out her frantic sister-in-law in the spirit of family looking out for family did not turn out as well as expected. Asya's husband, Samuel, confronted his older brother, Zacharias: "Well, I never imagined that in your home there would be a *bordello*!" he said. Flabbergasted, Zacharias enquired what he was talking about. "Oh, you know people. They meet and they chat," said Samuel, sharing the rumored gossip about the encounter between the judge and Raya in Vava's own apartment.

My father takes a break from his narration to sip his tea. Like an actor, the master raconteur has portrayed the parts of his mother, her "Mooskateer" friends, his father, and his uncle in his dramatic recreation of the family saga of his youth. When I had asked him to tell me stories from his young days in Vilna so I could better understand his background, I never expected to hear such riveting revelations about relations between relations. With a newfound awareness and appreciation of the complexities of large families, I wait for my father to continue with his true-life soap opera.

"Every now and then my parents, still on good speaking terms you see, would meet at Mother's apartment to discuss things about me," he says. "The next time they met, my father said to Mother, 'Vava, tell me: What is this story that I hear about you and your friends arranging liaisons in your home?' Mother explained how Aysa, terrified of possibly losing her license, had appealed to her to use her connections. 'Raya came up with an excellent plan involving her friend the judge. A little bit of money exchanged hands and *c'est tout.*' My father looked at her and said plainly: 'You should not have interfered. You should not have helped them in that way.'"

Zacharias, usually a mild-tempered man, was infuriated. He didn't approve of the way his younger brother Samuel conducted himself or his family business. Zacharias had bailed him out on several occasions and found it reprehensible that Samuel would treat him and his former wife with such disrespect, indulging in degrading gossip, and having the *chutzpah* to malign his own sister-in-law after she had helped his wife avoid a tricky situation. It was not his idea of how family should operate.

"The next day, after their talk, Mother went over to Asya's place to give them a piece of her mind, Vava style," my father says. "I don't know what transpired, but from that day on, Uncle Samuel never spoke to Mother again. He also suddenly stopped being nice to me. Every day, after school, I would go to Uncle Samuel's office to meet my father, who came from the city council offices, right across the street, with a book for me to read or to take me out to the Hotel Europa for a treat of hot chocolate with whipped cream and lots of cinnamon and sugar. But Uncle Samuel simply ignored me, like I wasn't there in his building at all. That was my life in those years: school and sitting in my uncle's long, dark office, the big portrait of the famous Yiddish writer Peretz hanging on the wall, and me waiting for my father, while my uncle walked by without even a 'hello.'"

In the early autumn of 1929, Zacharias Jutan, president of the World Association of Jewish War Invalids, Widows and Orphans for Europe, left for America on an important fundraising mission. "Oh, it was such a big event, splashed all over the Vilna newspapers, that my father was off to America to meet all the important people and to collect lots of money," my father says, his voice reflecting the pomp and ceremony. In New York, the children of his uncles who had left Vilna and settled in America met Zacharias at the docks. They in turn introduced him to more cousins and relatives. Zacharias sent an illustrated guidebook of New York by mail to his ten-year-old son back in Vilna. "Hours I would spend with that book, studying the big city, the streets, and famous buildings of the impressive metropolis of New York. Such joy I had, so many years later, when I first traveled to America, arriving in New York and I recognized the buildings I remembered so well from that book my father had sent me. And then, the same time my father was there raising money, the famous Wall Street collapse happened. My father, the doctor, the president of the association, the esteemed councilman, in order to eat a meal, had to wash dishes in a Bronx restaurant. What a humiliation! What disillusionment!"

Zacharias returned to Vilna a broken man with bitter memories and hardly any money, not for the widows, not for the orphans, and not even for himself. America, the famed Golden Land as many believed it to be, with its streets rumored to be paved with gold, turned out not to be the country of riches he thought he would find, but a country of false fantasy, where one day you were a millionaire and the next you were a pauper or, even worse, a man jumping to his death from the top of a tall building. "Yah, my father came back a sad, disappointed man," my father says, shaking his head. "But he was lucky. He recovered. My father's new brother-in-law, Mr. Tunkiel, Aunty Rachel's brother, who had married into a wealthy family and was made managing director of a private bank, helped him get back on his feet. But when it came to Mother, it was a different story. She was not so lucky. She had nothing but heartache from her new husband, Sor."

His parents came to an agreement that at the age of thirteen my father would leave his mother's home and live with his father and his stepmother in their new home on Ludwisarka Street in the center of town. The second-floor apartment, which had a surgical office and waiting room for the woman he still called Aunty Rachel, was near the entrance to the University of Stefan Batory and faced the magnificent Napoleon's Palace. "Because Aunty Rachel did not cook, my father and I used to lunch every day after school at the Hotel Europa, a beautiful, big, classic, old hotel. They knew me there—the teenaged schoolboy who met his father for lunch during the week."

Rachel, a pediatrician with a deep concern and caring for children, tried her best to educate her stepson. By his own admission, as kind and motherly as she was to him, he remained disdainful and unappreciative. "In my young mind, Aunty Rachel did not deserve my feelings of gratitude for all the nice things she did for me, so I was deliberately ungrateful and unkind to her," he says. After all, he rationalized, she was not his true mother, to whom he owed his sole allegiance. Nor was she, in his adolescent eyes, as glamorous, creative, or excitingly dramatic as the outspoken Vava. "I recall Mother saying something I never fully understood at the time. I was eight when I heard her mutter: 'It didn't help her. I wished her to have stones, and so she had a miscarriage.'" At the time, my father couldn't imagine why his mother wished for his father's new wife to have stones. Perhaps it was the reason she was so fat, he thought, because of all the stones stored in her body. Later he understood. His mother had wished the woman who married her former husband to be barren, wanting her son to be the only heir of Zacharias Jutan, the prominent citizen of Vilna.

Vava got her wish. "I was to remain an only child forever," my father says.

The Student

✦

Vilna, Poland, 1930–34

In our search for a father's love, we try to find it in religion.

Israel Jutan, the only son of Jewish councilman Zacharias Jutan, was sent to an all-boys Catholic high school, called in some European countries a *gymnasium*, and which my father pronounces as *gim-nah-zi-oom*. It was situated on Dominikanska Street, opposite the Dominican church, a five-minute walk from his Uncle Samuel's advertising office and apartment, where he would meet his father in the afternoons.

The priests in the school instilled in their pupils a love of Latin, a respect for history, and an appreciation for the beauty of the Polish language and its literature. While the majority of the Catholic students were attending their obligatory religious services, the eight Jewish boys in his class of forty pupils were taught Jewish history by a special tutor. My father took his studies seriously, especially languages. He could produce a Latin proverb for most any occasion. His facility with languages and his fondness for solemnly commenting on life with Latin quotes, like a judge issuing his sentences, made him appear extremely knowledgeable in my young eyes. Having studied high school French rather than Latin, I can recall only one phrase from my father's list of favorites: *De gustibus non disputandem:* "When it comes to taste there is no point in arguing," he translated. I came up with my own saying: *With Mr. Piat, non disputandem.*

My father enjoyed his academic studies. Sports, however, was a different story. His mother, concerned for her son's physical safety, had refused to allow him to participate in rough activities, so when his high school gymnastics teacher give him the position of goalkeeper on the soccer team, he figured it was a mean spirited punishment for being so weak in sports. "Against all expectations, particularly my own, I got accustomed to that position and proved to be a good goalkeeper. I learned to keep my feet moving, my eyes on the ball, and my hands ready to grab whatever the enemy aimed my way." He also surprised himself by excelling in the 100-meter races, winning some sprinting competitions by sheer willpower, despite what he considered the handicap of his thin legs. However, the teenaged Israel Jutan preferred exercising his imagination far more than his muscles. A more worthwhile pursuit, he believed, was the aim of scoring points on paper with far-reaching words.

"Our school was named after Adam Mickiewicz, one of Poland's renowned national poets, whose early-18th-century poems extolled the pride and passion of Polish nationalism, inspiring the fight for independence. We had to read and study the marvelous book *Pan Tadeusz* by Mickiewicz in which there was even a story about Jankiel, the Jewish fiddler, who was invited to the royal court to play at the baron's castle for weddings and other ceremonies. The story was especially meaningful for me and the other seven Jews in our class, because it validated our existence. It made me happy that a celebrated Pole had paid tribute to a Jew in a story written for all to read. What pleased me more was that it was the priests who taught us about Mickiewicz, this lover of Jews."

My father's thirteenth year was spent learning the rituals required for his *bar mitzvah* with his fellow Jewish students, and thinking about members of the opposite sex, whom he would meet briefly at parties.

"I kept wondering about my father's saying that I was 'the chosen of the chosen' and Mother's pronouncement of my being 'lucky in love,'" he continues. "But how could I be lucky in love when I was such a pale, serious little boy with a slight stutter, skinny legs, thin eyebrows, delicate hands, and no shapely muscles?"

Socializing with girls was a new venture for the shy boy. He recalls one particular nighttime party of a school friend of his, Izaak, who was six months older. Izaak's mother, a small, pretty woman, greeted him at the door, handing him a glass of lemonade and a piece of cake. Knowing none of the girls, he kept close to the other boys. When thirteen-year-old Izaak opened the pathefon, an early gramophone, and played the music of tangos and slow foxtrots and waltzes, Izaak's mother, noticing my father standing awkwardly off to the side, approached him. Ignoring his apologetic protestations that he had never learned to dance, the determined hostess began to show him how to do the slow waltz. "I was very embarrassed, trembling, shy, and nervous, with a dry mouth, but she took a strong hold of me, and I followed her lead," my father recalls. Once he had overcome his reticence, quickly picking up the steps of both the waltz and the foxtrot, she thrust him into the arms of Izaak's young cousin. Staring at his new dance partner, a girl his own age, he nervously moved in total silence, hoping nobody would notice his mistakes in the semidarkness. "That," smiles my father, "was my introduction to dancing and to teenage girls." Firmly resolving not to limit himself in his choice of dancing partners at subsequent parties, the budding Don Juan went on to coax many a hovering mother or observing aunt onto the dance floor to perfect his moves.

"My own *bar mitzvah* was not relevant for me. I did not have a party. First, it was too far for the boys in my class to come, and, second, I was not interested in all that Jewish rite-of-passage stuff. It was something I did purely for my father's sake. He insisted on it. Secretly, I knew it was really for Grandfather Reuven, but truthfully, my heart was not in it," admits my father. Preparing for his *bar mitzvah* entailed going across town to the poorer area in the Jewish section, crossing the narrow cobblestoned streets, and ascending the stairs of a ramshackle wooden building where an old Hasidic rabbi bombarded him with foreign phrases sung to a particular tune. Sitting at the rickety wooden table, writing down the strange Hebrew words in Latin phonetics, my father easily picked up the melody. The required Torah passage he learned from his helpful transliterations.

The simple *bar mitzvah* took place at the small, old *shul*, a short walk from his first home on Arsenalska Street, opposite the basement bakery where he used to get his breakfast buns in Garbarska Street with his old governess. It was where his father, the president of that intimate Orthodox synagogue, used to take him as a child for the High Holidays or on Saturdays for the Shabbat services. "You see, in that little *shul* I was not afraid," he adds. "What was there to be afraid of?" I ask. He looks at me in surprise. The synagogue, he explains, was a humble-looking two-story building, cozy and comfortable, like a normal home, very different from the imposing churches and cathedrals that had so intimidated him. "You see, I had been going to cathedrals with my governess from the age of three, before I ever stepped into a *shul*," he reminds me. "She was a devout Catholic, of course, with a big cross hanging from her neck. Every day, she would take me out for a walk to the little shops and cafés and bistros. On the way home, we would stop at the big, dark cathedral near Arsenalska Street, where she would pray. She instructed me not to kneel like her but to stay standing. While she closed her eyes to say her silent prayers, I did what she said—stood very still in that enormous place, looking up at the huge, pointy ceiling. Everywhere I looked, stone faces stared back at me: statues of dead barons and knights, all frightening to me. I had nightmares of them springing to life, chasing after me because I had not prayed properly to them. Soon enough, after our many visits, I already knew the prayers by heart."

When he was a little older, he would accompany his father on special occasions to the Great Synagogue on Niemiecka Street, (German Street) which could hold a thousand people. My father recalls a recent trip to Israel, where he saw a model replica of that Great Synagogue of Vilna displayed on a big table at the Museum of the Communities. An architect named Trotzki had donated it to the museum, having constructed it from memory of the papier mâché model of the synagogue he had once made as a child in the Vilna Ghetto. "It was perfect," my father says. "Every little detail exactly as I remembered. The cardboard model brought it all back to me. I stood there, and I cried." Struggling to hold back fresh tears, my father pauses. It seems as if he is taking a moment to pay silent tribute to a house of worship he visited only occasionally. But I know better. For my father, the non-observant Jew, the synagogue did not represent the religion that, through no choice of his own, marked him for death, but rather the cherished childhood memory of precious moments spent with his revered father.

His years from age thirteen to fifteen were lonely ones. Moving in with his father and stepmother meant moving away from friends who lived far from the commercial area of his father's new home. Even though he now spent more time in the company of his father, books became his new best friends. He tells me that the best part of his daily routine of school days was walking home from the house of his stepmother's sister, after having lunch there, the only boy, surrounded by aunts and his new stepcousins, all of whom were female. He enjoyed the long, solitary walk home down the steep hill to the *holtzmart*, an open-air marketplace, with stalls stacked full of cases of assorted fishes and boxes of fresh fruits and vegetables, the delicious wafting aromas stimulating his senses. His favorite place was the small secondhand bookshop, where he'd stop and browse. Sometimes he would buy books that brought the exciting wide-open spaces of North America, with its lore of cowboys and Indians, into my father's rather boring, urban Eastern European life. To him, their musty smell was the seductive fragrance of other worlds. Those books were his passports to the big, brave world that he knew lay beyond his beautiful Vilna.

At the time, little did he suspect that before too long, the outside world of foreigners would invade his world as he knew it, and change his life forever.

The Philatelist

✦

Vilna, Poland, 1929
Cape Town, South Africa, 1952–98

The stamps of approval or hate that we collect may be perforated around the edges, but they still stick.

"It was Mother who started me with my lifelong passion for stamps," announces my father.

On his tenth birthday, Vava gave her son an old book of Russian stamps, telling him about the Bolshevik Revolution and how important it was that her only child appreciate the historical value of the stamps of that revolutionary era. Her older brother, a violinist, the uncle he never had an opportunity to meet, had also collected stamps, she told him. Pointing out the stamps pertaining to the two significant years in her life, 1918 and 1919, she explained that the first was when she left St. Petersburg with his father to come to Poland, and the second marked the year of his birth, when she began collecting stamps for him.

"Of course at that age," he says, "I did not understand what she was trying to impart to me, but to please her I kept the old book with stamps printed in Cyrillic. One day at school, I saw two boys exchanging stamps and told them about my collection. Next day, I brought in my stamps and swapped some of my duplicates for their German and Polish stamps." Sitting in his Uncle Samuel's advertising office one afternoon, waiting for his father, he was busy glancing through his stamps when Samuel's teenage son, his older cousin David, approached him. "Follow me," he said, leading him upstairs to his room above the office in their apartment. From his bookshelf, David took out a big album and proceeded to display his book about Germany that bulged with pages for every stamp issued by the country up to 1925. David, a university student and fervent Zionist, was planning to immigrate to the still uncultivated Palestine, and had started collecting stamps on the topic of agriculture. Giving my father some of his duplicate stamps, David showed him how to use the tiny, black, glued corners called hinges to place the stamps in a new album. My father was hooked. Soon he was buying stamps from the old dealer at the stationery shop at the *holtzmart,* studying how to sort, research, value, and exchange the stamps through the mail, and competing with his schoolmates to see who had the most stamps. "For my *bar mitzvah,* Mother gave me a new stamp album," my father says. "When I moved from Mother's apartment to live with my father, before I packed that album together with my clothing in the suitcase, I counted every single stamp I had. My collection had reached 3,500."

At sixteen, Israel Jutan became one of the youngest members ever accepted into the local Philatelic Club. In 1937, his World War I overprints exhibit made its way to the Vienna stamp exhibition, where he was awarded a bronze medal. In just a few years, however, those precious stamps—a source of such pride and happiness—would become the cause of much heartache.

"It was 1941," my father says. "One afternoon, a Lithuanian policeman and a man dressed in a long black leather coat arrived at my father's apartment asking for me. The civilian spoke to me in German, and the policeman translated everything. He introduced himself as a stamp collector who specialized in overprints of recent war years. A Vilna stamp collector had told him about my specialized assembly of 1914–1920 overprints, and he wished to see it."

My father was shocked by the unexpected visit. When he hesitated to bring out the album, the stranger's polite request turned into a threat. If my father did not surrender the album he would be taken to the police station for an investigation. And then, the German hinted in a menacing tone, his parents might be put in the position of having to exchange the collection for their son.

"'You won't need these stamps anymore,' he told me. 'Rather, hand it to me now, and we'll be friends—or have it be confiscated by the authorities,'" my father says in the accent of the Nazi.

"There he was, with a policeman. And there I was, home alone, a young man of twenty-two. What could I do? Of course, I handed my album to him," my father recalls, his voice betraying indignation. The German official gave him a receipt and took the collection, saying that if my father should ever need assistance, he could be found at the Gestapo office.

For a few nights after that surprise visit, my father did not sleep at home, for fear that they would come again and confiscate his other collections. Deciding to take matters into his own hands, he appealed to an old non-Jewish school friend to safeguard his other collections. At the time of the Nazi occupation, he managed to go to his friend's house to retrieve some of his stamps, which he traded with a stamp dealer for food. Taking great risk to leave the ghetto a second time, he returned for the rest of his stamps, and was horrified to discover that his friend and his collection had vanished.

"It still upsets me to recall that very first stamp incident," my father says. "How easy it was for that German stamp collector, knowing the value of my award-winning collection, to rob me with a polite threat, because he knew we Jews at that time had no recourse. I never in my life expected a stamp collector to be a bully. A football player or a boxer, perhaps, but a stamp collector, dealing with such delicate, fragile objects? No. That is how ignorant I was. That man was a Nazi, indoctrinated with propaganda and hate, and he was used to taking what he wanted. In those times, whatever you owned could be confiscated. It was a lesson for me," he says. "The material things we collect with such enthusiasm and pride, such love and attention, can and will often be taken from us. Sometimes we will be forced to give up those things we value most, so we understand that we can continue, we can live without them. You see, from the history books the priests gave me, and the hard knocks the Nazis gave me, I learned that the one with the most brute force, the biggest weapons, and the most determination is the one who dominates. That is how it is. Ugly but true. Legitimate ownership means nothing to a thug. They know your weakness—that you place your life and those you love above all else. Yah!"

My father lets out a long sigh before resuming.

"It tells you something about me, that after the war, when I was liberated in '45, near Lauenberg, Germany, I straightaway went to look for stamps after first securing for myself some clothes left abandoned by Germans. I was happy to find some stamp collections, too. A few months later, when I was looking for a job in another town, Bydgoszcz, I spotted a stamp shop and went inside to enquire about selling the collections I'd found. To my horror, I recognized one of the customers standing in that shop. It was the same German official who had stolen my prize-winning stamp collection during the occupation. I stood frozen, not knowing what to do. My heart was pounding, my head felt light. I almost fainted. I could barely ask for a glass of water. The German, in the meantime, left the shop. After a few minutes, once I had finished drinking the water to ease my nerves, I asked the shopkeeper if he knew anything about the man who left. 'Yes,' he told me. 'He is a *Volksdeutcher*, soon to be evacuated from here to Germany. He sold me a nice stamp collection.' I asked the shopkeeper where the man lived but he didn't know."

For a week after that, he paced up and down outside that shop on Twarda Street, hoping the German would return. Obsessed with watching the shop and its clients, he deliberated about going to the militia with his report. But whom would he complain to, the army or the administration staff? And what proof did he have to show? He didn't even know where this man lived. It was 1945. My emaciated father had barely survived the war. Seeing that man again brought him right back to that first upsetting incident, where he had felt so helpless, so robbed. Overcome with rage, he began plotting how to get his retribution. His mind urged him to pursue justice with a vengeance, but his body was too weak from the years of deprivation. He recognized that the authorities were already overloaded with more critical post-war problems, such as the influx of thousands of refugees, relocation challenges, fights in the hostels filled with displaced people from the Eastern frontiers, and attacks and robberies on Jews by the right-wing Poles in the streets. Moreover, the unsympathetic new Polish administration had openly expressed their disappointment that the Nazis had not finished their intended job, leaving them to deal with the "elements," their code for Jews. The level of hate and prejudice among the locals was now even greater than before the war. After much consideration, my father realized the futility of reporting the unprovable theft.

"Seeing that man brought back a flood of feelings," my father continues. "Such regret I had over the loss of my precious prize," he says. "All the injustice I had experienced! But then, slowly, stoicism took over. I began to see that Destiny, with a capital D, was like a giant umbrella over my head. Destiny in collaboration with Fate. That combination of D and F is what allows me to go ahead in life, sometimes to stumble, sometimes to run faster, not always on a smooth surface, but still reaching the milestones of my life of the next birthdays to celebrate, the new friendships to establish, the old illnesses to conquer, the vacations to plan and the losses to put behind me. Even when I suffer from financial losses hitting me hard in the pocket, and I have had my share, trust me, my D-F philosophy is a driving force, urging me to continue. '*Abi gezunt!*' As long as I am healthy. Most important. Nothing else is worth the worry. All this, I learned the hard way—

through my losses. So I decided, then and there, after the war, to resign myself and accept that I would never see my collection again. I would not let myself cry over that collection."

What began as a childhood pastime would become a lifetime passion for my father. He may have been robbed of his precious collection, but no one could take away his lasting knowledge, experience, and joy of collecting stamps. After arriving in Cape Town in 1951, he lost no time in scouting out the stamp shops and spent his lunchtimes pursuing his hobby with his previous ardor. Steadily, he gained a reputation as an expert on stamps and, in 1952, appeared in a cover photo and frontpage news article in the "Talk of the Times" section of a Cape Town magazine. In 1953, he published the first bilingual *South African Stamp Album*, aimed at younger collectors, selling over 2,000 copies. His weekly column on stamps in *Die Jongspan*, the Afrikaans newspaper's special youth section, led to a regular column in the prestigious *Cape Argus* paper for which he won an award from the South African Philatelic Federation. "Stamp collecting," he said, "is the hobby of kings and the king of hobbies." Writing for children, he encouraged them to pursue the royal hobby that would educate them about the world: "I am the world's greatest traveler. I use every land, sea, and air conveyance, even submarine, balloon, and rocket—and sometimes even pigeons carry me. I frame the horrors of wars, the blessings of peace, and the hardship of emigration. I reflect the symbols of art and culture, natural resources, the development of industry and trade, agriculture, and all human endeavor. Yet, I am only a postage stamp. Such a small item, but what a vast world of knowledge." The enterprising Mr. Piat soon turned his hobby into an educational and lucrative sideline, organizing clubs for junior philatelists, even arranging for them to attend traditionally adult-only stamp conventions. Introducing his band of substitute sons to a world beyond their provincial hometown, he encouraged his *bar mitzvah* boys to spend their pocket money on the first day covers of the newly formed state of Israel, teaching them that if they collected wisely, their stamps could be worth a fortune some day. It was important for

Jews, the Holocaust survivor taught them, to have both transportable material assets and a permanent physical homeland.

I imagine that stamp collecting was a kind of meditation for my father. Requiring slow, meticulous and precise care and attention, the activity must have been calming for one who could be so instantly riled. Sitting for hours, listening to the radio, undisturbed in his study at home, the king would quietly occupy his time with his hobby. In the regal act of placing stamps from different countries next to one another in little books or envelopes, Mr. Piat was creating tangible albeit miniature proof that his dream of international peace, at least on paper, could be achieved.

"These we call 'veergins,'" he explained, showing me the unmarked stamps and pointing out the artistry and idiosyncrasies of the various stamps he spread out in display on his desk. He had given me a beginner's stamp album for my tenth birthday, hoping I would share his philatelic passion. Regrettably for him, his offspring did not inherit his patience or compulsion to collect and carefully sort such flimsy, fragile things. I had watched him for years pick up the stamps with his tweezers, examine them under the magnifying glass for irregularities or flaws, insert them carefully in their transparent album sleeves, and research their value in books and magazines from all over the world. Endowed with far too much nervous energy for that kind of focused attention, I preferred making a mess with paints to putting things in order. Besides, I felt sorry for the stamps, cooped up inside their preassigned pockets in closed albums. "Ugh, Shame!" Wouldn't those stamps be happier on the edges of envelopes, flying off to all corners of the world?

When it came to his side business of selling used stamps, the king of the king of hobbies had no compunction about putting his two daughters to work. My sister and I were forced by his royal command to join him in the tedious task of soaking, drying, and bundling piles of used stamps torn from mounds of old postcards my father brought home from various sources in overflowing garbage bags. Any virgin stamps found were to be reused as postage. In my father's world, nothing went to waste. Not even time. Idle hands were put to work. Before recycling was even a word or a fashionable concept, Mr. Piat, the *greeneh*, the Yiddish word for greenhorn or naïve new immigrant, had already taught his daughters how to think and act green to potentially bring in more green, as in money. When I moved to America, my instructions were clear. I was to stick as many stamps of every denomination as possible on the letters I sent back to South Africa. I knew the fate of those poor stamps. Torn, soaked, dried, and bundled, they'd be sold to the highest bidder.

I may not have picked up Mr. Piat's fervor for stamps, but for better or for worse I inherited his abhorrence of waste and his mastery in conservation and recycling. For Mr. Piat, every scrap of paper was precious. His desk drawers were crammed with assortments of envelopes, ballpoints, and all sizes of rubber bands, even collections of broken pencils stuffed into salvaged cigar boxes given to him as gifts. God forbid we should run out of stationery supplies! Napkins from restaurants and correspondence paper from hotels and even airplanes came home in his pockets. (In those distant days when letter writing was the common form of long-distance communication, airplane companies offered lightweight, logo-imprinted stationery for their passengers to use.) Every inch of any letter I received from him would be covered with his neat handwriting crawling up sideways along the pages to employ all available space. War had trained Mr. Piat to live by sheer wit and extreme efficiency. He gave his girls strict orders: "Switch off the lights!"; "Finish your food!"; "Take short showers!"; "Borrow books from the library!"; "Reuse the paper!"; and "Don't waste the water!" I graduated *cum laude* in the art of frugality and saving.

"Who would have thought that when Mother gave me my first album and David gave me his old collection that I would start an adventure with a hobby that would bring me so much joy and also so much suffering?" muses my father. Now I understand his love affair with stamps. They were a link to his mother and her family. They were his tiny picture passports to exotic lands he thought he would never visit. His treasured stamps had proven to be extremely valuable in times of trouble. Easy to collect, easy to hide, they could buy you a crust of bread or your family's freedom.

After my father's death, my sister and I returned to Cape Town to clear out his apartment—a Herculean task, given his fondness for collecting and his aversion to throwing things away. We now had to decide what to keep, give away, or sell. Wading though his various collections of stationery, photos, books, *New Yorker* magazines, old cameras, broken radios, bills and receipts, and other paraphernalia, I came across a gift I had bought him for a recent birthday. When I had first caught sight of it hanging in a little gift shop, I was ecstatic. What a coup—a single item combining two of my father's great loves! It was a dark blue satin necktie covered with pictures of postage stamps of Marilyn Monroe, the movie star he adored.

For my sixth birthday, my father presented me with a brand-new plastic doll with short platinum blonde hair, brown eyes, and long lashes that opened and closed if you tilted her head just right. He had bought that particular doll, he told me, because she resembled the angelic Marilyn Monroe, whose picture hung on his office wall. I should definitely name her Marilyn, he said persuasively to the girl who wished to please her daddy. I imagine he felt a kinship with the pinup girl's inherent loneliness and craving for recognition. Maybe he admired her tenacity and capacity for reinventing herself, for rising above her humble beginnings to the stature of sex goddess and movie icon. Perhaps he loved her so, because of how unashamedly she revealed her emotions, flaunted her sensuality and exposed her tender vulnerability. Whatever it was, I regret not asking him about his infatuation with Marilyn. I just remember that when he heard the news of her death on the radio he broke down and cried and mourned her loss for days.

When I found the tie hanging in the wardrobe of his seaside apartment it was still in the ready-to-wear knot he'd made. Holding it in my hands I could not bring myself to give or throw it away. It had its own indeterminable sentimental value. I brought home Mr. Piat's Marilyn, knot intact.

The Zionist

✦

Vilna, Poland, 1934–39

Evil triumphs only when we are robbed of our words.

By the time my father entered his adolescence in the 1930s, Europe was a wave of *isms.* Nationalism, Socialism, Marxism, Communism, and Zionism were sweeping the continent, and charismatic leaders with visions of idealized societies were casting their spells in written and spoken words, rallying groups together—most often against other groups. In Poland, anti-Semitism seemed more popular than ever, perpetuating the longstanding tradition of targeting Jews as the convenient scapegoat for any political or economic problem. For Polish schoolboys, it became a national sport.

The eight Jewish boys in my father's high school class soon put into practice the lesson of the Latin proverb *in unitate fortitudo*—"in unity there is strength"—figuring out that the best way to protect themselves from the daily bullying was to stick together. They arranged to meet after school, walk home, study, and complete their homework as a group. The solidarity effort paid off in security and in test scores, with each of them placing in the top ten of their class. Education had always been highly valued in their Jewish homes. "People can take everything away from you, but not your education!" repeated my father when I was in school. With an education, you could make a living anywhere in the world. That, he knew, was important, especially for a Jew.

A few of the more aggressive Polish boys, those who had taunted their Jewish classmates by stealing their food and squirting ink on their clothes, got wind of the special after-school study group and asked to be included. My father and his friends deliberated about allowing them in and devised a plan. "We said to those bullies: 'We'll tell you exactly what we are doing so that you will also be well prepared for school work. But on one condition: You must be our guards! If anyone threatens or attacks us, you will have to stand up for us and protect us.' The bullies agreed. Soon the whole atmosphere changed. We would stay after school in the classroom and work with those boys. Everyone was pleased, including the priests. So we made our bargain, and it worked well for us," my father nods, smiling.

Only one Polish gentile boy in that study group was genuinely friendly to my father: Jerzy Hajdukiewicz, a tall blond fellow, the son of a banker, who lived near him in Arsenalska Street. They would walk home together from school, discussing their shared interests of stamps, reading, and politics. One day, Jerzy invited his new friend to his house. When they arrived, a maid opened the door and showed them in. Immediately, Jerzy went over to his mother and greeted her by kissing her hand. When she stretched out that same hand toward her son's new friend, my father did what he knew to be the customary, polite thing. He took her hand and shook it. Coolly, she asked him where he was from and what his name was. "Israel Jutan," he replied. She turned to her son, and said promptly: "Jerzy, you have to go upstairs now. You don't have time to entertain your guest, so I'm afraid he will have to go home." With a polite "thank you for coming," my father was shown out by the maid. The door was shut firmly behind him. The next day at school Jerzy informed my father that he could no longer play with him. His mother had said that anyone who did not know the proper etiquette of kissing a lady's hand could not come to her house. My father's initial embarrassment soon turned to upset, then blame, when it dawned on him that it was because of his last name that he was not welcome in their home. He was angry with Jerzy for not telling him about the hand-kissing custom and even angrier that his mother's veiled anti-Semitism prevented him from visiting his friend. Nevertheless, my father tells me, they still managed to remain friends without going to each other's houses. It was Jerzy to whom my father would later turn for help in hiding his precious stamp collection and who would disappoint him a second time.

My father was walking back from school one afternoon when a rowdy group of Polish boys ambushed him, beating him mercilessly. With his jet-black hair, soft pale skin, and largish nose, Israel Jutan had what was widely considered a typically Jewish look. Unfortunately, his school uniform with the Catholic school crest on the arm of the jacket was of no help in preventing him from being attacked and called names by the young thugs who punched and kicked him into the pavement, yelling, "*Zyd parch,* Jewboy! You killed Jesus Christ! You murderer, you! We'll make you pay for that!"

Passing by on the other side of the road, another boy, bigger than my father, saw the attack, ran over and jumped in to fight off the bullies, sending them scurrying away. Helping my father back on his feet, he lent him his handkerchief to wipe his bloody nose and asked what had happened. My father was taken aback when his rescuer, who didn't look Jewish at all, said: "You can't let this keep happening. You must belong to a club of fighting Jewish boys. We Jews cannot allow ourselves to be victims of these bullies any longer. Don't you agree?"

The boy introduced himself as Mishka Smolgowsky and accompanied my father back home across the Green Bridge to Kalwaryska Street, where Zacharias and his new wife now lived in a big one-storey house in the poorer section of town. His humanitarian father had established their new surgical offices on the ground floor to make their medical services more accessible to the poor and needy. It turned out that Mishka, my father's defender, lived nearby, in a large apartment over his father's restaurant, at the entrance to the Green Bridge near the river Wilja. The newfound neighbors soon became fast friends.

It was Mishka who introduced him to Betar, the right-wing militaristic Zionist youth movement spearheaded by Ze'ev Jabotinsky. My father eagerly joined Mishka as a member of the Masada offshoot of Betar, a group of intellectual, scholastically inclined students, mostly coming from professional households. The new cause gave him a sense of passion and purpose. Immersing himself in the books at the main Jewish library, he eagerly read about the lives of Jewish thinkers and leaders, learning the differences between Socialism and Revisionism and gleaning as much information about the history of the Zionist movement as he could. Who were Weizman and Herzl? What did Bialik have to say? What was the Balfour Declaration? "A whole new world opened up for me, thanks to a bunch of adolescent anti-Semitic Polish thugs," my father remarks. Soon enough, my father's leadership qualities were recognized and he was made secretary of that group. At fifteen, he ardently embraced Zionism like a new lover.

"Zionism fascinated me. A homeland for the Jews," he says. "After all the prejudice and terrible pogroms we suffered in Russia and Europe, it seemed the logical conclusion for ending our misery at the hands of those who wished to kill us." Reading all about Ze'ev Jabotinsky's Revisionist Party, he heartily embraced the idea of Jews defending themselves and fighting back instead of being helpless victims. Enthused, my father was happy that he was part of the militaristic youth movement that emphasized self-defense and military training. Compared with the majority-favored Socialist ideology, the Revisionist party and its Betar youth group were considered violently militant, for in Poland in the 1930s, he explained, it was a radical idea for Jews to be armed and dangerous. Exasperated with being perpetual victims of anti-Semitic violence, the zealous followers of Jabotinsky aligned themselves with their leader's belief that Palestine, including both sides of the Jordan River, was the ancient sacred birthright of the Jews to be fought for and declared a Jewish homeland for the Jewish nation. The exodus to liberation from oppression and intimidation necessitated having their promised land become a sovereign homeland, a country where Jews from all over would be welcome and gain citizenship. A national home would be the manifestation of their desperate dreams. Believing that Palestine was that hope of salvation and refuge, they made "Next year in Jerusalem," that ancient Passover prayer, a call to political action. Fueled by utopian ideals, eager young Jews from Europe and Russia left their old birthplaces of prejudice and persecution and set forth as dedicated pioneers to transform a mosquito-infested Mediterranean desert into an oasis of orange orchards. Armed with guts, grit, guns, and a fierce determination to rid themselves of their disempowered past, they willed a new country into being.

My father's cousin David, who had inspired his youthful philatelic efforts, now encouraged him to take on a leadership role in the Revisionist Zionist party, in which he himself had gained a reputation as an influential speaker. My father would travel to where David was delivering his speeches propagating the revolutionary cause of "two sides of the Jordan," just to watch and learn the art of oral persuasion. "I took note of David's decisive hand movements, penetrating gaze, and punctuated oratorical style of using short sentences to drive his point home. We called it *tzu der zach*—to the thing. David would get right to the heart of the matter. A great speaker. Very inspiring."

For my father, being a leader and planning the educational and entertaining programs for the weekly meetings of the different age groups was a full-time occupation. "Also a welcome addition to my social life," he adds. With his friends Mishka and Ziamka, he designed programs to keep the group of more than eighty teenagers involved in a variety of interests and activities. During the week and on Sundays the young members of Betar would meet on the second floor of an old three-storey office building where they were educated about Zionism and the historical development of their political movement. Their activities included training in military exercises by special instructors, learning basic Hebrew, and attending parties in Vilna and picnics in the nearby forests.

"Such wonderful hours we spent, boys and girls together, with our organized roll calls, exercises of physical fitness, and summer excursions away from the town. Twice a month, on a Saturday evening, we'd gather together for times of storytelling and songs, acting and music. Our happiest events were the farewell parties we made for those lucky enough to get emigration passes or study certificates for Palestine."

There was a great commotion in the town when the controversial founder of the Revisionist party, Ze'ev Jabotinsky, visited Vilna in 1938. "Even though the Yiddish-speaking population was passionately divided into different political and ideological factions from the extreme left to the far right, everyone was caught in the same excitement to see this important figure, the man of the hour, in person. In Vilna, where every third person was a Jew, even the Gentile population was talking about his visit."

My father's Betar group, Masada, went in full uniform to the Porubanek Airport to greet Jabotinsky. Flying blue and white banners, the cavalcade of cars and buses drove to the Polonia Hotel in the centre of the city, where Jabotinsky occupied the main suite for two days. On the morning of the second day of Jabotinsky's stay, my overjoyed, hero-worshipping father was appointed to stand guard outside the door of the hotel suite of his esteemed leader. Proudly, nineteen-year-old Israel Jutan stood with his group of flag holders on the side of the stage where Jabotinsky was greeted with wild applause. In what my father remembers as a stirring, thought-provoking address in Yiddish, Jabotinsky called out to the Polish community to evacuate themselves from Poland and begin marching to Palestine: "*Vilner Yidn, ir zitzt oyfn volcan. Farlozt Poyln! Gayt nach Palestina!*" That is, "Jews of Vilna, you are sitting on a volcano! Leave Poland! Head for Palestine!"

But Jabotinsky's warnings about the dangerous successes of the rising Nazi party in Germany and the growing anti-Jewish laws and boycott of Jewish shops and factories in Poland fell mostly on deaf ears. To many of the moderate minded Jews, he appeared to be a raving fanatic. The next morning, bold banners in the Jewish leftist press screamed: *EVACUATION—NO!* A month later, spurred by the rousing words of Jabotinsky, my father joined more than a thousand Jewish war veterans and young fellow Betar members on a march of solidarity. Following the route of illegal immigration to the ships docked in the Black Sea, they walked as far as the border of Romania. There they were halted by the Polish police at the urgent request of the British Foreign Office, alarmed at the prospect of more Jews potentially entering their colonized Palestine.

"It became clear to me that it was increasingly dangerous to be a Jew in Poland," my father says soberly. "Already there were expulsions of Jews and beatings of Jewish youths executed en masse by the *endeks,* the radical Polish nationalists, both at the university and openly in the Vilna streets. The university authorities instituted discrimination in the form of prearranged seating that prohibited Jews from sitting during lectures. Everyone else—the Lithuanian, Polish, and German students—were allowed to sit except us Jews. We were forced to stand with our backs to the wall while taking notes. Yah, they made it very uncomfortable for us. Under these bad conditions, it was difficult to concentrate in class, so I spent much of my time in the library. But those restrictions only made me more determined to excel academically and participate with more fervor in my Zionist group."

The Boyfriend

✦

Vilna, Poland, 1937

In finding one's love, one can lose one's mind.

A whole new world of romance and intrigue had opened up for my father when he joined Masada. As an only child and student at an all-boys school, he was unaccustomed to the whirlwind life of boys and girls mingling together. Suddenly, he found himself the protagonist in the ploys and plots of love-crazed girls obsessed with snagging partners. After two years as secretary of Betar, he had risen to the rank of deputy-commandant, joining what he calls the *troika* of leadership working to increase membership, often competing to see who could impress the most girls. His good friends Mishka, who resembled the young film star Robert Taylor, and Ziamka, who looked like Marlon Brando, were magnets for the girls and had no trouble attracting new members. They realized that enrolling the fairer sex was the key to enticing more boys to the movement. "You see, it was the policy of us boys in the head command of the group to be nice to all the members, especially the girls. We couldn't afford to lose any members of the movement," he smiles.

"I used to get secret letters from three girls at the same time, even from Mishka's sister, two years younger than me, who would secretly put love letters on my desk or in my jacket," my father smiles. "My own affections soon turned to Lilka Lewinowna," he adds, "a tall, pretty, shy brown-eyed sixteen-year-old whose father had the only toilet paper factory in Vilnius and also made the filter paper for do-it-yourself cigarettes."

I've always been amazed at my father's remarkable capacity for remembering people's names, but even more so by his interest in and attention to their professions. Was it a Vilna custom to take note of the family occupation of a prospective suitor or bride's family, because it possibly indicated their financial status? Or was it just his own personal curiosity about what people did for a living? Whatever the reason, my father obviously thought it good business to make other people's business his business.

His courtship of Lilka consisted of his walking her home once a week after the Betar meetings. She would invite him in for some tea and cake, and then they would sit and hold hands, listening to music on the radio. Lilka never allowed him to go further than a hug or a kiss goodbye. Gentleman that he was, he respected her wishes.

One day, after a Saturday matinee cinema show, my father spotted an acquaintance of his walking with another tall, beautiful girl. Approaching them he started up a conversation, wanting to know more about the girl for whom he felt such a strong attraction. The object of his desire was named Wilma and she attended a private school and lived far away from his suburb. After turning down several of his invitations, she finally agreed to accompany him to the romantic musical film *Rose Marie,* starring Jeanette McDonald and Nelson Eddie.

"Wilma was absolutely beautiful. She had a straight nose and full voluptuous lips and long reddish-brown hair that flowed around her delicate face," recalls my father. "I was very much attracted to her.

But she was aloof. Even when she let me dance with her in her room to the music of the tango playing on the modern record player, she kept her body distant." Their platonic friendship lasted a few months. When Wilma began making excuses for not being available, my father commiserated with his friend Ziamka, who kept secret what he already knew: Wilma was dating their friend Mishka. Eventually, one of the girls in Masada broke the news to him. Angered, my father confronted his good friend about stealing his girlfriend. Defending himself, Mishka told him that it was Wilma who had pursued him, not the other way round, repeating what Wilma had told him—that she felt my father was too serious and too involved with the organization and his Zionist ideals. His friend's words stung. Upset and hurt at the loss of his beautiful girlfriend, he decided to go straight to the source, wishing to hear from Wilma's own luscious lips why he was not the favored one. Evasive at first, Wilma finally admitted that my father was too reserved and formal for her liking. He was devastated. This was his first romantic rejection and the idea that he had lost his girl to his close friend Mishka, who had rescued him from the bullies and introduced him to Betar and Zionism, only confused his crushed feelings. Ever stalwart and pragmatic, he consoled himself with the notion that there were always other girls to attract his attention. Perhaps not as beautiful as Wilma, but certainly there must be others willing to go further than a kiss.

Her name was Vera Lerman. She was blonde, tall, always well dressed, and not a part of the Masada circle. The daughter of one of his father's circle of doctor friends, she lived in another part of town, in a huge apartment in an eight-story building, the only one in Vilna with an elevator. My father went to visit often, warmly welcomed because of Zacharias's status and good reputation. My father sighs when he talks about her. "Vera, with her upper-class looks and manners, was the one I really hungered for in my heart. I remember when we met. It was the summertime. Every summer, from the 15th of June until the end of August, my family would go to our country *dacha*, about fifteen kilometers from Vilna, in the forest near a river. The peasants in the village would rent out their rooms for us, the *letnyakes*, the summer people from the big towns. On Friday evenings, the trains used to bring all the parents to spend the weekends in the country houses and on Monday mornings they would go back to work again. My father used to stay on as the country doctor, working out of his own surgery. As a result, we had a lot of fresh eggs, bread, cheese, butter, and chickens—payment from the peasants for his medical services. My stepmother, who worked during the week in the hospital with the children, came to join us for the weekends."

Vera vacationed with her parents in the same little village, staying just a ten-minute walk away. "I was very, very much in love with her," my father reminisces. "I suppose if I think back now, she was my first true love. But it was not to be consummated as I would have liked. She never allowed me to make love to her. We would take long walks along the riverbanks, find a place nearby, and take off our clothes. We would lie down next to each other and move our bodies close together innocently to enjoy the feel of our naked skin touching each other," my father smiles.

Unexpectedly, he breaks into laughter. Is he mocking the pretentiousness of sexual purity or ridiculing a lost opportunity? Perhaps it is the chuckle of retrospection, as the older, wiser man finds humor in the clumsiness of adolescent lust and conservative morality. Whatever it is, my father keeps emitting little grunts of amusement. With a smile of a wily country cat remembering the treat of milk after a day's catch of mice, he tells me the story of their peasant landlord's daughter, Yadviga. "Let me see, I was fifteen, so she was about seventeen. It was Yadviga who introduced me to the whole story of lovemaking. One day she took me aside, saying she had something to show me. We often examined natural curiosities together, you see, because coming from the city, I found farm creatures like frogs, rabbits, and chickens all very interesting. I willingly went with her to see what she wanted to show me in the barn, and followed her up the ladder into the hayloft, to the back corner, where it was dark. That was where my lessons in the barn began with the older and wiser Yadviga, and me, the good student, of course. Yadviga was a convincing and eager teacher. She told me it was alright to do what my mother had forbidden me to do long ago."

He was around seventeen-years-old when my father met Malka at his Masada group. As he mentions her name, it's clear from his tone that the woman with the Hebrew name for queen is about to play an important role. Malka's father, he tells me, had a big electric supply shop near a monastery in the center of town. "Although he was a rich man making lots of money from his electrical business," my father comments, "he led a rather simple and boring bourgeois life. From his busy shop to his untidy home and back again, that's how it went. No music, no art, no books, no culture. Nothing but work and more work," my father says. "All they talked about at their home were material things and, of course, food and money. This Malka was an indulged girl, you understand. She had the best of everything. Beautiful clothes and beautiful shoes. But, to her favor, she was also generous, donating money to the organization, and always offering to pay for everyone's food if we went out as a group. All the time she would say to me: 'Don't worry, I have the money. I'll pay.'"

On one of their Masada-organized group outings, they were hiking in the nearby mountains when Malka tugged at my father's arms and said: "Let's go up a little further. I know a nice place where we can watch the birds a little higher up. Come with me!" He knew from their previous conversations that Malka loved nature and the outdoors, enjoying hiking and taking long walks by the river or lakeside. With only ten minutes till the end of the hike, he was worried about missing the rest of the group and getting lost if they lagged behind. "Don't worry," she assured him. "We will be back in time. It won't take long." Holding my father's hand, the athletic Malka pulled him up after her as she clambered over the rocks. In a few moments, they had climbed to the mouth of a cave. "I told her I was claustrophobic and didn't want to go into the cave," he continues. "But she kept urging me, 'No, don't worry, it will be fine. It isn't really a proper cave. Come here, see? It has an opening. You can see the sky through this hole up here. Look how beautiful it is. Just take a look. The view is marvelous.'" Hesitantly, my father stepped inside, noticing that the cave was like a grotto, with a hole in the roof through which sunlight filtered down like a spotlight. The floor was a hollow rock, covered with a soft layer of moss and grass. Further along, a wide opening on the side of the mountain revealed a beautiful vista of forest below. Turning around, he noticed that Malka had laid herself down on the soft, natural blanket of moss. Stretching out her hand to him, she whispered, "Come! Lie down next to me." Unsuspectingly, he did as she asked, wondering what more there could possibly be to see from that horizontal position. Lying close to her, he caught a whiff of the salty sweetness of Malka's moist face, mingled with the dampness from the cave. All his concerns about being left behind on the trail vanished as Malka rolled toward him and started kissing him gently. "Well, you understand what comes next, of course," my father smiles at me. "I was a teenage boy in a cave alone with a young, sweaty teenage girl. Malka. Beautiful, rich, generous Malka. What could I do? Of course, I obliged."

My father pauses. After such a rush of reminiscences, the pause seems longer than a lover's moan. I dare not break the reverie with questions. An old man with his memories of a young romance is like a mother nursing her baby. One should not come between the two. "She was right," he concludes, still smiling. "The view was marvelous."

In just four years, the members of Masada would be faced with a different view. In September 1941, they would be imprisoned within the confines of the high walls of the Vilna Ghetto under German occupation, with the windows of the buildings clamped shut and boarded-up. My father was working as an administrative clerk in the ghetto labor office when he glanced up from his paperwork one day to see Wilma standing in front of him. Beautiful as ever, but very subdued, she had specifically sought out my father to ask for his help getting assigned to a work unit. Remembering his fondness for the girl who had rejected him and broken his young heart, he managed to get her a job outside the ghetto. With the new employment card from my father, she was able to protect her mother and get a ration of food. A few weeks later, she came to his desk to offer her thanks. She informed him that she had found a better, more permanent job as a cleaning girl for some of the German army officers. Several months after that, rumors began spreading about a high-ranking German Wehrrmacht officer who had fallen in love with a Jewish girl from the ghetto who worked in his apartment. The affair was discovered by the Gestapo. The officer and the girl were later found dead together, having killed themselves in a suicide pact. The girl was Wilma.

The Writer

✦

Vilna, Poland, 1937–38

For us to rewrite, first we must remember.

In the spring of 1937, the same year my father graduated from high school, Zacharias Jutan had a heart attack. The cardiogram results showed that he was suffering from a heart condition called *angina pectoris,* and a long rest was prescribed. It was decided that, rather than return home, it was better for him to lie in comfort at the nearby apartment of Uncle Samuel in Niemiecka Street, where Aunt Asya had a large surgical office for her midwifery practice. Every day for about a month or more, my father would make a special stop to visit him there. Seeing his usually busy and active father in so much discomfort, restricted to lying prone on his back, filled him with pity and remorse. It seemed like added insult to injury to think that his father was confined to a bed in his brother Sam's house, the same brother who had snubbed him, and caused his father grief.

"Despite my concerns over my father's convalescence and my own busy activities of stamp collecting and youth group meetings," my father continues, "I am proud to say I managed to do well in my matriculation exams." Following his father's dream for him to go into medicine, he applied to Columbia Medical School in New York. However, he was still unsure about what he wanted to do with his life, and began to have mixed feelings about leaving Poland. Earlier, it had been his ardent wish to visit America and the skyscraping metropolis of his youthful imagination, but now, New York seemed so far away from his familiar surroundings, and he was quite certain that he did not want to be a doctor. A doctor, he thought, was always occupied with duties, with no time to be involved in his children's lives, their interests and dreams. He was determined not to follow the pattern of his father.

Most of the original group of seven boys in the initial leadership of Betar had already left Poland for Palestine. He had considered going, too, but at that time British authorities had announced that quotas for Poles entering Palestine were full for several years, and he knew immigration there would be problematic. Nonetheless, my father put in his application to the Zionist office in Warsaw—seeking the necessary permission to apply either to the University of Jerusalem or the Technion of Haifa—and sent along his qualifying papers to the Technion and Columbia, waiting to hear from both universities.

The dilemma of deserting his father weighed heavily on him. How could he leave his father so sick and troubled? What if his father were to die while he was far away studying in a foreign country, with no way of knowing until it was too late to say goodbye? "In all this thinking," my father confides, "I suddenly became aware of the power of something I now call 'institutionalized love.' Yes, of course, there was the love from me to my father, but I began to question the nature of that love. Does a child love a parent out of duty? Out of appreciation for the memories of consideration and effort given to the child by the parents? And is that bond strong enough to make a son sacrifice his life out of devotion to his father? I loved my father because he was my father. Perhaps he loved me because I was the only son and child he had. At the time of my last year of high school, all I knew was the duty of an only child to love his ailing father and the fear of leaving him. For all these reasons, I was reluctant to turn my back on Vilna and my sick father and set sail for a completely new life."

By the time he was accepted at the Haifa Technion in Palestine, Poland was under the rule of the Soviet authorities and there was little hope of leaving the country legally. My father decided to let fate take its course. Unwilling to waste a year, he enrolled at Vilna's Stefan Batory University for the degree of Humane Letters, now called a bachelor of arts. He found it ironic, that after the war, when he needed proof that he had graduated from high school, the only institution able to provide the necessary paperwork was the Haifa Technion, a school he had not even attended.

"What prompted me to study literature were several small articles I had written not only for my school paper but also for a Polish daily called *Kurjer Wilenski*. At home my father impressed on me the importance of being well informed about world events, so I was an avid reader of the newspaper to which he subscribed," my father explains. An image immediately springs to mind: my father napping on his bed, fully dressed, a newspaper spread wide over his face to shut out the light. "*Chupping a dremmel,*" my mother would call it, the Yiddish expression of catching a little dream to describe his after-work naps. Even in his sleep, it seemed, my father wished to breathe in the distinctive smell of newsprint ink. After all, newspapers were an important feature in his life: They provided him with several careers, informed him of the latest international events, dried his recycled stamps, proclaimed the successes of his wife, daughter, and himself, and became the medium for his stories of remembrance to reach and touch people of all faiths.

Already from the age of fourteen, he was contributing stories to his school newspaper, *Wallpaper,* where pieces of paper with handwritten or typed articles and stories were stuck up on a long, horizontal board on the wall of the school corridor. By sixteen, my father tells me, he had become the editor. Without knowing it, I had followed in my father's footsteps, becoming editor of my high school magazine at the same age.

His initials, "I.J.," for Israel Jutan, marked his submissions to the daily *Kurier Wilensk* and the national Jewish paper in Polish, *Nasz Przegland.* In the summer of 1935 my father was awarded a trip from Vilna to Warsaw to participate in the youth correspondents' Jamboree of the *Maly Przegland,* the Friday supplement to the newspaper, edited by the famed Dr. Korczak. The founder and director of a Jewish orphanage in the nearby health resort of Otwock, Dr. Korczak was also a best-selling author. His imaginative children's stories tracing the adventures of King Maciek the First and his children-soldiers and children-citizens, were based on the innovative, child-oriented democratic organization of his orphanage.

"After the war, I read about Dr. Korczak's insistence on remaining with his Otwock orphan children at the time of liquidation of the Warsaw Ghetto," my father says. "They say that one of the Nazi officers in command of the transport to the Majdanek and Auschwitz concentration camps recognized Korczak's face from the cover of a storybook he had read to his own son. He offered to hide the Polish author in his home in Vienna, but Dr. Korczak refused the gesture to save his own life. He chose instead to stay with his treasured Jewish orphan children until the end, when they were all killed together in Treblinka. On the anniversary of Korczak's murder, Israel commemorated him with a special postal issue. As a stamp collector and philatelic columnist, it pleased me greatly when other countries followed Israel's example in honoring him. On the tab of the Israeli stamp of December 1962, there is an inscription: 'Janusz Korczak, friend to children, father to orphans: 1879–1942.' I salute his memory," my father says.

One day, a fellow contributing journalist from the *Kurier* took my father aside. "He mentioned to me that my initials and Jewish-sounding name might hinder my chances at furthering my career as a writer," he says. The journalist suggested that if my father didn't want to be stuck writing little sidelines and trivial articles, he should consider writing under an assumed name or adopt a pen name. "I took the hint," my father adds. "I thought long and hard about a suitable pseudonym.

Then it came to me. 'I have it! The perfect name for myself! It will be Ksawery. Ksawery Piontka!'"

At sixteen he had discovered a book written by a Polish writer named Ksawery Pruszynski. *Palestine for the Third Time* described the author's third visit to Palestine and how glorious it was for him to see the dedicated Jewish people create a Garden of Eden out of a sand-swept wasteland of a desert. "It is very possible that the writer's inspiration came in response to the slogan devised by some anti-Semitic Poles, saying, 'Jews! Go to Palestine!' which was first written as graffiti on the walls, then displayed on fabric banners hanging from balconies and eventually printed in their own Polish newspapers," my father says. "I believed Ksawery suited me well, not only because of that wonderful Polish writer whose writings had impressed me so, but also because of how aristocratic it sounded. The surname I chose is written in Polish as Piontka, with an accent mark under the letter 'a.' It means number five, which is also the highest grade achievable in school—the best score. I wanted to be the best, you see? So that is how I was known at the newspaper. They called me Ksawer, Ksawery, Ksav—all variations on the same noble name."

"*SCHREIBT UND FARSHREIBT*! Write and record!" my father shouts suddenly like a prophet on a mountaintop. "Yah! This was to be my credo for the rest of my life," he says, explaining that the phrase he called out was uttered by the writer Simon Dubnow, an eminent historian, while being dragged to his death by a Gestapo officer, a former student of his. My father took the martyred author's command to heart. On Holocaust Remembrance Day, he would submit his essays to local daily newspapers that would publish his wartime memories. When my father became secretary of the She'erith Hapletah, the Holocaust survivors' organization in Cape Town, he was among the first to call for the city's few scattered Holocaust survivors stemming from Poland to Rhode Island and from Russia to France to talk openly about their experiences. Later, he began advocating his idea for a book of collected stories of their different wartime accounts to serve as testimony for posterity. In 1995, on the fiftieth anniversary of the defeat of Germany and the liberation of the concentration camps, *In Sacred Memory: Recollections of the Holocaust by Survivors Living in Cape Town* was published with a foreword acknowledging Mr. Piat for his inspiration and perseverance in helping launch the book. Every last witness's story must be written and recorded, he believed, so future generations have continuous and constant reminders of the long-term ravages of war.

This was the victory of paper over rock.

The Lover

✦

Paris, France, 1939

Love is the quest, the question, and the answer.

At the time my father was feeling so uncertain about his future, his mother sent him a ticket to come and visit her in Paris. "It was a perfect opportunity to escape Poland for a while and reconnect with my mother," my father recalls. "Of course, the thrill of seeing Paris was not to be overlooked. So I went in June 1939."

Having left Poland for a brighter future, Vava was by this time the chief designer for a small couture clothing factory, living at 19 Rue de Coeur, near Les Halles, a pleasant part of Paris, only a few minutes from the grand boulevards with their elegant boutiques and designer shops. Mother and son would go out together, mostly to her favorite music halls and movie matinees. Paris proved to be a city of firsts for my father. It was the first time he ever saw a black man or heard negro spirituals sung; the first time he saw bohemian artists, men wearing long hair and little berets; and the first time he came across what he called "sidewalk ladies," whose provocative, sultry stroll in fishnet stockings and sensuous flesh bulging from their skimpy clothes made his heart race. For a young man broadening his horizons, this visit to his mother—and her world of cultural stimulation—was an unforgettable experience.

"I saw the legendary Maurice Chevalier and Josephine Baker, the exquisite Negress," says my father. "Ah, Paris! The center of earthly delights—the sights, the smells, the flashing lights in the sordid bordello district, and for me, a boy in my prime, a young aspirant reporter with ravenous eyes, it was like the Garden of Eden. Everywhere I turned, some kind of forbidden fruit was hanging, waiting to be tasted."

One delicious encounter was with a friend of his mother, a Jewish woman from Poland named Eva who was working and living in Paris. "Eva always had a smile on her face, a good sense of humor, and joking eyes," he says. "She was about thirty-four maybe, with darkish skin, hair, and eyes. She reminded me of what I imagined Cleopatra to look like—something exotic. She told me that my mother had instructed her to give me a good time in Paris. And that is exactly what she did."

He then tells me the story of how, after a night out dancing, the sultry Eva brought him home to his mother's apartment and introduced him to what he calls "the rapturous mature lovemaking of an experienced older woman." On a subsequent outing to a dance, Eva let it slip that the evening of sex education had been his mother's idea. Apparently, Vava had decided it was time for her son to be expertly coached in the art of lovemaking. Believing her friend Eva to be the perfect, gentle guide, Vava set the whole thing up, deliberately staying away from her apartment on the appointed night when Eva treated my father to a surprise fantasy night of exquisite sexual intimacy. "Mother of course never mentioned it, and I never spoke about it. I never let on that I knew about her little conspiracy with Eva," my father says. "But she gave me an early birthday present I will never forget." At his birth in Vilna, Vava had declared her son would be lucky in love. In Paris, twenty years later, she did her best to set her son up well for that good fortune.

Gazing into the distance, my father adds: "Yah! For all Eva taught me that night, I am forever grateful to her." Then, raising his brow in mock fatigue, he smiles, "And all those women who appeared later in my life, they too have the magnificent Eva to thank."

When my father told me the Eva seduction story, I admittedly was taken aback. This was not the kind of graphic story I expected to hear when I asked my father to tell me about his past. Yet, in a strange way, this relished anecdote of his amorous night of passion in Paris with an older woman allowed me to know both him and my liberal-minded, unconventional grandmother that much better. It had been my original intent when I approached my father to share his life stories with me to get a sense of who and what came before me, of what his family and life had been before the war. Now, I was beginning to get an idea. This unusually intimate conversation gave me a chance to understand my father beyond the limitations that kept us locked in our predefined roles, me, forever the child, and him, forever the authoritarian father branded a "Holocaust survivor," with its own associated definitions. Revealing such a story to a daughter went beyond what my father referred to as "institutionalized love." In talking to me so frankly, I felt for the first time, that he was treating me like a peer, a fellow journalist, deserving of the truth, even if it was a lot more naked than I had expected. By sharing so frankly, my father had granted me permission to see him as a complete human being, a flesh-and-blood mortal, stuttering and stumbling his way through love and sex. In letting down his guard, my father had let me in. My father, the raconteur, possessed that rare ability to comfortably cover all topics, from the profound to the profane. I felt fortunate to have the kind of father-daughter relationship, unusual, as it may seem to some, which allowed us to share ourselves in the fullness of such revealing personal stories.

As a Holocaust survivor, stripped bare to the bones, he had been habitually deprived of any privacy, physically exposed for many years to public humiliation. Had the conditioning of those barbaric, undignified dehumanizing circumstances perhaps in some way made it easier for him to transcend otherwise standard discretionary reservedness when it came to talking about bodily functions or matters others would consider private? Or was he like his mother, who apparently believed that expressions of the heart, often finding its language through the pleasure-seeking body, were to be explored and enjoyed rather than concealed or suppressed? And where did I fit in, caught between cultural crosshairs—that of my father's more sexually liberated European mentality and my prevailing Anglicized society's more repressed, prudish mindset? Besides, if I am to hear of the horrors, why not also listen to the pleasures? Why shy away from the subject of sex, when it's one of the ways the lonely body seeks love and connection? Perhaps my father's outpouring of recollections of lovemaking helps compensate for the memories of more desperate times, when his desires for a woman's body gave way to the consuming cravings for a stale crust of bread. I have heard it said many times that evil is the absence of love. What would our lives be like, I wonder, if we focused more on becoming better lovers than perfecting the skills of making a killing?

In our quest for deeper understanding, why place limitations on our discussions? What is there to protect but our innocence? Didn't the Holocaust serve to take that away?

And if we are to become wiser, then let us ready ourselves as individuals to face and acknowledge the full, broad spectrum of our human nature, from our elevated, uplifting spirituality to our most primal and basest of bestial instincts.

My father made no bones about his attraction to beautiful women. I was very aware of it, growing up. He would openly admire them on the street, on the screen and at home. It seemed to be part of his natural enthusiastic appreciation for anything of aesthetic beauty, like a fine piece of art, or elegant stamp, or well crafted story. When it came to my mother, Mr. Piat put his short wife on a very tall pedestal. Her smile, talent, humor, and charm dazzled him. Not many traditional men of his day would have comfortably accepted their wives keeping their maiden names or traveling around the globe pursuing their artistic career. When her fans and other strangers mistakenly called him Mr. Rosenthal, he took the misunderstandings in good stride and continued to serve as the devoted promoter and organizer of shows for his "local celebrity" wife, whose personality shone brightly, both in and out of the spotlight.

Ladies with affection to spare were equally attracted to the sensitive, romantic man with the dark past, especially after my mother's death. I know, because every year I would get calls from different women enquiring when Mr. Piat, the charismatic and available widower, was arriving in Boston that summer. I imagine that to him, the finest of these females represented the elements of elegance, gentility, warmth and grace needed to bring beauty to a predominantly sordid, violent, indifferent world too often ruled by crass, delusional warmongering men. Women could sense that he appreciated what they had to offer and that he took pleasure in giving them the time and attention to make them feel special. No doubt they were smitten by his European accent and charm. "I just listen to them," he once confided in me with a twinkle in his hazel eyes as we sat at my kitchen table, talking about his romantic conquests as a widower. Revealing the secret of his success, he said to me: "They pour their hearts out to me, and I listen. I show them I care. They understand that I am interested in their story."

Back in Paris, when Eva and my father first met, he had listened to her sad story of jilted love, forsaken promises, and loneliness in her first months of arriving in France. Now, I realize that I too am rekindling the love between my father and myself, renewing our closeness, just by listening to his reminiscences. My father closes his eyes, sighs, and leans back in his chaise. It seems our brief excursion in Paris is over. This last memory of exotic Eva has left a smile on his face. I'm not sure which keeps him warmer, the blazing afternoon sun outdoors by the pool or the glowing memories of a candlelit night of ardor and amour in his mother's apartment on his first trip to Paris.

c.1922. Vava (nee Goldman) and son.

c.1938. Zacharias and son in Vilna.

c.1923. The Jutan family portrait. Bottom Row: L to R: Asya and Samuel (standing) and son, David Jutan. Zacharias Jutan is seated slightly right of center, with my father, Israel to the right. Center Row: Ethel and Reuven Jutan are seated 3rd and 4th from the right. Back Row: Anushka, (in white stole) stands 2rd from the right.

1952. Adderley Street, Cape Town.

1954. The Pavilion, Sea Point.

1956. Posing for a professional portrait.

1958. Beachfront Park, Sea Point.

ISRAEL JUTAN a.k.a. XAVIER PIAT

1938. The Student, Vilna.

1945. The Survivor, Lauenberg.

1946. The Editor, Jelenia Gora.

1948. The Reporter, Paris.

1952. The Philatelist, Cape Town.

1953. The Interviewer, with Danny Kaye.

XAVIER PIAT AND CHAYELA ROSENTHAL

1945-1947. Jelenia Gora

1949. Paris

1950. London

Chayela (center, in beret) and Xavier (leaning out the door) with British Utins at train station.

1974. My father, my sister Zola and I, and my mother, at the opening of my first art exhibition, Cape Town.

1976. Father of the Bride.

With Love

Dad

Sept '95

PART II

✦

War

The Daughter: A New Life

✦

Jerusalem, Israel, 1973

It had always been my father's expressed wish for me to visit Israel. My father had been overjoyed when the dream of a Jewish state, first put into words in 1896 by Austrian journalist Theodore Herzl in *Der Judenstaat,* became a reality in May 1948, just three years after the end of World War II. Still stuck in postwar Poland at the time, he celebrated when Palestine was finally granted its independence by the British to become a homeland for the Jews. The new country was renamed Israel, evoking the new identity bestowed upon the Old Testament's Jacob after his transcendent spiritual dream in the desert. "For thou has striven with God and with men, and prevailed," was the meaning behind the name given to my father at his birth and now, to the phoenix nation, reborn from the proverbial blood, sweat, tears, and ashes.

Wishing to instill in me his own Zionist passion, my father encouraged me to join the newly formed Betar Zionist youth group in Cape Town when I was thirteen. Not daring to betray his authority of conviction or defy his strong will, I submitted to his zeal to follow in his footsteps, and, like father like daughter, also became a leader in the organization. In the 1960s of revolutionary social changes rippling through the Western world, for us non-rebellious Jewish South African adolescents—a minority of the white minority—a cause of passion, purpose, and politics satisfied our hormonal hunger for connection and a greater sense of belonging. Gathering at summer camps by the seashore and winter seminars by the lake, we sat around campfires, sang our heartfelt Hebrew songs, discussed the complicated issues of the modern state of Israel, and fell in puppy love with other teenagers whose parents had read from afar about the near death and new birth of a nation.

A trip to Israel was my college graduation gift from my father, who viewed travel as enlightening education. The country that had been a visionary's ideal in my father's youth had become, just one generation later, an international hub of tourists, a thriving whirlpool of entrepreneurs, and a successful agricultural model for the Middle East, attracting pioneering Jewish immigrants from affluent countries and offering shelter for refugees escaping from oppressive regimes. In the days when hitchhiking was still acceptable, I stuck out my thumb, relied on the kindness of strangers, and explored the tiny Jewish homeland from the bottom of Eilat's coral reefs by the Red Sea, to the lake of Galilee, and up to the top of the northern chalky cliffs of Rosh Hanikra near the border of Lebanon. Young, thin, tanned and twenty-one, I walked in wonder along the Via Dolorosa and in and out through the crammed, winding stone stairs of the aromatic Arab markets in the golden Old City of Jerusalem. Seduced by the vibrant sounds and sights of Israel, I enrolled in Ulpan Etzion, an absorption center for new immigrants in Jerusalem, where I slept in student dorms, studied Hebrew and socialized with other young Jews from Argentina to Uzbekistan. Like a released prisoner, I was high on freedom. For me, there was no need for drugs. It was enough to soak in the exhilarating energy from a testosterone-infused tourist-swamped Israel, a young country still riding high on the crest of its miraculous victory of the 1967 Six-Day War.

Leaving his Cape Town winter, my father came to visit and share part of my July summer in Jerusalem. Together we visited Yad Vashem, the Israeli Holocaust museum, where I stood in silence at his side in the dark Hall of Remembrance, with its flickering eternal flame that burned in memory of the millions of murdered European Jews. I wondered what and who my father was remembering but did not dare to disturb his solemn contemplation. How could I have known that decades later I would become the torchbearer myself, a guardian of the pilot light of remembrance that burned incessantly within him?

In October of that same year—1973—on Yom Kippur, I was visiting my Canadian boyfriend on a kibbutz when I heard an unforgettable sound that was to change my experience in Israel. The entire country had shut down in religious observation of the holiest day in the Jewish calendar. "Inscribe us into the Book of Life," the nation prayed together as one, asking for forgiveness from the long list of transgressions. Suddenly, the prolonged, piercing sound of an amplified alarm shattered the serenity. Rushing out of the synagogues in shock, people scattered in dismay and confusion. I didn't know what was happening, but everyone else who lived there did. The sirens screaming across the country were the all too familiar wailings of war. Within minutes, the ground around us shook with a continuous, heavy, thunderlike rumble. It was the roar of fighter planes taking off nonstop from the airfield adjacent to the kibbutz. The news came fast. It appeared that the citizens of Israel had been caught off guard. Egypt and Syria had unleashed yet another onslaught of intended annihilation attacks. The Yom Kippur War had begun.

I rushed back to the language institute in Jerusalem where my fellow students and I continued our Hebrew lessons, expanding our vocabulary to include words pertaining to war and getting firsthand knowledge about blackouts and nighttime curfews. As newly recruited war volunteers, we woke up before dawn to replace the bakers from the nearby bread factory who had turned overnight into soldiers. My anxious parents called long-distance from South Africa, concerned about my safety, asking if I wanted to come home. "I'm staying," I told them. "Don't worry. I'll be fine." How could I abandon Israel at that critical time? It was already starting to feel like my new home. What I would not and could not articulate to them was something I had only just recently distinguished myself: My secret, perverse desire to experience the danger and devastation of war. Something within me needed to identify with my parents in some small way, to feel closer to them, to relate more deeply. War, after all, was my inheritance. Thus far I had felt it only vicariously through association with my parents, but this time, in Jerusalem, I was presented with the real thing. Even if it meant just watching from the sidelines, it was a taste my wounded psyche craved, that of the bitter herbs. To be there, in the holy land, the land of strife, was enough. *Dai*: the Hebrew word for enough that sounds like die. Why? Why this pernicious, persistent deep-seated proclivity for suffering, this thirst for feeling the pain of loss that runs so deep in my soul? So that I, the privileged living, could smell the breath of death around me, to remind me of where I came from? I didn't know the answers. I just knew that an integral part of me resonated with being in a war zone. Jerusalem was telling me to stay.

Remaining in war-torn Israel, I watched the streams of armed vehicles, the highways teaming with anxious young men and women in camouflage uniforms, Uzis slung casually on their shoulders like a friend's hugging arm. I heard the stories of young boys taken prisoners of war in Egypt and knew with a familiar ache that they would be prisoners of war forever. I met the parents who lost first one son, then another to the cause of keeping a country alive for future generations. Even their daughters in the army were ready to risk their lives, for every person born in Israel knew their legacy was that of battle. There, in the midst of war, in Jerusalem, the holy city of many religions, I began to see how we, who call ourselves the chosen, keep choosing survival and resurrection, even in the face of constant attacks by those who keep choosing us as their victims, marking us for death.

In that year of my personal liberation in Israel, and the country's enslavement to war, I recognized something about the tribe into which I had been born. We are the ones, who, each year on the Day of Atonement, keep praying to God for the blessing of another year of life so we may celebrate our very existence, no matter what, no matter where. Scattered around the globe, speaking our different languages, indulging in our petty differences and discriminations, we are nevertheless the same ones who continue to pour the sweeter-than-sweet wine, lifting our glasses to make the toast not to our health, as other cultures do, but to our living. *L'Chaim!* To life! Eighteen. One, side by side with the vertical infinity sign of the perpetual loop of loss and life.

The Translator and Reporter

✦

Vilna, Poland, 1939

Nothing truly prepares you for war, but war prepares you for Nothing.

Official papers arrived in Paris summoning my father to an immediate return to Poland, now busy mobilizing for impending war. He cut his trip short and hurried back home.

With the Soviet occupation of Vilna in 1939, Zacharias Jutan had slowly returned to health and begun working again at the hospital where he met some young Jewish doctors affiliated with the army. Through those connections, he was able to arrange an interview for his son to obtain work as an English translator at Napoleon's Palace, now the headquarters of the Soviet army's administration. After being scrutinized and inspected by five different army officials, my father was taken to meet with a Russian officer, who expressed delight at his highly desirable facility with English.

"You are ideal for us, young man," the officer announced, writing my father's name down in the attendance book as Israel Jutan. After completing his assignment translating the rather difficult military terms and diplomatic phrases into English, my father was asked by the officer to teach him some basic conversational English phrases, like "How do you do?" and "Pleased to meet you." Soon, he found himself the appointed English teacher for about six to ten men, including majors and colonels, all eager to improve their skill in English because of their increasing communication with Americans.

It was my father's good fortune to have had as his English teacher at the Adam Mickiewicz High School the only woman among the mostly male clergy staff, a young girl from England who had come to Poland to teach. "She was wonderful," he says. "Young, pale, with reddish hair. All of us boys would walk around during our break times and talk with a falsetto accent in the 'propah English of the Queen!' I even wrote a creative essay on the 1937 coronation of the king and queen in English for my matriculation. I was lucky. Languages came easy to me, and I enjoyed learning them. Perhaps it was part of my wish to travel to foreign places."

My father was pleased at the relative ease of his assigned army job of monitoring the radio and translating the Russian, German, English, and French messages coming through the airwaves. It did not require him to be out on the field practicing shooting, even though he had mastered those basic military skills in his final years of school and at Masada. On his free Friday evenings and Saturdays, he spent time together with his Betar friends and Malka, who now was his steady girlfriend.

"Nobody seriously expected war," my father says casually. "I ascertained in my radio work that France was very well prepared with the Maginot Line, even though England was not. Then, suddenly, events started to happen quickly. Austria was annexed by Germany, and Zaolzie, part of Czechoslovakia, was taken over with great patriotic fervor by Poland, claiming it had always been theirs. Even when Germany took over Czechoslovakia, Poland—bolstered by the assurances of the Allies—felt confident that she faced little danger compared with

Czechoslovakia. After all, with our horses ready, our men mobilized, nothing could happen to us. That is what we all believed. The slogan among the Polish soldiers was, 'We will not even give them a button off our pants!' Then came September 1, 1939, and war was upon us."

The first of September. Exactly forty years later, on that same date, my mother would succumb to ovarian cancer. I couldn't help but wonder if those cancerous cells that eventually overtook her insides began their insidious entry the day Poland was invaded, the day war became their new reality, the day her life was destined to change forever.

During the seventeen days immediately following that fateful September day, German troops swept through Poland, occupying half the country. September 17 saw the collapse of the rest of Poland to Russia, which then occupied Vilna. When the battling ended, my father, who was living in the army barracks, demobilized himself from the army, threw away his uniform, scratched out his name from the officers' guild, and returned to civilian status. Not wanting to stay at home for fear of being caught by the Russians as a Polish soldier, he asked Malka's parents if he could stay with them. They agreed, giving him a room for himself. After about ten days, the occupying Soviet authorities nationalized all the bigger shops, including Malka's father's enormous electrical wholesale supply store. Because her father was a working electrician himself and had always been kind to his employees, they vouched for him, persuading the Soviet authorities to allow him to remain on as foreman. In comparison with other prosperous business owners whose companies were stolen right from under them, with little or no compensation, Malka's father had it relatively good.

"It helped that I was staying with Malka," my father says. "A Russian officer was now stationed in Father's home and had taken over two big rooms, which meant less space for everyone else. Father's position deteriorated rapidly. Previously, he had been active in the government of Poland, but now with that option gone, he remained sick, lying most days in bed. To help him keep a low profile, his medical colleagues signed papers effectively stating that he had not been professionally active for the past several years. The political upheaval brought a time of great uncertainty. We all were gripped by enormous fear."

The Russian Communists also took over the Polish daily newspaper. Distrusting the Poles for their expressed resentment of the takeover and their refusal to accept Communist beliefs, they were keen to find a young reporter, preferably someone Jewish. My father, with his Polish press name of Ksawery Piontka, fit the bill. It did not seem to matter to them that he was a Zionist, especially in the first months of occupation. His assignments were to write articles about university life, sports, and cultural events, including cinema, art, and theatre. Under Russian Communist rule, Vilna focused its attention on the upcoming cultural festival in Moscow in which the ethnic groups from the conquered territories, now part of Russia, were to be represented. The ardent Soviet authorities, extremely skilled at producing lavish communal patriotic shows, organized a special music contest at city hall where a winner would be chosen to represent Vilna in Moscow. It was here that my father, covering these cultural events as a young reporter, first heard the singing talents of a pretty sixteen-year-old named Chayela Rosenthal.

"Chayela played the part of a young worker doing her job with a good spirit, singing about her joy of working. Her performance was stellar. The song, written by Leyb Rosenthal, her older brother, an established poet and writer, became an instant hit on the radio. She sang the song in Yiddish, which was now officially recognized as an ethnic language and sponsored by the new government. In my first article for the *Youth Truth,* I wrote about how well she performed and what an honor it was for this petite, vivacious, young Jewish girl to be chosen by the Cultural Association to represent Vilna at the International Festival of Folklore Music and Dance, to be held in Moscow. Of course, at the time I was writing about her," my father smiles, "I could not know that fate would bring the two of us together. I just remember being impressed by her talent and joyful presence that emanated from the stage."

Even though Jewish cultural life seemingly flourished under Communist rule, a reactionary wave was being directed at the Jewish refugees who had flocked to the perceived safety of Vilna in fear of the Germans. For the Jewish and Zionist political parties, the situation was particularly dangerous. Jews running toward Vilna and away from German-occupied Poland were targeted and hunted down by the Russians. Menachem Begin, who later became prime minister of Israel, and other major leaders from the Zionist Revisionist party all feared for their lives. Aware of the dangers, Malka's father confronted my father, his new tenant. 'Listen,' he said to me. 'These are bad times. Nobody knows what the future holds. We need to know what your intentions are with our daughter.' I answered him as best I could: 'Well, at the moment I am Malka's boyfriend. I don't know about the future.' He looked at me, patted me on the shoulder and said: 'Okay, okay. Don't worry. Whatever will be, I will always make a living and whatever it is, you will be part of it.' I thanked him for his generosity. I was grateful for that."

The Soviet authorities, increasingly concerned about potential sources of rebellion, began to regard the organizers of the Zionist meetings and gatherings as a threat. They directed their backlash sentiments toward what they called "enemies of the people"—Polish army officers and certain Jewish leaders. With their secret service commando NKVD units, forerunners of the KGB, they actively sought to purge these alleged anti-Communist movements. Rumors and reports in the newspapers spread the alarming news of escalating arrests of suspected leaders or radicals, who were sent to Siberia and far-away territories in Asia. Anyone thought to oppose Lenin-Stalin ideology was targeted for swift reprisal and punishment. The rightwing leaders of Betar clearly were not fans of the Russian ideology of Socialism or their extreme Communist propaganda and they feared for the safety of their prominent spokesmen. Worried that my father's cousin, David Jutan, a high-profile activist in the Revisionist movement, was at risk of being imprisoned or exiled to Russia, they knew he had to be hidden. But where?

"In our basement," says my father. "We concluded that the best place to hide him would be in the cellar of my father's apartment house in Kalwaryska Street. After all, we had a friendly 'tenant,' the Russian officer, who lived there. We relied on his trust. This hiding place would be only temporary, because David had managed to secure papers for a transfer through Soviet Russia to get to Palestine." In the middle of all this political intrigue, David and his girlfriend, Sara, managed to get married in a ceremony that took place in the beautiful Choral Synagogue. According to my father, all the important Jewish dignitaries and personalities attended the celebration.

In those days of fervent political affiliations, the tension and conflict experienced by the Jewish community came not only from the foreign invading powers, but, as is still all too common, from within the community itself. Members of the various political parties battled aggressively and vociferously for the domination of their particular ideology. Arguing violently, Jews fought with one another, often betraying one another to the authorities. In the climate of fear induced by the occupation, the squabbling took on serious, often fatal consequences. My father recalls that after a raid on the Jewish right-wing Zionist offices instigated by the Jewish Communist groups and youth movements supporting the Marxist ideology, David Jutan and his new bride, Sara, along with Menachem Begin and his wife, Aliza, and a few of their friends were quickly spirited away once more, to spend several nights hiding in the safety of the cellar of Zacharias's home. Soon, through all sorts of complicated manipulations of falsified papers, the newlyweds managed to get visas to leave Poland for Palestine.

"My family preferred not to dwell on what could have happened had we been found hiding the state's 'enemies' in our cellar. Violence from anywhere is bad, but it's worse when it comes from your own people. And in those perilous times, you never knew who could become your enemy and turn you in," my father says. "Visas. You see, everything depended on getting the right paperwork," he explains. "People could leave Vilna via Moscow. The American Joint Distribution Committee aided by providing funds to enable many prominent Jews to leave. Certain consuls went beyond their duty to provide visas to other countries, too. There was so much behind-the-scenes scheming and planning going on to help people get out, it's impossible to describe."

Much later, I learned about some of those few good men, concerned citizens like the young American editor, Varian Fry, who helped smuggle European artistic talents Marc Chagall, Max Ernst, Hannah Arendt and Jacques Lipchitz to freedom, and diplomats like Bingham, Sugihara, and Ho, who assisted the frantic Jewish refugees in their efforts to leave. These men of conscience and courage followed their own ethical code, boldly defying their governments' restrictive quotas or mandates, often to the detriment of their own professional and family status, some even to eventual personal economic ruin. Literally taking matters into their own hands, they worked tirelessly around the clock, writing out hundreds of visas, day after day, to save as many Jews as they could under the crucial time constraints. By issuing illegal visas, they helped save thousands of lives.

"What was so important about David and Sara having to leave quickly?" I ask. Snapping back at me with a scowl, my father says: "This is not good. I must talk without being interrupted, and then you will ask me questions later, and I will write down the answers for you." I watch his struggle for control, his frustration and irritation. In his world, I realize, everything is a battle for survival or domination. Usually, his outbursts silence me. Not this time, though. I trust my instincts and ask my question again. "Well, I was losing a cousin, my best friend," he acquiesces. "He was like a brother to me. When David went, it seemed as though a part of my life had gone with him. I don't think I realized it at that time, but I really felt his absence, and I missed him very, very much."

The Prisoner

✦

Vilna, Poland, 1940–41

There is more to life than the "I" can see.

Under Soviet domination, life in Vilna was hard but at least safe. The Jewish population swelled to a record 70,000, counting all the Jews who fled Warsaw and other German-occupied territories. The influx of Russians coming into Vilna looking for places to stay caused an acute housing shortage in the city. By the end of 1939, strict regulations were being enforced, with the order going out that people with more than one domicile must reregister at only one place.

In the middle of 1940, Malka's father once more took my father aside for a friendly chat. My father replays the conversation: "He said to me: 'Look. I don't want to be unpleasant about this, but we need to register you as living here with us and not with your father at his place. It is only fair to the system. Besides, the committee of the apartment has been bothering us with questions, and they can make trouble for us, which we do not want.' After the talk, I decided it was better for me to be registered at my own father's house anyway."

The outcome came along in an unexpected manner. This time, it was Malka's mother who came to talk to my father: "I know what's happening between you and my daughter," she said. "She doesn't want me to tell you, but I must. She is pregnant. There! Now you know. Now you have to make a decision."

My father, shocked and dismayed, immediately went to his father to discuss what he had just learned. Zacharias asked if he had slept with Malka. My father nodded. "And now she is pregnant?" his father asked. My father repeated what Malka's mother had told him. For the ethical Zacharias, there was only one way to solve the problem—the honorable way. "Then the only thing you can do is marry her," he declared.

Israel Jutan was not keen on the idea of marrying Malka. However, he valued his father's advice to do the right thing, so arrangements were made with the rabbi to perform the marriage ceremony but to postpone the official registration. A small wedding took place at Malka's house, with a little wine and the traditional breaking of the glass. And so it was that at age twenty-one he became a rather reluctant husband.

And then came another unexpected event. Around June 24, 1941, my father heard the unusual sounds of explosions. The deep, rumbling drone of German Stukas, the low-flying airplanes, filled the sky, and bombs began falling on factories and military barracks. Suddenly his beloved city, Vilna, was under attack. One bomb fell near the Green Bridge, close to where his father lived. As soon as he heard the explosions, my father ran from Malka's house where he was now staying again, straight to his father's house to check if he was alright. Not finding him there, my father concluded he must have run somewhere else, either to his brother's or his sister's residence. Only Aunt Rachel, his stepmother, was at home, agitated, because she could not go to work at the hospital.

A tremendous panic broke out in the town. With great consternation, the citizens of Vilna saw the Russian soldiers rushing everywhere, on the run. My father couldn't believe his eyes. The mighty Soviet Red Army could be seen on every form of vehicle—trucks, cars, bicycles—all on the road, fleeing Vilna and heading back to Russia. The telephones stopped working. People were scurrying wildly about in the streets. Quickly, my father ran to find his friends from Masada, and they reached a unanimous decision. If the Germans were moving in they had better move out. Malka told him she wanted to stay close to her parents and that the boys should go ahead without her. Hastily gathering some belongings, my father and his friends met up and joined the march of people evacuating the city. On the streets leading out of Vilna toward Minsk, the young men merged with the fleeing mass that had already become a steady flow of hundreds of people moving on horses, foot, and bicycles.

Desperate to escape the terror of the advancing Germans, people had appeared from everywhere, carrying *peklach*, parcels, packages, bags, and luggage, all shlepping their belongings on their backs, donkeys, baby carriages, wheelbarrows, and makeshift carts. Herded together, they moved as a unit, surging forward alongside the Russian soldiers huddled in their military vehicles. Every so often, when they heard the low, whining rumble of the approaching German airplanes, they would dash off the road to cower in the fields. Like monster mosquitoes, the droning enemy planes swooped down, dropping their exploding bombs on the roads behind and in front of them. But no one dared stop moving forward. Even at night, they kept on walking. After a day and a half of nonstop walking, the fleeing group saw an alarming sight on the road in front of them. Hordes of people were staggering toward them. Soon enough, they learned the bad news from those haggard strangers: The Germans were ahead of them. Trapped in the middle, there was nothing for them to do but turn around and walk back. By the time my father and his friends returned to Vilna, the Germans had settled in and taken command.

That July the Nazis put into effect their ruthless mass-eradication program, seizing thousands of Jews in their homes or on their way to work, ordering some to pack a small suitcase of essentials, under the guise of being sent off to work. Those Jews were never seen again. Their family members, left behind, assumed their loved ones had been shipped off to the east to work. In reality, many had been taken to the forests of Ponar, also known as Ponary, about six miles outside Vilna. Once a vacation resort area, Ponar had been turned into a mass-killing field by the Germans. There, the Jews were forced to undress and then shot execution-style, their bodies tumbling into gaping round pits that had been previously excavated by the Soviets in anticipation of storing large fuel tanks. My mother's father, Nochum Rosenthal, the publisher of a daily Jewish newspaper, *Der Ovund Kourier,* the man after whom I was named, was taken there and murdered in one of the first roundups. According to official reports, the torture, degradation, and mass killings in Ponar took place from 1941 until the end of the war, when in the last days just before liberation, a small group of prisoners, bound in ankle chains, were ordered to get rid of the evidence and forced to burn the remains of tens of thousands of victims buried in the sandy pits of Ponar.

"In the first week of September 1941, thousands of Jews were imprisoned at nearby Lukiski Prison for the alleged shooting of a few German soldiers," my father continues. "The shooting had actually been carried out by some Lithuanians, but it was used as a pretext for getting rid of many Jews, including public officials, women, and children. The rest of us were forced to leave our homes and belongings and enter the Vilna Ghetto. They cordoned off about six small winding streets in the old Jewish section for all the Jews of Vilna to live in," my father says. "Two ghettos were established, one larger and one smaller, for skilled and unskilled workers. Within a month, everyone in the smaller ghetto was murdered, including cousin David's parents, Samuel and Asya."

The routine persecution and killings continued. Public proclamations, solely addressing the Jews—warnings, demands, restrictions, and prohibitions in German, Lithuanian, and Polish—were plastered all over the buildings and in the newspapers. "The Germans were extremely well organized and methodical, speedily obtaining information about who in the town possessed valuables or desirable objects. Whatever material goods could have been sold or bartered for food or help from the Gentiles, they simply took away from us. They had only been in Vilna a fortnight, when they had learned about my stamp collection. That is when the Gestapo man came and robbed me of my prize collection," my father says.

A few days after the stamp-collection incident, he had hurried over to his high school friend Jerzy's house in an attempt to hide his remaining stamp albums. He trusted that this friend, whose mother had spurned him, would feel obliged to help. Jerzy, at first trepid, eventually gave in to my father's pleas to safeguard his albums. A public announcement was made shortly afterward ordering all Jews to hand over household goods, including radios, telephones, typewriters, fur coats, and other valuables at designated areas. No receipts were given for any of the confiscated items. The Germans had a plan for everything. They would strip the Jews of their belongings, one by one. They would prohibit contact with the Gentiles. Any form of communication with the locals in the outside world was strictly forbidden under threat of death. "Everything became a life-and-death situation," my father remembers. "Fear was everywhere, not only for us Jews."

My father knew that to obtain some extra food he would have to get his stamp album back, since stamps could be sold on the black market. Knowing full well that he was risking lives, his own and those he dealt with in the bartering, he was desperate and daring enough to take the risk. One day he joined a work unit going out of the ghetto, after ascertaining that their work assignment was near where Jerzy lived. Approaching his friend's house, he quickly slipped away from the group and knocked on the door. When Jerzy opened the door, and saw who his visitor was, he was struck with terror. Hurriedly, Jerzy gave him the album and some food, all the while begging his former schoolmate to leave.

My father remembers the incident vividly: "He was so nervous, either of being caught talking to a Jew or just of having me there, that he kept repeating: 'Please, for the love of God, go! Leave us in peace—but go, go now! I cannot do anything for you, please go!' I explained to him that I could not leave just then. I would be caught. I had to wait until the unit returned so I could go back with the group into the ghetto. Jerzy told me he had to go somewhere and didn't want to leave me alone with his old granny. I looked at him and said: 'Jerzy, my dear friend, what is the story with you? We have known each other for so long, and now you look at me with scared eyes and push me out of your house? Is this how you treat an old friend, a friend you trusted with intimate secrets and romances and your deepest thoughts?'

"With a nervous panic in his voice, he answered me: 'Well, this is life; this is life. If they find you here, I will be dead. I don't want to die. Please understand, I don't want to die. I'm sorry, I just cannot help you. You must understand.' But I didn't. I expected a friend to help in desperate times," my father says, shaking his head. "I was very upset and disappointed when he pushed me away. Jerzy was a scout, a proud Pole who wanted to be an officer. In my mind at the time, he revealed himself as a faithless coward the moment he succumbed to the Nazis' anti-Jewish ordinances. But as I talk about it now, so many years later, I feel I was wrong to judge him so harshly. He had done what he could for me. He had hidden my stamp album for me. I had no right to expect more. After all, look at his environment! There was no love or affinity for a Jew in his home, nor in thousands of other Polish homes. It was the Catholic priests, I believe, who led them to blame and hate all Jews for what they called a crime, something we never committed in the first place. When those boys on the streets shoved me, accusing me of killing Christ, I didn't know what they were talking about. 'I don't even know this person, so how could I kill him?' I kept shouting at them. What did any of that ancient history have to do with me or my family? But at that time of Nazi occupation, the threat of punishment for assisting a Jew was real, so of course Jerzy was truly afraid for his life. To help a Jew in those days demanded enormous courage or moral conviction."

My father pauses.

"And incidentally, you did not ask what was so important that I would risk my own life and his, too, by leaving the ghetto work group to go to his house. I will tell you. It was my only copy of a *World Stamp* catalogue." Taking a deep breath, my father nods his head, letting out a long sigh: "Yaaah!" as if that one long release of breath could dispel his own regret and past harsh judgment of a scared young man, a former friend.

How marvelous it would be, I think, if in just one huge sigh, we could relinquish a lifetime of sorrow, heartache, prejudice, condemnation, and disappointment, letting it all disperse and evaporate into the air. From my Hebrew lessons in Jerusalem, I recall that *ruach,* the word for breath and wind and air, is the same as that for spirit, viewed by Kabbalists as the animating element of the soul. I think of how we begin and end our physical life with a breath. Air. Breath. It is our precious life force. Like a contagious yawn, my father's sigh forces me to take one of my own. It feels good. Now I know why my mother used to sigh so much. She was letting the past go, little by little.

What would I have done in the same situation, had a friend come to me asking for help? Listening to his description of war, I find it hard to fully absorb. As a free citizen of the democratic United States, how can I possibly understand another time and place where ordinary, innocent people lived, literally holding their breath, in constant fear for their lives? Thankfully, I never experienced terror of that magnitude and am grateful for that. I want to believe that under dire circumstances I would do the noble thing, regardless of fear. Truth is, I have never been tested, and I'm also grateful for that. "There but for the grace of God go I," has been my motto. The only thing I feel certain of is that I cannot judge or criticize others if I have never been in their position.

For the many who did not help in those perilous times, there were nevertheless some quiet, unsung heroes—ordinary, often humble citizens, some religious, some not—who bravely aided Jews and others at grave risk to their own family's lives. I believe it is important to remember that. During the Holocaust, when the worst, the most vulgar of humanity's depravity was unleashed, there were also those gentle souls who exemplified the best of humanity in acts of dignifying kindness. We may never hear of their stories, and many of them will remain unacknowledged and uncompensated. But they were there. For them, it was not about the monetary reward. It was not about following the immoral orders of others, but obeying the dictates of their own noble hearts. Theirs was the true valor.

I spoke to one of those gentle saviors. In September of 2003, while in Vilnius, I attended the official ceremony held in the grand Napoleon's Palace of my father's stories to honor those Christian citizens, some living and some posthumously, who helped save Jewish lives. Moved by the sight of those frail elderly people receiving medals sixty years later, I wanted to speak to them and hear why they helped Jews despite the real danger of Nazi retaliation. With the aid of a translator I asked a small, old, shriveled woman, one of these "righteous Gentiles," what made her hide a Jewish woman and her young son, who was now the president of the Cultural Association of Lithuania and the organizer of my visit to Vilnius. Shrugging her shoulders, she smiled, let out a sigh and said in a soft voice: "I was young. I saw what was happening around me and knew it was wrong. I could not stand by without doing something. It was simple: I had to do the right thing."

The Husband

✦

Vilna, Poland, 1941–46

Some loves shine bright like the sun;
others, like falling stars, disappear into the night sky.

"How was it that everyone went along with the German proclamations and rulings?" I ask my father, even though, as a former South African growing up in the intimidating police state of the apartheid regime, I should know the answer.

"Ugh! It was all made clear to us," he explains. "By force. By decree. By pointing of the gun. By taking from us gradually, methodically, all we owned. You must understand what it is when hundreds of soldiers, not only Germans, but Lithuanians, too, with boots and guns are surrounding you, and you are just a civilian. We Jews were law-abiding citizens. We were used to obeying the rules. The Germans were now the authority in charge, making the rules. In the first instance, we had to turn everything over to the Jewish Committee. They were collecting ransom to free ten Jewish hostages taken by the Germans. Our finest men of distinction—the rabbi, the president of the committee, the banker, the chief doctor, all important people, leaders of the community—were taken in the first days. The Nazis announced that they would kill them if they didn't receive a certain amount of gold, silver, and money for their release. We believed their threats. Kidnappings were nothing new to us. In medieval times, rulers frequently captured Jews for ransom. The same mafia tactics are employed throughout history. No different with terrorists today. Brute force to induce terror to spread fear."

The fearful Vilna Jews responded rapidly to the orders of the surrender of goods. Obediently, they stood in long lines in front of the office of the Jewish Committee, waiting to give generously of their accumulated treasured valuables—heirlooms, silver candelabra, rings, jewelry—anything to save the lives of their leaders. In the end, they were plainly robbed. The men they thought they could save with their carefully collected, sentiment-laden, handcrafted possessions of gold and silver were murdered in cold blood with machine-made lead bullets. "What fools we were," my father says. "The Germans first took our ransom; then they killed the hostages, claiming that the value the Jewish community placed on the hostages was clearly not high enough for their lives to be spared. They knew how to add salt to our wounds."

The Nazis' list of restrictions on activities by Jews grew progressively more prohibitive and punitive with each new proclamation. Forbidden to walk on the sidewalks, Jews had to walk on the cobbled streets. They could not walk in pairs, only single file. Systematically, incrementally, Jews were stripped of their riches, their rights, their dignity, and their humanity. It was the Nazis' meticulous master plan of subjugation, degradation, and eventual annihilation.

War was a free license for sadism. Vicious verbal attacks against Jews were broadcast on public radio for the Polish and Lithuanian population. Happy to conspire in trapping and taunting Jews, the Lithuanian police and their Polish helpers eagerly helped the Germans they regarded as heroes for forcing out the despised Bolsheviks, whom they associated with Jews. My father recalls that if a Jewish man walked by in the streets, the locals would grab him, point a gun at him, and order him to clean the street with his bare hands, while they stood by and laughed, joking and cursing, often kicking him when he was down on his knees. If someone resembling a Jew was standing in line for a bread ration, the locals would push him or her to the end of the line. Often the victim would be forced to walk back home in silent rage, empty-handed. For the Vilna Jews, already forcibly removed from their homes and deprived of their possessions, there was at every moment of every day, at every corner of every street, always the threat of attack and violence.

My father and his group of Jewish friends decided that it was not safe to remain in Vilna, where the *chapoonehs*, the catchers, waited like vultures. Thinking that in the countryside there might be fewer nasty German soldiers and angry Lithuanians ready to pounce, people were going in search of work from the Polish peasants who might need extra laborers in the rural areas.

"I joined a group of sixty boys and men, and we went about forty kilometers from Vilna to Biala Waka where there were peat patches," my father says. "The payment was in food only, and the working conditions were bearable, although for those of us not accustomed to hard work with a spade in the field it took some time to get over the unfamiliar back pains and calluses. On Sundays, when we had half days off, our families would visit us. Malka would come with her mother only. Her father was afraid to visit in case he got caught on the way."

One Sunday, during one of those visits, my father looked at Malka and noticed something. "Wait a minute," he said. "You don't look very different. What happened to the pregnancy?"

"Oh," she said. "I aborted it."

"What? But why, why, why didn't you discuss it with me?" he asked her, shocked.

"Oh," she said lightly, "I talked it over with Mother, and we both agreed it was the best thing to do. I needed to do it quickly, so I went in and it was over, and that was that. It's all taken care of now. No need to get upset."

Malka's casual manner riled my father. But the more he pondered the situation, the more he rationalized that, given the circumstances of war, it was probably the logical thing to do. However, something kept bothering him. Shouldn't Malka have been quite large by now? Young men in those days were not so informed about pregnancy and birth as they are today, and he hadn't paid too much attention to changes in her body. Suddenly he began to wonder whether the whole pregnancy story had been true in the first place. What if it had all been a bluff? What if she had tricked him and manipulated him into marriage? More and more convinced of Malka's deception, his former loving feelings began to wane, and he no longer felt as kindly disposed toward her. "Even though she was officially my wife, I was now just a husband out of duty," he admits. "But because her family, which was now mine, had been so kind to me, I resolved to continue to help them as they had helped me. But toward Malka my heart had become stone."

My father continues: "When we were later taken to the camps, we lived in separate barracks: I with men, Malka with women," he says. One day he heard a rumor that she was in love with one of the men in the same work group. When she came back that evening, he confronted her, asking if what he heard was true. She told him that she did love that man, and if they survived this nightmare, she might want to stay with him. "But at the moment," he says, "she wanted to be with me as well. She said she felt very confused and scared. I did not know how to answer her."

Later that night a girl ran up to the men's barracks, knocking on the window and calling out my father's name. "When I came outside, she told me that Malka had disappeared and had perhaps committed suicide. I ran with her to various outbuildings to look for Malka. We finally found her in the toilet outhouse, hanging by a belt over one of the toilets, but still alive," he recalls.

"I untied her and carried her to the clinic, to Dr. Jaszpan. When I asked her why she had done such an awful, foolish thing, she looked at me sadly and said that she just couldn't take it any more. The girls in the barracks had scolded her, telling her how badly she was behaving. She said she felt terrible when she knew I had found out about her love affair. So, she tried to end it all for the good of everyone. Of course, at that moment, I comforted her and told her I would forgive her, that time would be kind to us all, we must just wait it out. But later on, back in my barracks, when I had time to reflect, to think about this rationally, I wondered if that was also just another of Malka's dramatic false alarms. It was staged to look like she was hanging, but I remembered she had tied the belt around her chin, not her neck. When I checked with Dr. Jaszpan, he confirmed he had not noticed any marks or bruises on her neck."

My father never said a word to Malka about his suspicions. It was not worth making an issue about, he explains. At the dissolution of the camp, the men and women were separated and taken to Tallinn, Estonia's capital and port where they were loaded onto a ship and brought back to Poland. My father's destination was the Stutthof concentration camp, while Malka was sent to another. He decided once again to let fate run its course and dictate the future of his loveless wartime marriage.

I had known about my father's first marriage before he divulged his secret to me. The first time I heard about it was on the eve of my own wedding. My father's step cousin Luba had made the long trip from Melbourne, Australia, to Cape Town and had invited my fiancé and me to a special celebration dinner, just the three of us. I was biting into a tasty piece of steak when she asked if my father had told me about his first wife. "His first what?" I repeated, my fork hanging in the air. Quite nonchalantly, Luba informed me that during the war he had been married briefly. It was an impetuous marriage, she said. No children. She just thought I needed to know, she remarked. Most of my parents' past was still a secret to me, but I never suspected that kind of newsflash. About to embark on my own journey of marriage, I thought it best to leave further investigation of that intriguing subject for later. I never told my father that I knew about his first marriage. That would now be my secret. I also felt certain that for my father there would be only one truly beloved wife—my mother.

Now, hearing about Malka from my father himself, I sense that he is ashamed of his first marriage. It was not a marriage of choice but rather one of coercion, convenience, and concern—perhaps even guilt. It seems he regarded it as a trick, a manipulation. Maybe that, in part, explains why Mr. Piat, the attractive widower, chose not to remarry after my mother's death, despite the plethora of women willing to offer up their bodies and surrender their last names to him.

What makes one the particular *besherte,* or destined one, the soul partner and another not, I wonder. Do we really get to choose the partners in our life, or is it written in the stars? Is it love, or is it luck disguised as timing? Is it providence, karma, or a mishmash of all that conspires to bring two souls together, or intervenes to keep them apart? A strange image pops up in my mind of an old, overworked, harried bureaucrat, a manic matchmaker, a wedding-planning casting agent–type *yenta,* sitting up in the clouds with broken spectacles, teased hair, and a ticking stopwatch. She's shuffling through cards of pre-assigned matches, trying her best to maneuver clueless couples together down here on earth. When the cosmic alarm goes off she drops invisible seeds of dissension into their minds to split them apart. Then she reshuffles the cards. Maybe she can explain to me the mystery of how strangers become lovers and then those same lovers become strangers again. And if it is truly all preordained by God, or what my father refers to as fate, then how can we really consider anything that happens a mistake? And what of my legacy of divorce that I am discovering? What of my own marriage? Has it become one of duty or love? And how would I be able to tell the difference? As I listen to the man who set the stage for how I learned to relate to love, I wonder what more I will learn about my own heart.

There's more to the story of Malka, he tells me. About three months after the war ended, my father was alone in his apartment in Jelenia Góra. His new love, Chayela Rosenthal, with whom he was now living, was away performing in the Displaced Persons' Camps. Hearing a knock on the door, he opened it to find Malka standing there with a friend. He was shocked. He had presumed she had been killed by the Nazis.

"I got your name from the Jewish Committee," Malka said, staring at him. "I've heard all about you, what you are doing these days, and who you are with. I have come to ask you for a divorce and a proper *get*."

She also asked him for some money, clothing, or whatever else he could give her. Whatever he had available, he handed over to her. They then went together to the Jewish Committee where the rabbi in attendance greeted and ushered them into his office. Gravely, he asked my father if he still wanted to be married to Malka.

"No," came his swift reply. Malka gave the same negative response.

"Then I, as a Cohen, had to say three times that I was divorcing her," my father says calmly. "I spread my fingers apart in the sign of the Cohen and followed in my father's way." The rabbi and the two of them signed some papers, which Malka took, folded, and tucked in her purse.

"We looked at each other," my father says. "We had signed our farewell. I extended my hand to her. She hesitantly put out hers. We shook hands and wished each other well. We said goodbye, and that was the last time we ever saw each other."

That night, my father says, he went back to his empty apartment and contemplated all that had happened to him. He thought about how he had stayed behind in Vilna to be the good son to his sickly father rather than leave for America, his dream. He reflected on the obligation of duty and the nature of love and how the two can often be confused as one. He had stayed with Malka to be the good husband and the good son, honoring his father's advice. He had tried to be a good son-in-law, to repay the debt he felt he owed his wife's family for their kindness. He even thought about the different kinds of love his father Zacharias might have felt for his two very different wives, Vava and Rachel, and his filial love for Reuven.

Falling asleep in the early hours of morning, he woke up certain of one thing.

"I was happy to be alive," he says. "I was grateful that I was now in love with the most delightful, talented, and endearing girl, the young star of the Vilna Ghetto theater, the woman I knew I wanted to share my future with," he smiles, "and have children with. Yah! Your mother."

Many years later, during one of his first trips to New York to visit his old Masada buddy Ziamka, who had immigrated to the United States, he learned that Malka had married an American, had a daughter, and was living in the U.S. Taking a chance one day, they found her phone number and called her. Malka refused to speak to my father. Perhaps she associated her first husband with times of tragedy, of shame and remorse. Perhaps even guilt and deceit. "Please," she told Ziamka, "do not mention his name to me ever again. I cut this period out of my memory."

Several years later, on a subsequent visit to the States, he met a former Vilna girlfriend of Malka's at a Holocaust gathering and asked her the unanswered question that had nagged him for many years. Had Malka ever carried his unborn child? The friend admitted there had never been any pregnancy. Malka, she said, had considered Israel Jutan a good catch. The rest was a ruse. Angered at first, he felt vindicated at this confirmation of his earlier suspicions and consoled himself with the thought that at least the marriage of convenience had worked for them both, perhaps even helping to save their lives.

Some years later, when my father heard from Ziamka that Malka's daughter, her only child, had died tragically at a young age, he was moved enough to want to write to her and send his condolences. Ziamka persuaded him not to. Sometimes the dead, he was advised, whether it be a person or a relationship, needs the respectful space of silence.

The Witness

✦

Vilna Ghetto, Poland, 1941

Bearing witness is the work of more than just one person.

When the German announcement came that all Jews must leave their homes and take up residence in the ghetto, situated just ten minutes from Malka's house, my father made sure he got there early enough to secure a good place in one of the buildings.

"I entered the gate on Rudnicka Street, opposite the Catholic Church of All Saints," he says. "My instinct pushed me to enter the first apartment house on the right side of the street. Already people were there in the yard with whatever bundles they could carry, occupying rooms on the ground and first floors. I quickly ventured up to the second floor. When I entered a room, about thirty by twenty square feet, I met the tenant whose parents owned the shop on the ground floor. The SS and Lithuanian police had occupied it and turned it into their guardroom at the gate. Malka was to share my corner in the room. Her parents and younger sister went somewhere else. My father was able to get a room in the same building as I was but on the ground floor, because he couldn't walk upstairs."

Soon the furniture was removed and that one room with its exposed wood parquet floor became a sleeping place for twelve and sometimes more when new people arrived desperately looking for a place to rest. The mattresses and cushions, which some people had dragged over there, were placed upright against the walls during the day. In the beginning there was no electric power for cooking and no wood or coal for the stoves for heating until the busy ghetto administration, known as the Judenrat, arranged for more wood supplies to prevent people from further dismantling windows, fences, and doors to use as firewood. When the occupants of the smaller ghetto were taken away and killed, people from the larger ghetto were permitted to take some of the possessions left behind. My father was allocated a bunk and a small mattress for which he built a stand containing shelves to store utensils and clothes.

Food was scarce. A public kitchen was established where people could get a few rations, some soup, and tea—"hot water to warm up your stomach," my father says. Usually the first meal was at midday. Those who worked outside the ghetto were given some soup and a piece of bread by their employers. In due time, home restaurants were established, where for a certain sum of money one could even have a party of ten for dinner or a *simcha,* a celebration for a special occasion. This was thanks to the *shtarkeh,* appropriately named "the strong ones." They were the fearless, street-smart, business-minded men who obtained contraband by dealing and negotiating with their former Polish neighbors and by bribing German soldiers. The *shtarkeh* arranged for supplies to be snuck in and out of sewers and secret places, to bring in more food and other products necessary for survival.

With the passing of time, the Judenrat could barely provide adequate food for their workers to stay alive. To cope with his constantly gnawing hunger, my father pretended that he was put on a strict diet.

"What astonished me," he says, "was seeing my formerly portly father, who'd been so sickly and was already much thinner, now walking daily to his work without the use of his cane, which for the last four years had constantly been at his side."

When the Nazis ordered the registration of all those who could work, Zacharias had been helped by his wife's brother, Mr. Tunkiel, the banker, to find better work outside the ghetto in another city. "A German policeman took him and his wife, Rachel, on his double motorcycle with the small seats on the side and drove them out of the ghetto to a town called Lida, where they both worked as doctors. When Lida was liquidated, the same policeman, for the same fee presumably, brought them back to Vilna," my father said.

What my father didn't tell me was that my grandfather had provided detailed testimony to the Red Cross Observers as witness to the atrocities he had seen in Lida. He described the brutal Nazi mass shootings of citizens of Vilna, including key figures of the Jewish administration, executed in the prison courtyard in Lida by the Gestapo. I read about Zacharias's role as eyewitness from an article found by my newfound cousin, Lizzie, when she and her partner Martin visited me in New Jersey in April 2006. While researching the Jutan family at the Yivo Institute in Manhattan, they came upon a reference to the tragedy of Lida in a tiny footnote in a book, which read: *See the entry of March 1942. In the Yivo Archive (Kaczerginski-Sutzkever Collection) there is an eyewitness account by Zkharye Jutan.*

Surely if my father had been told that story by his father he'd have passed it on to me, his chronicler. Could the reasons Zacharias did not tell his son what he had witnessed have been the same as those preventing my own parents from telling me what they had seen? Was it the sheer horror of it all that overwhelmed the senses and gutted the emotions? Zacharias had witnessed his Vilna friends and acquaintances, men and women, ripped apart at close range by dumdum bullets that later rendered some of them unidentifiable. I imagine the caring physician so dedicated to saving lives would have suffered greatly having to stand by helplessly, watching the vicious murder and callous cruelty of innocent civilians around him. I believe he would not have wanted to burden his son with more painful emotions. He must have recognized that the prescription for survival at that time was inner strength and outer resilience. Every ounce of fortitude was necessary medicine for endurance. Zacharias, the responsible doctor, was determined to survive, to remain strong enough to help others when he could.

My grandfather's testimony found its way to me regardless, reminding me of my legacy of bearing witness. That this remote piece of documentation came through my father's distant relatives makes it clear to me I am not alone in this journey. Chapters are still unfolding. Circles are widening. When I least expect it, when I most need it, more evidence appears, more graphic stories, more synchronistic events to add yet more pieces to the unfinished puzzle. That is the story of history. There is always more to rewrite.

My father continues. "All postal connections with the outside world were severed from the first week of the establishment of the ghetto in 1941. Radio contact was illegal, but the underground resistance still took risks to listen to smuggled radios to notify people of the war's progress. We Jews had little knowledge of the Nazis' plans. Never knowing when the next *aktion* or attack would be, we were constantly in fear. We just knew it could come at any time."

He recalls one particular Yom Kippur night in the Vilna Ghetto. Although they had grown accustomed to eating little, the Jews still fasted according to the tradition. They were eagerly awaiting sundown, marking the end of the fast and the beginning of the traditional small feast that celebrated the conclusion of the most holy day in the Jewish calendar.

"The evening prayers were just about to start when the wooden gates of the ghetto burst open and in stormed a group of SS men with the death-skull insignia on their uniforms" my father recalls. "With the collaboration of the Lithuanian police, they started to round up men, women, and children from the streets, synagogues, yards, and cellars. They kept shouting: *'Raus, raus zur Arbeit!'*—out, out to work! Herding the bewildered people together at gunpoint, they forced them to run toward a square where another company of German soldiers and Lithuanian police, with machine guns aimed, were waiting for them."

In the evening darkness, the strict blackout regulations were forgotten. For the first time, the streets of the ghetto sparkled with the flickering lights of many candles, flashlights and automobile lights from the trucks the Germans brought in to remove the sick and the elderly from the hospital. The pandemonium grew worse when the Nazis began using their rifles and bayonets to beat those who didn't or couldn't move. If people ran too slowly, they kicked them with their boots. Unperturbed by the growing tumult and pleas, the ruthless SS killers, whose trained mission was murder, brutally dragged people from their homes and aggressively shoved them toward the ghetto gates at the end of Rudnicka Street. The silence of that Jewish holy night was pierced by a cacophony of jangled screams and wild cries of Nazi SS men repetitively barking their orders, terrified children screaming for their parents, anxious mothers calling for their families, and old men, still draped in their prayer shawls, wailing their prayers. "I could hear the frightening cries of the panic-stricken crowds from all around, and they only increased my own feelings of doom," my father says.

As it dawned on people that the German soldiers had come to take them not to work, as their orders said, but probably to their death, they frantically began to look for places to hide. Secret passages, prepared in advance, were quickly opened and closed again when filled. My father managed to escape from the street where he had been caught in a group. Trying to keep in the shadows, he ran swiftly to the block where they lived, to join his father in the attic of their building, their previously designated hideout.

"Fifteen of us were crammed into this small space. We didn't utter a word. We didn't dare make a move. Just squeezed together in silence. Through the thin walls, we heard heavy steps and Germans shouting," my father says. "We kept ourselves silent as we heard the Nazis shouting curses at the two elderly ladies from the nearby apartment who were too ill to move by themselves. We heard the awful sounds of the women as they were dragged and thrown down the staircase. A mother hiding with us nearly choked her two-year-old daughter, pressing her hand tightly over the child's mouth to prevent her from making a sound. We were sweating profusely. My father's hand was clutching my right shoulder. I couldn't tell if it was for reassurance or from fright. After some time the mumbled cries and noises outside subsided. We heard some movement from the floor below, then footsteps outside our door and unrecognizable muffled talk. A knock came, then another, on the wall leading to our hiding place. Fear gripped my entire body. This was it! We had been betrayed! The Germans would take us away! Nobody moved. I held my breath. I could hear my father whispering some prayers.

"We waited, not moving, our beating hearts trying to jump out through our throats. My father's hand was no longer on me. He was doubled over, bent down in one of his cardiac attacks. I tried silently to help him. Then we heard a distinct shout in Yiddish: 'It is over! The Germans have left the ghetto!'"

After a while, they crept out, one by one, from their hideouts. A neighbor, who had escaped the slaughter, greeted the group that had hidden in the attic. They moved Zacharias onto a bed and gave him his pill. Down in the streets, they could hear people talking about the *aktions,* or surprise roundups. Rumors were sweeping through the ghetto. Some still believed that it was an *aktion* to gather people to do work somewhere, but others were talking about far worse intentions. One thing they all agreed on was that the Nazis had deliberately planned to execute this roundup on the most sacred of Jewish holy days.

"That Yom Kippur night, full of turmoil and despair, seemed to be the longest night," my father continues. "I could not fall sleep. At dawn, weary and exhausted, I was on my way again, being counted as I joined my group heading for our assigned work at the German barracks at the airport."

The next day in the ghetto was a flurry of people going in and out of the buildings, checking to see if loved ones were okay. Some wandered like lost souls, not knowing what to do, their family members having been snatched up. Children were left without parents, parents bereft of their children, a wife without a husband, a brother without a sister.

At the administration centre, officials tried to register the missing, to restore some kind of order, but to no avail. Everyone was in shock, dazed by the brutality that had brought such devastating loss and mocked their prayers to be inscribed for another year in the Book of Life.

On that one autumn day in 1941, the Nazis took away over five thousand people from the Vilna Ghetto. A few days after that Yom Kippur, one of the survivors of the massacre managed to make his way back to the ghetto. He told a tale no one wanted to believe was true. Describing how they were driven to Ponar Forest, outside Vilna, he recounted how the Nazis and their Lithuanian assistants taunted and beat the men, women and children during their forced march towards the pits. He spoke about all of them being subdued, and ordered on the spot to undress and stand naked in front of one another. Standing at the rim of a gaping pit, they were shot by several Nazi machine gunners, their bodies tumbling down into the large hole in the earth that now became a mass, open grave. Further waves of bodies covered those already murdered on the same spot, until the hole filled up with dead bodies. The last group of remaining Jews were given shovels and ordered to cover the mass graves with the sandy soil before they too were shot at dawn, their bodies left on top of the pile of corpses. This man, although wounded in his thigh, had survived by throwing himself in the pit after the first shot was fired. He lay there, pretending to be dead, while the drunken SS men and Lithuanian soldiers inspected the results of their day's shooting. After lying under the heaped corpses and soil for many dreadful hours, he managed to crawl out from under the pile of bodies during the night and make his way out of the forest to a nearby village. There, a local woman was compassionate and brave enough to give him shelter, treating his wounds and arranging for him to reach a group of Jewish laborers on their daily assignment in the fields. Slipping in amongst them, he had pretended to be one of the laborers returning in their group to the ghetto. The story, too gruesome to be absorbed by most, spurred some young activists, like Isaac Wittenberg, Abba Kovner and Vitka Kempner into action. For them it was a call to arms. Vowing never to go to the slaughter like lambs, they began to plan for an uprising, organizing and training a group of resistance fighters, called partisans, many of whom would eventually escape to the forest.

After this brutal *aktion*, the Vilna Ghetto went into deep mourning. The imprisoned Jews expected that the German soldiers could and would prepare more Yom Kippur nights for them, with the willing cooperation of the Lithuanian police. The closely monitored prisoners, like trapped animals within the confines of the walled, guarded Vilna Ghetto, had limited access to the outside world. Surrounded by a hostile local population, they understood the gravity of their situation. They were at the mercy of the murderous Nazis who showed no mercy.

The Clerk

✦

Vilna Ghetto, Poland, 1942

A story well told can save a life.

Soon after the violent Yom Kippur raid, someone in the ghetto labor bureau warned my father that the Germans were looking for him. Within days of arriving in Vilna, the Gestapo had taken over all the important public institutions, quickly setting up base in Napoleon's Palace, which the Soviets had evacuated when the German tanks rolled in. In their haste to escape, the Russians had carelessly left administrative papers lying around. There, in the palace, the Gestapo found my father's name, Israel Jutan, inscribed in the logs of his former English student, the Russian officer. They traced his name through the offices of the Ghetto Arbeitsamt, or labor bureau, in which every Jewish person had to be registered. Now he was on their list.

"Everyone had to be registered because without it," my father explains, "one could not get food rations. Most importantly, you needed to be registered to have a chance of working outside the Ghetto, which of course, could help you stay alive. Fortunately, this friend of mine from Betar who worked at the bureau told me the Gestapo were trying to find me."

Many of the ghetto policemen were chosen from within the ranks of the Revisionist party, the organization my father belonged to, because they already had the militaristic training required for maintaining order. Since the names of those working within the Arbeitsamt were never disclosed to authorities outside the ghetto, my father reckoned that it would be safer for him to stay in the ghetto working within the administration than continue to go to work as Malka's father's electrical assistant and risk being caught on a labor pass outside.

In short order, my father was introduced to Solomon Gens, the senior manager of the ghetto Arbeitsamt, who knew and respected his father, Zacharias. Solomon was the younger brother of the chief of the ghetto police, Jacob Gens, a captain in the reserves of the Lithuanian army, who had been a language teacher at Kovno Jewish High School. Appreciating the gravity of my father's threatened situation, Gens offered to employ him as a recorder of events, a clerk, within his office. With that position my father got a food card, which he could use to obtain potato and bread rations.

It was Jacob Gens, my father informs me, who helped save my grandfather. Zacharias, sent on an underground expedition to buy saccharine needed at the ghetto hospital, was spotted by a Lithuanian policeman who arrested him and sent him off to the infamous Lukiski prison, known as a one-way ticket to death. Jacob Gens, learning about the prominent doctor's imprisonment from another Lithuanian policeman, went immediately to the prison, traced someone he knew from his past affiliation with the army, and paid the necessary bribe to get Zacharias out of prison and back to the ghetto.

"My father returned with broken ribs and a bloody face," my father says. "In the prison, the Lithuanian policemen had beaten him savagely with a metal chair, causing him to be hospitalized for two weeks. Luckily, my father recovered."

In July 1942, Jacob Gens was appointed "ghetto representative," which put him in charge of all ghetto negotiations with the German authorities. My father remembers attending the monthly meetings Gens held in the large auditorium downstairs from the administration offices with the "brigadiers," those leaders of work groups employed outside the ghetto for the Nazis's war machine.

"Gens proclaimed that the basis of existence in the ghetto must be 'Labor, Discipline, and Order.' His view was that work would be our salvation. All residents must be productive," my father says. "Gens used to end his speeches by saying, in his loud, German-accented Yiddish: '*Mir veln zey iberlebben!*'—We will outlive them!" He even made plans to safeguard the children by organizing children's work units called the "Transport Brigade." Groups of orphans, seven to fourteen years old, were employed by the ghetto administration to operate dozens of wheelbarrows and handcarts for transportation purposes, helping to keep them from being easy prey at roundups.

"I knew of Joseph Muszkat, a former refugee from Warsaw who Gens put in charge of the Transport Brigade, from his position as the leader of the Masada organization in Poland," my father says. "Muszkat told my father who then told me, that Gens was secretly involved in army training for the ghetto police, preparing them to become partisans, freedom fighters in the forest." In my father's opinion, Jacob Gens was a good leader, a man of principles and great charm, who made friends easily. "Even his subordinates got on well with him," he says. "He was married to a non-Jewish Lithuanian woman, but he still maintained his strong secular Jewish identity and Zionist leanings. Jacob Gens, with his agility with languages, was someone who commanded respect and trust, even from the Germans."

Responsible for delivering thousands of Jews to the Nazis, Gens was also a controversial figure. Many of the Jews in the ghetto regarded him disdainfully as a dictator, mocking what they viewed as his imperial ways. Because of his leadership position that necessitated dealing with the Germans, he was blamed by many ghetto inhabitants for what they believed was his cooperation with the Nazis. What most people could not understand, my father points out, was the rationale behind Gens's deliberated actions. It was his calculated strategy to buy time and save more people by negotiating with the enemy. If sacrifice was a foregone conclusion, let it at least be planned. Better to cooperate and have some control than none, over who and how many were selected to die, for if left to the ruthless Nazis, it would just mean more random murderous rampages, more widespread disaster and fear, and many more deaths. When it came to delivering numbers of people dictated by the Nazis, Gens used his discretion and discernment in making difficult choices, often sacrificing the weak and sick for what he saw as the good of the whole community. This military-trained man no doubt understood that, in the end, it was all a question of strategy and everything was to be negotiated.

It was crucial, Gens maintained, to create a sense of order, normalcy, calm, and continuity in the midst of the horror-filled chaos and uncertainty of ghetto life. To boost the flailing morale, he believed in resurrecting the cultural activities of art, music, and entertainment that was so vital to Jewish life. To that end, Gens resolved to get an active theatre up and running in his ghetto by obtaining the necessary permission from the German authorities. By presenting regular, full-scale productions, often original musicals and concerts, the theatre would provide needed employment for people in the arts and temporary emotional diversion for the deprived ghetto population.

Many in the Jewish community expressed their outrage at the prospect of entertainment in the ghetto. Demonstrating their vehement opposition to what they firmly believed was inappropriate frivolity, groups of angry, indignant objectors smeared posters on the walls: "On a graveyard you don't play theatre!" However, Gens prevailed. The theatre was formed and concerts were staged. Starved for cultural transcendence, many of the ghetto inhabitants attended the shows, despite the knowledge that their German tormentors were sitting in the same audience, often in the front row, right next to Gens. Eager for escape of any kind, families, torn apart during the day, sat together in the darkened auditorium, watching performances that made them laugh and cry and forget for a brief moment their nightmarish circumstances. There, they were reminded of the dignity and decency of a cultured life, where one could be uplifted by an actor's passionate turn of phrase and a singer's refrain of hope. My actress/singer mother and her lyricist/playwright brother played key roles in what is today regarded as the cultural and spiritual resistance of the Vilna ghetto.

Most of the ghetto Jews, ignorant of Gens's good intentions and intense behind-the-scenes bargaining with the Nazis, saw those who worked side by side with the enemy as the enemy himself—guilt by association. Regrettably, as a clerk in the administration, distributing work passes, my father also incurred the wrath of those people he was not able to aid directly. During those traumatic times, those who were in enviable positions of relative power, like my young father, were often the target of resentment and malicious rumor, slander and, later, unfair accusations of causing deaths by their failure to help. When he could use his influence to assist, especially those he knew, he certainly did. Many years later, on a visit to America, he was pleasantly surprised when a man named Michael, the husband of a former Betar friend of his, insisted on thanking him for saving his life in the ghetto.

"I was embarrassed by his profuse gratitude, but when he mentioned the particulars of the story, I was reminded of how important it was at that time to know the right people in the right places," my father recalls. "Past connections could mean the difference between life and death." Michael was working outside the ghetto in the Byala Vaka labor camp, when he learned that his wife and baby boy were taken away to the Vilna Ghetto. His foreman agreed to give him the necessary work permit allowing him to travel to the ghetto and back for a quick visit, for everyone knew that a Jew found walking on the road or in the street without a *shein*, the yellow labor pass, was as good as dead. The next day, Michael was stopped by an SS man at the ghetto gates and told he could only visit his family if the SS man kept hold of his work certificate until he returned. Thrilled to be reunited with his family, Michael nevertheless worried about retrieving his *shein*, without which he could be killed. His wife knew who to turn to—her old Betar friend Israel Jutan, a clerk in the labor bureau.

"A few hours later," Michael reminded him, "you came to our place in the ghetto and asked me to bring you a bottle of vodka or schnapps. I did so. When I saw you again the next day, with a smile on your face, you gave me back my *shein*. I was able to go out and work again. You might not remember, but I offered to compensate you many times, and you refused. You said to me: 'What are friends for if not to help each other?' I have blessed you many times for saving my life."

"It all came back to me," my father says. "I had gone to the gate and recognized the SS man as the one called Weiss, the overseer of the ghetto for the first year of its existence. I then went and told the story to Joseph Glazman, who had been head of our Betar Zionist organization and was now chief of police. He had many dealings with Weiss and knew exactly what was needed: a bottle of vodka. With the Nazis, everything was to be traded, bought and sold. Glazman made the trade, and that's how I got the *shein* to give back to Michael. I was lucky to be in a position to help an old friend. In those days, it was not always possible to help people, and, when we could, it was a small victory for us all."

Rescue one person and you save the entire world, goes the Talumic saying. *Tikkun olam*: Hebrew for "repair the world," a basic tenet of Judaism. War taught my father that in the giant web of strangers, one's very life hangs on a thread made up of a multitude of tiny acts of kindness from those we treat as friends.

The Scribe

✦

Vivikonna, Estonia, 1943

The one who records dictates how history is remembered.

"'Keep yourself busy!' That was always my motto," my father reminds me. "When the Vilna Ghetto was finally liquidated in September 1943, I didn't want to take the chance of being without work."

My father always kept himself busy, expecting the same from his daughters, constantly finding chores for my sister and me to ensure that we were gainfully engaged in purposeful activity, too. "If you had a job to report to, you were useful," he clarifies. "All during the war, I kept telling myself: 'I must just make myself handy. They will not shoot a worker.'"

When the Germans cleared out the Vilna Ghetto two years after it was established, it is estimated that only a couple of thousand survivors remained of the more than sixty thousand there at the beginning. Most of the victims were murdered in the forests near Ponar. The remaining Vilna citizens were sent as "volunteers" to forced-labor camps in Estonia. My father and his wife, Malka, were transported in the same group.

After two days of travel, they landed in Vivikonna, near a coal mine and the Kiviolli factory that produced petrol from the coal. About a thousand of them were put to work laying railway lines for a new railroad to connect the coal mine to the factory. This would enable the Germans to transport the coal and make it into fuel, desperately needed to keep the war going. Vivikonna was in the tundra of northern Estonia, where the bitterly cold climate and late autumn rains turned the ground into a giant marshland. The barracks in which the citizens slept were built atop sturdy poles with tall, narrow staircases to keep the wooden houses off the wet, soggy earth.

"You cannot imagine how it is with an icy wind coming down on you and your only protection is the miserable thin clothes made from cotton and only a pair of shoes, no socks. In the freezing cold you must, with your bare hands, put the railroad lines of steel and wood together, for the whole day, day after day. Oh, how I would dream about better, warmer days," my father says to me as we sit in the warm sunshine by the pool.

I am struck by the incongruity of the situation. The man who endured such cruel hardship and dehumanizing degradation, now lies in his swimsuit by the pool, bronzing himself in the sun and talking somewhat serenely about the death and destruction he had witnessed. Is this what we might call poetic justice? Is the moral to it all—that everything is subject to change, and that possibly, given enough time, suffering, even evil can be transformed and expiated?

One day, during the *appell*, or roll call, when the prisoners were lined up in formation, standing outside to be counted, one of the German SS men called for someone who could write in German. Pointing to where my father stood in his row, the Jewish leader of the group, the *eldster*, said: "That prisoner knows how to write well in German." Knowing by now the importance of fast action, my father quickly stepped forward out of the line. That is how he obtained the job as *schreiber*, the official scribe or recorder of the camp, and was spared the hard, backbreaking manual labor of laying down a railway line in the cold.

"I was very happy for my stroke of good fortune," my father smiles. In late November, a call came for about two hundred and fifty people to go to a new camp to operate a cement factory. That same *eldster*, a very efficient man, who, with his easy command of the German language, had made friends with the camp commandant, requested to be in charge of choosing that select group of people. "This man, with his rotund stomach, was a good organizer," he says. "He used to be a school principal in Vilna, and of course was used to taking command and giving orders. He remembered me from one of the youth-movement meetings, so he chose me to be his secretary, and I was instructed to write the list of people he planned to take. I put Malka's name on the list as well. After all, I was still her husband, even if we were estranged and I didn't trust her. It was the right thing to do."

When the group arrived at the new camp, they couldn't believe their eyes. Stretching before them was nothing but a wide-open space with barbed wire and endless land as far as one could see. That night, the group slept on the cold, bare ground. A day later, building supplies arrived. Now it became clear why the *eldster* had been specific about whom he had chosen. Wisely, he had picked people who were good with their hands—a carpenter, an electrician, a man who had been a supervisor of certain industries in the ghetto, a shoemaker, two tailors, and women who could cook and clean.

"We built the actual camp ourselves, from nothing," my father says. "That schoolteacher oversaw the construction of the buildings: a large bathhouse, outhouse toilets, a kitchen, and two big double-storey barracks—one for men and one for women. Within two months everything was completed." Watching all the ongoing construction stood the Estonian guards and three SS men. One of the SS was a commandant by the name of Johann Klee. "An absolute sadistic tyrant," my father says. "He used to put his Jewish prisoners on roll call, where we would have to stand out in the winter for hours on end, while he took his time counting us twice, three, and even four times. He would beat people just for fun and steal food from their meager food supplies, even though he had an entire kitchen of his own."

From where that camp was set up, twenty kilometers from the harbor town, it was possible on a clear day to see all the way across the ocean to Finland. To my father, Finland represented the promise of freedom. He had heard that the Jews in Finland were treated kindly, even during their occupation. Staring out toward the ocean, he would often daydream about escaping, fantasizing how to get himself across the waters to a place where he could be free. He had already made it his business to befriend some of the Estonian guards, attempting to learn their language. He would interact with them, courteously initiating simple conversations, always with a smile. Soon he was able to count in Estonian and say, "How are you?" and "Where are you going?" and other phrases. One day, one of the guards informed him that for one gold coin, or ten rubles, it was possible to arrange transportation to Finland. My father had already heard rumors about a man in the camp who had hidden gold rubles on his person. The man was a lawyer—a small, gentle, refined man who even in the shoddy, ragged uniforms they were forced to wear, managed to look elegant and composed. My father immediately approached the man, asking for a meeting in the office. Out of earshot of others, he told the lawyer what he had heard about getting to Finland, to freedom. Mr. Rubinsky, the lawyer, listened to him in his calm, dignified way and made no response.

"I couldn't understand why he even hesitated," my father says. "My God, if I had the money, I'd be gone immediately." He kept trying to persuade the quiet lawyer, pressing him on: "Hey, come on! What's the matter with you? We should go. As soon as possible. It's our chance to escape. It's no secret you have rubles. What are you waiting for? Let's grab our chance for freedom. Don't you want to get out from here?" But Mr. Rubinsky simply shook his head. With soft-spoken determination, he asserted that he simply could not go. His wife, he explained, had escaped from the Vilna Ghetto and managed to find her way to Yugoslavia to join her father, who was chief rabbi of a town there. "I know in my heart that she is alive," he declared, "and she is waiting for me to rejoin her there."

"Against love, one cannot argue," my father concluded, watching his hopes of escape to Finland evaporate into the Baltic fog. So emboldened by his love was Mr. Rubinsky, so convinced of his intended reunion with his wife was he, that he went to see Commandant Klee.

"Would you consider giving me permission to write to my wife who is in Yugoslavia?" he asked the commandant. "She is not Jewish, and I wish to write how well your camp is run and what a good commandant you are. She has some good connections. Maybe a promotion could happen for you. Who knows?" Commandant Klee must surely have been astounded at the bravery of this request from the seemingly timid Rubinsky, who no doubt was well aware that it was strictly forbidden to give signals or send letters. For whatever reason, whether it was because the request was delivered in such a genteel manner or whether some rubles had found their way to Klee's pockets, he agreed and the letter was sent.

After the war, during a visit to Prague, in a refugee camp crowded with displaced people who against all odds had survived the elimination of the Jews from Europe, my father was amazed to recognize his former Vivikonna camp mate. "I could not believe it," he remarks. "Rubinsky had survived the Holocaust! The first thing I asked him was, 'Did you ever hear from your wife?'"

The lawyer's face lit up. He told me that his wife was alive and with her father, and that he was on his way to Yugoslavia where she was waiting for him. I recognized what strength his love had given him. His desire and belief to be reunited with his wife was so firm, so unshakable, that what he had believed had actually come true."

This story my father tells me of love, commitment and the power of promises makes me wonder all the more: What prophetic power lies within the declarations we make and the trust we put at stake, to one's self or to another, or even to the Invisible Grand Master Planner? Can a simple vow to oneself or a pledge to another change the course of one's life? Can the act of honoring one's word dictate one's destiny? Could it be that in the moment of commitment, when faith is affirmed, fate is then sealed?

Mr. Rubinsky and his wife worth more than rubles is an example of how, in the matter of survival, we are able to endure the worst of conditions not so much because we care for our own personal lives, but rather because we care so deeply about those to whom we have given our hearts, our life and our word.

The Letter Writer

✦

Newton, Massachusetts, 1994

We sit on the shores of our own private Babylon, weeping our tears of exile.

"It is much easier for me to tell you small incidents that I recall—events and activities that happened—than to describe the day-by-day brutalities and indecencies. The labor camp in Port Kunda that we built ourselves may have been more comfortable than the rest, but because of Klee we could not enjoy our relative comfort. Commandant Klee was a monster," my father says. "So when I talk about a beautiful camp, or I complain about a monster of a man, please understand that I am trying to make the unreal real. As best I can, I will describe extraordinary events as if they were normal. Maybe, in understanding, you will find a way to forgive me for my own past cruelties, which I see now with age were from my times in the camps."

Tears spring instantly to my eyes. Are they for me or for my father? So absorbed by his stories am I that the outlines separating us become blurred. The moment hangs heavy. Old childhood wounds buried by time twinge again in vague remembrance. What can I say in response to this sudden confession? Yes, Daddy, you were cruel to me. You let your anger spill onto me. You punished me for things others did to you. You hit and humiliated me and made me cry. Sometimes you even laughed at my crying, and that hurt more than anything. But, after summers spent listening to my father's recounting of dreadful years of trauma, loss, and deprivation, I cannot bring myself to say any of that to the old man who sits by my side. As a child, I was too young to know that the damage that caused my father's tirades was not done by me. But not young enough to escape the damages I felt by his demonstrative expressions of displeasure, disapproval, or disappointment. Not too young to absorb the guilt and shame I breathed in from the air singed by his searing rage that could be enflamed at any moment and without warning. At this stage of my life, those emotional wounds have become faded scars. What can I say in response? Perhaps it is enough merely to listen. Maybe that's where forgiveness can be found, in the gracious act of listening. Maybe this is what both our hearts had desired and our souls required: a period of reflection and rapprochement.

This is the second time my father has asked me for forgiveness. The first came the summer after we began working on this book. I came upstairs to my bedroom one afternoon, and found, there on my bed, waiting for me, a plain white envelope with my name on it. It contained a letter from my father, describing how he had been thinking about an old letter I had sent him from Jerusalem, and now had a revelation about the harsh, punitive ways he had raised me. "Please forgive me," he wrote. "I never meant to hurt you or cause you damage. It was because of all I suffered during the war."

I sat on my bed, alone, stunned, reading the letter over and over. Then I began to cry. I had not known until the moment I read those words how long I had been waiting, aching to hear them. I had spent much of life feeling pity and compassion for my father's past indignities and sufferings. Now, for the first time, I wept for my own.

In the unexpected release of tears, painful childhood memories came flooding back: the sharp snap of his belt on my bare bottom, the cruel yanking of my ears, the insulting slaps across the face, his ignoring my pleas to stop, his ordering me to stand with my face pressed to the corner of the wall, his sneer at my humiliation, his mocking of my shame. "Kiss the hand that smacked you!" he would order, stretching out his right hand toward my tear-stained, snot-dribbling face after he had smacked me for whatever childish transgression I had innocently committed. "Now, say you're sorry! Louder!" Turning my eyes away from my wrathful god, I'd kiss his hand and chant my well-practiced staccato-soprano verse of "I'm sorry, Daddy. I'm sorry, I'm sorry, I'm sorry!"

Sitting on my bed, clutching the letter, I felt my whole body begin to heave and shudder, shaking out the remembered hurt and pain. The heat of the tears rolling down my cheeks surprised me. I couldn't recall feeling that sensation before. Were tears always this hot? Even my nose was crying. "Ugh, Shame!" What a blubbering mess. You're a grown woman, I thought to myself. Get a grip! Just as I was berating myself, thinking how foolish I was to be crying so hard over a few simple words in a letter, I was struck with an epiphany: I had associated crying with my father's mocking. Crying meant giving my father that edge, that satisfaction of seeing me beaten, vanquished, ashamed and I could never let him or any man have that victory over me. I dared not show that side of me, that vulnerability. It would cost too much: My dignity, that sense of tough self I had worked so hard to maintain. "You're such a strong woman," friends would always say to me, and I would take it as praise, feeling smugly validated for my forthright and practical manner of going about things. Suddenly I realized that what I regarded as a strength might actually have been a weakness. Being the strong caretaking woman came with its own high price: It didn't leave room for anyone to take care of me. Who would know if I needed them, when I couldn't even allow myself to ask for help? And how would I reach out to ask for comfort if I couldn't even let myself feel my own hurt? In not letting myself cry, I shut myself off from my own compassion. I had lost an essential part of my female self—that tender part of me that allowed for the fragility of being human—that softhearted girl who wished to be held and hugged with love I could trust.

Alone in my room, I sat on my bed weeping, more and more, letting the snot dangle and drip and the scalding tears dribble down my face without even trying to wipe either away. I was crying for the little daughter who had loved her father so deeply despite his petty tyrannies and harsh cruelties. I was crying for the teenager who had hardened her heart, and relied on her intellect. I was sobbing for the young woman who had avoided plunging to the depths of inherited sadness for fear of drowning in such overwhelming grief and sorrow. I was weeping for the middle-aged woman who had grown up not knowing the comfort of crying in someone else's arms or that I deserved to have that kind of loving embrace and warm solace, especially from a man. And I was wailing, finally, at last, after all those years of putting on a happy face, wailing in heartbreaking grief for my father and mother and their inexpressible loss.

When my tears eventually subsided, I tried to remember my correspondence from years ago that had elicited this letter of apology from my father. At the time I wrote the letter, I was twenty-one, living in Jerusalem, and convincing myself that the huge physical distance I put between us would help reduce the emotional tempestuousness of our relationship. There I was, trying to heal and liberate myself in a country itself wounded and slowly recovering from the Yom Kippur War. Living on my own for the first time, a stranger in a far away strange land, away from the familiar, brought new perspective into my life and past. Summoning the courage to put my reflections into words on paper, I wrote to my father, telling him about several recent insights I'd had concerning the damaging effects of his cruel, physical punishment on me, as a child. I questioned sending the letter, worried about the risk of estrangement from the most important man in my life. It would be the first time I would directly confront him about how his volatile temper had affected me. I imagined it would upset him greatly. But wasn't he the very one who had taught me the importance of speaking out for one's beliefs, to stand up against injustice? How could I honor his teachings if I did not say what was in my heart? He, after all, was the one who told me the story about the nineteenth-century French intellectual writer he so admired, Emile Zola, whose name he gave my sister.

Zola had risked his life and career by writing a letter to the president of France accusing the French army of anti-Semitism and wrongful conviction of a Jewish army captain named Dreyfus. His famous *J'accuse!* letter became frontpage news and a political turning point in what became known as the Dreyfus affair.

I sent my letter.

I wanted to believe that the relationship with my father was such that I could always speak my truth to him and he would accept me and hear what I had to say. He didn't reply. Instead, my mother wrote back saying how pained my father was to read what I had written, and how disappointed they were in me that I would accuse him of such things after all those years.

Then, twenty years later, the return letter in my hand. *T'shuvah.*

With time, my father had recognized how the travesty inflicted on him might have spewed over onto me. Confronting his own inner demons spawned from those external demons that had so cruelly invaded his life, he had taken responsibility for his harshness and reached out to me in a plea of reconciliation. For both of us, the wicked, weak, and wounded, his letter offered resolution. It brought the healing I had needed—an apology from father to daughter. The past excusing itself to the present: The path of forgiveness, the way of accountability, the road to liberation for us both. The letter I held in my hand was his atonement, a truce. To me, it was a testament of love.

Now, sitting face to face with my father by the side of the pool, hearing him talk about the monster Klee and asking me for forgiveness once again, I recognize that there is still more to heal, more to cleanse, for myself as well as for my father. All those things I did not ask him about, things that defy comprehension, things that had probably twisted and distorted themselves into punishments directed by a parent at an unsuspecting child, now lodge in my mind. Dad, the incessant horror of the SS brutality, how did you stomach it? Dad, the stench of the excrement and urine in the trains and latrines, how did you stand it? Dad, the sheer physical exhaustion of sleep deprivation and hard work, how did you push through it? Dad, the constant hunger, the continuous aching for food, how did you deal with it? The constant terror? The abuse, cruelty, injustice? The anger and despair? The helplessness and shame? The loss. The sadness. The waste. The terrible waste of it all. How did you live with it, day after day, year after year, never knowing what was next? Daddy, what's it like to be a skeleton?

But I sit quietly. This is not a time for questions. It is time for a response. Those questions will go unasked.

Swallowing the lump that has formed like a stone in my throat, I gaze back at my father. In a voice that surprises me by its gentleness, I find the words to say that all is forgiven, and, yes, through his stories, I understand him better. That is why we are sitting together, day after day, to record his memories, I tell him, to right the past and rid ourselves of the burden of wrongs committed. I am here, after all, as his scribe, to help as best I can put the past to rest. The emotional little child in me wishes to jump up and spontaneously hug him, but I remain seated in my chair, next to the tape recorder, preserving the facade of an impartial interviewer. The strong woman.

There is something about the dignity of space, the respect for humbling distance. Perhaps this is how I become the adult in the presence of my father, by holding my ground and staying rooted where I am, not leaning toward him. This is how, in this moment, I honor us both. We take a few moments to wipe away the tears that spring too easily from years of loving each other by sharing each other's pain. I used to struggle to hold back my tears in front of my father for fear of ridicule. No more. Now I let my tears of release flow freely and without shame.

The Schemer

✦

Port Kunda, Estonia, 1943–44

In the plot and plan lies the fate of a man.

"If there is such a thing as a devil or a monster, that was our Commandant Klee," my father continues, taking us back to the Estonian tundra. "He was a real thug, a tormenter, a sadist—a true criminal. He made our lives a living hell. So, because I have always been one to try and make life easier for myself, not wishing to endure too much pain or suffering, I busied myself day and night thinking how to rid ourselves of this evil man.

If only there was a way to get him shipped to another camp. If only we could complain about him somehow. But who would listen, and what complaint could we make? That he was beating us for no reason? Ha! Those things would have gotten him a commendation or a medal of honor from the Nazis!"

Every day my father schemed how to get rid of Klee. One day it came to him in a flash, and he brought his idea to the *eldster*. What about an anonymous letter, in German, to the Nazi authorities reporting that Commandant Klee was not doing a good job, because he has taken to bed with him—and was now living with—a Jewish woman? Reckoning it was a risk worth taking, the *eldster* agreed to participate in the scheme. They wrote the letter in the name of a concerned Nazi sympathizer from the town, and addressed it to the SS headquarters in Germany, an address my father knew from his administrative work. They gave the letter to one of the friendly Estonian guards, exchanging a pair of socks and some spare rations of food for a promise to send the letter.

Life in the camp continued with the majority of prisoners working at the cement factory. Some of these groups worked in the mines alongside Estonian communists, taken prisoners at the time of the Nazi occupation. These miners were continuously complaining about the Germans, eagerly anticipating the day their Russian Communist comrades would come and "kill all those bastard Germans and shoot those traitor Estonian guards." And so the days passed, each day as before: the early morning roll call, the constant shifts of hard labor, the meager food gulped down in hunger in the evening, and the restless sleep at night of two men forced to share a small bunk in a barrack housing one hundred men. They forgot about the letter.

About a month or two later, three sleek black cars arrived and pulled up into the yard of the camp. The Jews immediately thought that something had gone wrong, anxious about this unexpected SS visit that usually implied trouble. They watched the SS officials walk briskly across the yard, through the kitchen, in and out of the barracks, inspecting everything. The next thing they knew, Commandant Klee was gone.

My father smiles. "The *eldster* looked at me. I looked at him, and we stopped our work in the office. 'Well,' he said to me, 'it just goes to show. Sometimes even a Jew can get lucky!' I started to clap my hands and began to laugh. I couldn't believe we had pulled it off. That such a small trick devised in my own desperate mind could yield such a reward! Yah! That night, we in the administration had a celebration in honor of Klee's departure. We raised our metal cups, filled with thin brownish soup that we pretended was wine, and toasted *'L'Chaim!'*"

In a wasteland of no true winners, my father and his fellow Port Kunda prisoners felt they had gained a small but very satisfying victory. With the reality of Klee gone came the uncertainty of who would replace him. They hoped and prayed that there could not be a worse fiend. The next day, Klee's replacement, Johann Bekker, arrived. They saw that in his favor he was far better looking than the ugly Klee. Soon after Bekker was put in charge, he summoned the official Jewish staff to his office.

"Who was there? Me, the *schreiber,* Mr. Rubinsky the lawyer, who was the official secretary, and Mr. Hayman, the *eldster*, the overseer of all of us Jews in that camp. Also Dr. Jaszpan, the camp doctor, a well-known diagnostician from Vilna, a friend of my father. We stood in a row in front of this new German SS man, who told us to sit down in the chairs. We could hardly believe our ears. To sit? A moment of *menshlichkeit*, decency for us? Very hesitantly, we sat down and waited for Herr Bekker to begin speaking," my father says.

Commandant Bekker looked at them all and said, "Klee has been sent to the front. I know about Klee. We all know about him. He was a drunkard, a thief, a thug, what we call a really low-class person. The truth is that Klee was a common criminal serving time in prison for assault. He already had a reputation for his temper and his violence, beating up other prisoners, so we knew what he is. It is my assumption that the only reason they sent him out here was that this isn't a big camp and it's not difficult to run."

Leaning over his desk, Herr Bekker explained that he had called them into his office to reassure them he was not at all like Klee. "Completely different," he claimed. "I am a pharmacist from near the Polish frontier. I have a nice home and a good business."

He stood up, walked over to the window, and looked out as if he could see his little village from there. Then he turned back to face his prisoners and continued: "One day the SS men came in and announced that they needed more people for the front and that I must sign up. I pleaded on behalf of my advanced age, my profession, and my family. They suggested that I join the SS instead. I was well known and respected. They assured me they would see to it that I would get an administrative job. Because they had been left with so many pharmacies on the Polish side of the border, just across the river, they needed me to teach other Germans how to manage a chemist shop. And so I became an SS man," he continued, "and I traveled back and forth from Germany to Poland, teaching others my skills. But in 1942, with the establishment of work and concentration camps, more SS men were needed for positions of governing and controlling those camps. They sent me off to a training camp for this sort of job. When I heard in 1943 about this small, out-of-the-way camp, where no one would come and snoop around and watch over me, I asked to be transferred here. So this is why I am part of the SS, and this is why I am here."

Herr Becker paused, offering a smile. The inmates waited in silence. Their bitter experiences had taught them to distrust anything a German in uniform said, however appealing it was. They could only sit and listen and hope that the twist of fate would turn out well for them.

"'I called you here to explain to you my situation, so that you may know where I stand and so that you may know where you stand with me,' Herr Bekker told us," continues my father. "'It is important for you to realize that we Germans are not all of us criminals. It is apparent you have suffered enough already at the hands of what I can only call ignorant and evil men, but I assure you I am not one of those, even though I wear the insignia on this uniform they gave me.' Then he said quietly: 'I will try my best to make this work camp as comfortable as can be. I give you my word.'"

Although their new commandant seemed sincere enough, my father and the rest of the group sat there for several minutes trying to assimilate this turn of events. The doctor was the first to stand up and voice his appreciation. The rest soon followed. Bekker stretched out his hand for a handshake, and, one by one, they shook his hand. For a moment the world seemed almost civilized. Could it be that an angel had been sent to replace the devil?

"Yah, Herr Bekker did turn out to be an ideal commandant for us," my father says. "So, while hell was all around us, those of us lucky enough to be part of the administrative staff of this camp, well, we had a little haven in the midst of misery. Bekker allowed us the freedom to conduct the business of taking care of the operations of our daily work without constantly checking our actions. We could read his newspaper that he left especially for us. The general camp *appell* was short and sometimes not at all. Throughout the entire time of Bekker's command, there was not one attempt to escape. Fate granted us a moment of respite and the intelligence of a kind and respectful gentleman."

Bekker constantly hinted that the war would soon end. It was apparent in his constant requests for assurances of their forgiveness. "It was clearly important for him how we viewed him. He wanted us to see him as an individual, not a pawn of the ruling political party. He would say to us in the office: 'Just remember, when all is over, that I was good to all of you. If the Russians come and take over, I will count on you to remember to vouch for my kindness.' And of course we nodded in agreement, because he truly was good to us," my father recalls. "Everything would have been all right, but for the timing of events."

At the time Bekker arrived at their camp, there was already an escape plan underway by a group of the camp inmates organizing a defense committee. One of the mineworkers, named Miller, who later became mayor of a town in Israel, had started an underground movement along with some of the Estonians. My father and the rest of the staff knew about the plan which was to leave Herr Bekker with his Germans while the Jews escaped into the mines. In preparation, Miller and his group had been covertly storing food and other supplies down in the mineshafts. They were setting up for the exact moment of evacuation, waiting for the Russians to come to Port Kunda. Hearing the sounds of Allied bombing in the distance, they anticipated the signal for the dash to hide in the mines coming at any moment.

Suddenly, three young men in SS uniforms arrived at the camp and promptly relieved Bekker of his position. They assembled the prisoners in the yard for the roll call, ordered them to take food for two days, then marched the group toward the railway station where they packed them into train cars bound for Tallinn, the capital of Estonia.

"We had no warning," my father says. "No time to issue the command for the planned escape or any defense. Nothing! It was just assemble, follow orders, or else. They caught us by surprise! Within two days, these young SS men had put us on a big boat to ship us off to Danzig. Total evacuation. Not one soul left. The day before we arrived in Tallinn, the SS had also evacuated Klooga. That was the camp in Estonia in which Leyb Rosenthal, your mother's brother, and my father and others from Vilna were placed. Up until the last minute, the Nazis were determined to continue their brutality, making sure they got rid of all the evidence of their crimes."

The Brother-in-Law

✦

Vilna, Poland, 1930s
Klooga, Estonia, 1943-44

One lives on in the words one gives to others.

Fate decreed that my father is the one to tell me the stories about my mother's family. Through him, I will learn about my mother's brother, Leyb, the uncle I never knew, whose round, serious face peered out at me from the small gray photograph, no bigger than a postage stamp, placed carefully under the glass of my mother's dressing table.

When my mother died of ovarian cancer at fifty-five, an age when some women today are just beginning to live out their best years, all I knew about her family or childhood were the smattering of one-liners and truncated anecdotes she left me, morsels strewn along the way like crumbs dropped in a Hansel and Gretel forest out of which I was to find my own way.

Once, when I was in high school, I found her sitting by the window at her dressing table, playing solitaire, whistling that soft, preoccupied, pass-the-time whistle of hers. I don't know what propelled me, but I said to her: "Mom, why don't you talk about your past?" She didn't answer me right away or even look at me, but just kept turning over the cards, one by one, putting them in descending order, one on top of the other. "When you're older; I'll tell you when you're older," she replied. I dropped the subject.

I got older. She got cancer. End of stories.

I was much younger when I asked my mother about the young man with the straight, combed hair, parted in the middle, the one whose gray face stared at me from under the glass of her dressing table. After a pause, she told me it was her older brother, Leyb. He was a playwright, songwriter, and poet, she said. With a group of puppeteers called Maidim, they put on marionette shows and political satires, and he let her do some of the voices for the puppets. He also wrote songs for her to sing. "He was killed, one day before liberation," she said, gazing at the photo. I remember that one sentence dangling like a sword in the air between us. My young heart ached for us both—for the uncle I never had and the brother she'd loved and lost. For the terrible timing, the injustice of it all. That was all she told me about her brother. Another incident I remember was back when I was maybe eight or nine years old, standing next to her in a sea of solemn faces, at a Holocaust remembrance day commemoration. She kept sighing and muttering something under her breath about her brother writing the partisan song the people there were singing and his not getting any credit for it. Too young to understand or to ask what or why, I was left with a distinct impression of my mother's disgruntled feelings of frustration and helplessness at the unfairness of something to do with my shadow of an uncle.

Other incidents came out the blue. I was about fifteen. We were standing in her bedroom. Unexpectedly, she began talking about the time she came home from Epstein Gymnazium, her Jewish high school in Vilna. "My mother was in the kitchen," she said, "just sitting there like a stone. From the corner of my eye I saw a chicken running around in circles without a head. She said the police had come to the house for my father, told him to pack a suitcase and then took him away. We never saw him again," my usually emotional mother said, dry-eyed. Shocked by her sudden revelation, I kept quiet, unsure of what to say or do. I didn't dare cause her more suffering by knocking on a door she usually kept shut tight. The thought of making my mother cry was worse than the image of the headless chicken that stuck in my mind, running around in a circle, wings flapping, blood squirting everywhere.

"At selection time," she continued, "I was with my mother. Dogs were barking. An SS man stood, pointing to the left, to the right, to the left, to the right. Now, he looked at my mother, and pointed to the left. Quickly, she told me to go to the right, to leave her, but I couldn't let go of her hand, I was holding on so tight. So she pushed me. She pushed me away from her, to the right. To the right meant life."

I could hardly breathe. I stood mute, my mind a blank. I had no frame of reference to what came before or after those incidents, or even where what she was recounting took place. Like the sudden giant gray fog that used to roll in from the ocean in the wintertime, up the hill past where we lived, blotting out the light so you couldn't even see your hand right in front of you, my mother's memory clouded the room. I tried to picture my grandmother, Fruma, but the fuzzy image of a stranger's face I once saw in a grainy photo long ago quickly faded away. There was nothing to hold on to. Not knowing how to respond, I just stood in silence, trying to scrape together my mother's words to store them away for later. What could I do about something I was not part of? How could I fix something so wrong? I could only do what I knew to do already: go to school, excel at my studies, practice my piano, write poems, win debates, get awards, star in the school plays, don't cause too much trouble and hope to make my mother proud enough of my accomplishments to fill up just a fraction of the empty space left by those who had played such a big part of her life and who had been absent from mine.

Sitting by the pool, decades later, my father now reconstructs for me the stories my mother told him about her family. In the Rosenthal family, he says, it was a great *simcha*, a joyful occasion, when a son was born in 1917 to Mr. Nochum Rosenthal, a quiet, short man who established a printing shop and published the popular Yiddish daily newspaper *Der Ovent Courier* in Vilna. Leyb was followed by his sister Mary and, later, Chayela, who was born in April of 1924. Leyb, a short, popular student at the Jewish Folks Gymnazium, was greatly influenced by cultural discussions of the many poets, writers, and journalists who often visited his parents' home. After school, Leyb worked at his father's daily newspaper, involving himself in the publishing trade. When the famous Yiddish narrator and writer Grosbart visited Vilna, Leyb was given the opportunity to read some of his poems to him. Grosbart's praise and encouragement for the gifted fourteen-year-old poet led to the publication of Leyb's first book of poetry. Soon Leyb's verses started to appear in Yiddish publications, and the well-known Ararat Theater commissioned him to write a few songs and short, light-hearted comedies. From 1935, at the age of eighteen, he moved to Lida, the southeastern town in the Vilna region that had a population of forty thousand Jews. There, he published the *Lider Folksblat* and became an accredited correspondent to a variety of Yiddish publications throughout Jewish Poland, writing under the name of Charif.

By 1936, his writings took on a more serious tone as he embraced a socialist philosophy, praising the communist volunteers as heroic fighters against General Franco's fascist regime in Spain. His outspoken views led to several arrests by the nationalistic Polish police who did not approve of his articles about the workers' struggles for human rights or his poems dedicated to the celebration of May Day. After a few days' incarceration, he would be released with a warning, and soon he'd be back on the streets again, fighting for his beliefs with what my father refers to as "his mighty pen."

As Leyb grew into a mature writer, his poetry reflected his concern for the Yiddish working class and the international proletariat. Believing in the liberation of the masses from the yoke of capitalism, his poems and articles pointed to the necessity of a united front of workers, a non-discriminatory party, whose aim was the improvement of conditions of life for all. Believing that a better way to propagate his ideas and thoughts to wider audiences might be through music, he started writing and composing popular songs that were soon heard and sung by many people. He also hoped the plays he wrote would provoke his audiences to action.

When the 1939 defeat of Poland by the Red Army led to the establishment of a Lithuanian Soviet Republic with the renamed Vilnius as the capital, Leyb, with his co-writer, a young, talented composer named Kiejdanski, devoted themselves exclusively to Jewish folklore and patriotic songs, praising the army, airmen, and working champions of the Union of Soviet Socialist Republics. The songs were played regularly on Vilnius radio, including what became a hit, his romantic love ballad *"Wos darf ich hobn mer, az du bist mine"* ("What more do I need when you're mine?"), co-written with a composer named Henrykowski. "On the radio, too," my father adds, "the special Yiddish hour often featured the singing talents of Leyb's younger sister, Chayela Rosenthal, the winner of the festival of the Lithuanian Folklore Songs, a competition I covered as journalist. In June 1941, Leyb, the prolific lyricist, and Chayela, already a teenage singing star in Yiddish, were scheduled to appear at the Folklore and Song Championship in Moscow. It would be Chayela's first trip outside of her hometown and she was most excited about her upcoming concert in Russia. But it was not *beshert*, not meant to be. On June 24, the German army invaded the city. Chayela never got to see Moscow."

In the earliest days of the German occupation, Nochum Rosenthal was one of the first to be taken away. In a roundup of about 5,000 Jews he was removed from his home, marched out of Vilna, shot, and dumped in the pits of Ponar. Two German soldiers and a Lithuanian policeman had come during the day and told Nochum to get a towel and some soap, announcing they were taking him to work somewhere else. That was the last time they saw him. Leyb, fearing the worst, disguised himself as a girl, jumped over their balcony and managed to escape by hiding at an uncle's house. He continued to avoid the many elimination roundups executed by the Nazis and Lithuanian special police, in which thousands of Jews were transported to unknown destinations, and many of Vilna's prestigious Jews were held as hostages to be exchanged for gold or jewels.

In the first week of September 1941, Leyb, his mother and two sisters, along with about 20,000 Jews left alive in the city, were evicted from their homes and forced to move into the cordoned-off confines of the Vilna Ghetto in the old Jewish quarter in the center of town. Without work permits they had to seek cover in basements and constantly change locations to survive. After some stability began to prevail in the ghetto, Leyb was helped by his literary friends to get a *shein,* a work permit, to keep his family safe. His reputation, popularity, and affiliation with the Vilna Literary Society stood him in good stead, and he was assigned to a unit whose purpose was to gather documents, books, works of art, and other important archives from the internationally recognized Vilnius-based research organization Yiddisher Wissenshaftlicher Institut (YIVO), or the Jewish Scientific Institute. His job was to make a list, in German, of the inventory. The Nazi's nefarious plan was to transport all archives and artifacts of Jewish historical significance from that institution back to Germany, where the literature would either be destroyed or kept as a relics of a vanished, exterminated society.

In secret defiance, Leyb hid some of the more valuable books and archives, sometimes giving them to select, trustworthy Poles outside the ghetto walls for safekeeping. The group with which he worked, the "Paper Brigade," mostly Jewish writers, poets, and journalists, some of them members of the Young Vilna Literary Club, also smuggled manuscripts and books within the ghetto, hiding them in canisters down in the sewers. It was a risky operation. Getting caught meant getting shot. Their goal was clear: to save their treasured literature in whatever manner they could. Even while he was working, compiling the lists, risking his life to hide the books, Leyb never stopped writing his poems and lyrics.

When Jacob Gens established a theater in the Vilna Ghetto, Leyb and his sister were given work permits and the perfect showcase for their creative talents. For Leyb, it was a period of important social and literary activity. My father remembers an article Leyb wrote for a ghetto newspaper called *Trep*, or Steps, describing the terrifying *aktions* in the ghetto. Working feverishly at night, often by candlelight, he wrote songs and revues for the theatre with the intention of inspiring people to maintain their determination to survive. *"Nisht gedayget, s'vet zine besser"*—"Don't despair, it will get better," was the motto that came forth. His catchy songs were sung by all the labor units outside the ghetto and by the people attending performances inside. *"Dos ghetto kind"* ("The Ghetto Child"), *"Suzi," "Vilna," "Ich vil tzaytn andere,"* ("I Want Other Times), *"Yisroilik,"* and many other songs, mostly sung by Chayela, entertained and uplifted their fellow prisoners.

"Yisroilik," one of Leyb Rosenthal's better-known songs, is still sung around the world by those who know and love Yiddish. The title, meaning "little Israel," refers to the endearing nickname given to many orphan boys in the ghetto, whose parents were taken away and killed. Left to fend for themselves, they survived as smugglers on the black market, often selling cigarettes or saccharin. In the first-person voice of the ghetto kid *Yisroilik*, the lyrics describe his sorry situation as he calls out to people to buy his wares. Barefoot, and dressed in an old, oversized overcoat and pants made from a sack, he defies people who laugh at him. Proud of his toughness, he admits to crying only when no one is looking. He didn't start out that way, he sings. Once he had parents who cared for and loved him, but now they're gone. Even though he's left on his own without a dime, he would rather whistle and sing his song than dwell on his sorrows. "Why talk about your sorrow, why think about your heartache—better don't talk!" That particular song of Leyb's became an anthem of Jewish survival, symbolizing the street-savvy, tough attitude of the small but brave child who helped smuggle messages and contraband goods in and out of the ghetto. Crawling through the sewers, slipping through fences, doing business

under the table, these scrappy street urchins helped sustain lives with their dangerous assignments of obtaining, stashing and transporting supplies for the Jews stuck in the ghetto.

For his one-act play, *"Einer fun Unz"* ("One of Us"), about the tribulations of a Jewish child hidden by a friendly Polish family, Leyb received an award from the Society of Jewish Literates. His haunting songs *"Shotns"* ("Shadows") and the popular *"Ich Benk Aheym"* ("I Long for Home") emoted the sorrows felt by the ghetto inmates in their distraught situation. When my mother sang that last song from the ghetto theatre stage, people told her that even the young German soldiers standing guard in the back of the ghetto theatre were seen crying, as they related to the Yiddish words, so similar to German, about missing home.

Chayela, playing leading roles in her brother's musicals, soon become known as the wunderkind of the ghetto theater. In Leyb's satiric musical parody "*Pesheh fun Resheh*," she played the part of a young girl, Pesheh, who reflects on the crazy situation of their ghetto life. Arriving in the Vilna Ghetto from the neighboring town of Resheh, Pesheh realizes that to stay alive she must not only have a strong character, but she will also have to pretend to be a family member of total strangers in order to get her work papers. Nothing seems normal, she sings, in a place where sisters pretend to be brothers, grandmothers act like children, and strangers fake being married. Leyb's play on words, witty songs and comedic interchanges on stage made it possible for audiences to see the absurd humor in their own dreadful circumstances and enabled them to laugh at themselves in the midst of their own inescapable suffering. Under such conditions, that artistic achievement was in itself a remarkable triumph of defiance.

Leyb had the opportunity to escape to the forests with his resistance fighter friends, the partisans, but he chose to stay behind, out of love for his sisters and mother, and the theatre. The partisans took his stirring songs of resistance with them into the woods. The march, *"Tzu, eynz, tzvey, drei!"* ("Ahead, one, two, three") kept them moving forward, his words instilling the promise of ultimate victory and vindication. Right up to the end of the ghetto in 1943, even when audiences sitting in the dark of the theatre auditorium were wondering if the next day would be their last, they sang along to the inspiring lyrics of Leyb's songs.

"On September 1, 1943, Leyb was sent away to the forced-labor camp, Klooga, in Estonia, together with many other remaining Vilna Jews being cleared out of the ghetto by the Nazis," my father says. "Undernourished, overworked, and suffering from exposure to the adverse weather conditions in that camp near Tallinn, Leyb still wrote his songs of hope and organized evening classes for his barrack, giving lectures on Yiddish classic writers. One of his last poems was *"Tzu mine Yiddishe Mammeh"* ("To my Jewish Mother"), dedicated to his mother who had been killed after a selection."

Again, the fateful date of September 1 pops up in my father's narrative. Intrigued by the synchronicity, I do the calculation. My mother died exactly thirty-six years after she and her brother were separated in Vilna. Thirty-six = eighteen doubled. Eighteen = *chai* = life. Two lives split on that date. First day of the ninth month. One and nine = ten. One, next to the empty circle. Me and my missing Uncle Leyb.

"On September 18, 1944, the commandants in charge of Klooga camp received orders to evacuate Klooga in the same manner as all the other camps in Estonia," my father continues. Facing defeat, the Nazis began all kinds of maneuvers to eradicate the remnants of Jews. They put the Klooga inmates onto a transport train leading to Tallinn, where a boat was commissioned to bring all Jewish labor forces in that area to the SS extermination camp, Stutthof, in East Prussia. "My father, Zacharias, who had been transported to Klooga after the Vilna Ghetto liquidation, was on that overfilled train destined for Tallinn. After the trains were fully loaded with people to be sent to the Baltic region, about 200 Jews were forced to stay behind at Klooga. Leyb was one of them," he says.

The Nazis had a different plan for those leftover Jews. They marched Leyb and the other remaining men into the nearby forest. There, they were ordered to build a platform from logs and forced to lie on top of the logs. More logs were piled on top of the men and then more men stacked on those logs. The Nazis shot them and burned them. A few Klooga prisoners had managed to run and hide when the trucks were being loaded and the camp was set afire. When they wandered out to meet the liberating Soviet troops, they came upon the sickening sight of the log pyres, the charred bodies, and the trail of carelessly strewn empty bottles of German beer.

Anger and regret rise up inside me. Anger at the Nazis for the brutal murder of my uncle. Anger that he was killed so close to liberation. Anger at my parents for not telling me about my inspiring Uncle Leyb while I was growing up. Anger at the world for standing by while innocent people were being tortured, burnt and tossed aside. Regret over not knowing more about the man who could have served as a role model for me. Regret that my mother had not taught me his songs. Regret that I had never heard her sing his songs while she was still alive.

As if reading my thoughts, my father adds: "For many years your mother was silent about her brother. She kept it inside her, the pain of losing her gifted, brilliant brother, such a clever writer, who had encouraged and promoted her talents, and provided the words for her to sing and act. You see, Leyb was more than a brother to her. He was her creative inspiration, her mentor in theatre. He was her protector when they took her father away. My heart would break for her each time she sang his songs. I admired her spirit, her love and devotion to her brother. After the war at a concert in Lodz, and at other concerts she sang for the refugees, she would stand on stage and proudly announce: 'This song was written by my late brother, Leyb, a victim of Nazi murderers.'"

The Daughter: A New Direction

✦

Newton, Massachusetts, 1996
Berlin, Germany, 2003
Vilnius, Lithuania, 2003

Even from the other side, the dead are still at our side.

The stories about my uncle and mother had a stirring effect on me, releasing a floodgate of creativity and disturbing my sleep. Swimming on the back of my father, I had landed at the harbor of my deceased mother. Standing on the docks, waiting for me with that beaming smile of hers, was the young woman I hadn't known, the mother I had too often mistakenly viewed and ignorantly misjudged as an overbearing, fussing, bourgeois, bridge-playing housewife. "Why are you writing a book about your father?" I could hear her melodic Yiddish accent in my head. "I was the star! Better you should write about me—and make it a musical. Music touches the emotions. People want to feel again!"

My mother's remarkable past as the star of the Vilna Ghetto theater had been kept secret for too long. It was wake-up and make-up time.

Make up songs. Make up a play. Make up for a forgotten uncle, lost talent and a missed mother. My Uncle Leyb, conjured by my father, loomed like a genie from another dimension. The brother-and-sister team who had uplifted so many lives during the war, now infused me with a renewed sense of purpose and passion. "Back to the theatre!" they cried. "Time for an encore!"

At three in the morning, they would fly in from their forsaken world to wake me up, nudge me out of my warm bed and prod me over to the computer at my desk. In the quiet hours, before the breakfast rush of three kids preparing for school and a husband leaving for work, they would inundate me with vivid scenarios playing out on my mind's stage. I heard the harmonies. I could see the characters. I wrote my visions.

◆ ◆ ◆

Vision

Scene: A bridge tournament set on a bridge in Heaven. A bright light shines on Chayela and Leyb Rosenthal, who play a game of bridge with friends. Chayela, the "dummy," is urged to return to the living to tell the stories she never told.

Scene: The crowded streets of the Vilna Ghetto. Across the stage runs a little barefoot orphan boy in a newsboy cap and large patched overcoat, the yellow star on a pocket. Weaving through the people, he picks their pockets and stashes away his supplies. When the books drop out of his baggy pants, he gathers them and disappears into the sewers. Song: "Yisroilik."

Scene: A young man in a dark cluttered room with shuttered windows and huddled bodies in the corners. Leaning on a wooden crate, he is scribbling furiously by candlelight, writing on papers that flutter around him. His sister, young, pale with dark braids, enters. She sings his latest poem. Song: "I Long For Home."

Scene: Cabaret in basement. Comedic actors rehearsing parody skit. Interruption by raid of SS. Song: "Pick A Little Victim."

Scene: The Selection place. Nazis shouting. Dogs barking. Armed soldiers surround a group of frightened Jews. A mother and her teenage daughter, holding each other tightly, are pushed into the spotlight center stage. Audio of soldiers marching, shouting "Left! Right! Left! Right!" Tug between mother and daughter. The mother pushes her daughter to the right side, while she is dragged off, stage left. Song: "Shadows."

Scene: Labor camp interior. A group of haggard workers sorts through mounds of torn, bloodied uniforms to be cleaned and repaired. The young girl, trying to instill humor, makes a joke. The kapo silences her. A friend defends her. An altercation between kapo and friend. The friend is dragged away. Song: "Uniforms."

Scene upon scene: Young lovers. Russian soldiers. Audition with Sol Hurok. Paris club. London train station. Finale: Ghosts walking among the living, singing in unison. Song "We Are Still Here!"

◆ ◆ ◆

In 1996, after a series of successful staged readings with a dedicated cast of professional actors bringing life to the ambitious full-length musical play I had written, it became apparent that a one-woman performance piece would be easier to take on the road and bring to more audiences. Borrowing a line from my uncle's song,*"Yisroilik,"* I rewrote the musical and gave the show a new title: "Better Don't Talk!" My Uncle Leyb, no doubt, would've enjoyed the irony. It's precisely because my mother didn't tell her stories that now I do. Human nature, it would seem, abhors a vacuum. The play would bring my Yiddish mother and me across the globe to old friends and new stories. Everywhere I went—Australia, Germany, Canada, England, and U.S.A.—people fell in love with Chayela, the tiny woman of enormous spirit. In South Africa, my mother's bridge friends told me anecdotes she had shared in confidence with them. In Melbourne, Vilna survivors remembered my mother's performances in the ghetto, one of them insisting on coming up on stage after my show. Clutching the microphone, he admitted to the audience of four hundred people that he had been one of those objectors I alluded to in my play, who had vociferously opposed the formation of the Vilna Ghetto theater with their disparaging posters. Looking out at the hushed audience that included curious students from a Catholic parochial school, he shouted dramatically: "I was wrong! I was wrong! Chayela and her brother, Leyb, were right." Fifty years later, he understood what my mother and her brother had known during that time: the triumph of the power of song and theatre over adversity. In their German-occupied Vilna, their everyday cemetery that even members of the priestly Cohen tribe were forced to walk in, my uncle's words in my mother's voice brought fellow Jews hope, courage, connection and amazingly, even the unlikely gift of laughter.

In the summer of 2003, I went on a German government–sponsored tour of Berlin as part of the Boston German-Jewish Dialogue group. Included in our itinerary was a visit to the Wannsee Museum, housed in the grand country villa overlooking the picturesque Wannsee lake. It was in that serene setting where, in 1942, fifteen top Nazi officials, many of them educated, cultured men with law degrees, had convened to devise their infamous plan for the "Final Solution to the Jewish Question,"—the total elimination of European Jews. Touring the museum, I was struck by the different nationalities and age ranges of the visitors who seemed keen to view the exhibits of the scenes of the crime, which our German Holocaust tour guide educators and preservationists referred to as the "topography of terror." Walking past the vertical Plexiglas displays documenting camps in Estonia, I was suddenly stopped short by a photo placed at eye-level. Something seemed familiar about it. Peering closer at the enlarged black-and-white image, I saw a stack of wooden logs interspersed with dead bodies. It was the scene at Klooga that my father had described! I could even see some tiny heads sticking out from between the logs. Leaning forward, I hoped in some perverse way to pick out from between the tiny round skulls the familiar face from the little gray photo under the glass of my mother's dressing table.

Was I crazy? I didn't even know my uncle. Even if I did find something resembling him, what would I do? Turn around and shout to the other tourists, like those students from the British school group: "Look! See? There, in between those pieces of wood, that's my uncle! Children, come over here. Look at what they did to him! Do you see the horrific, barbaric results of cold-hearted hatred? Can you understand that this came from a group of uniformed, intelligent men who sat here, right here, in this elegant mansion with its rose garden and its large windows that look out over this calm, beautiful lake?"

But I did nothing of the sort. I simply stared at a photo of some logs that represented the dead uncle I wished I had known. After a moment, I kissed my fingers and gently pressed them against the photo of Klooga and moved on to the next exhibit of vile cruelties conceived by men in that place of pristine nature.

It was on that same Berlin trip that Uncle Leyb came to visit me once more, this time in a charming medieval village outside Berlin called Tangermunde, a town today devoid of its Jews. Treated to a lavish lunch at a local restaurant, we listened to the featured speaker, a German librarian, talk about her commitment to maintaining the old Jewish cemetery and archiving news articles about local Holocaust commemorative concerts. More focused on the appetizing menu, I gave the scrapbooks and newspapers she passed around a cursory glance. Suddenly a bold headline grabbed my attention: Mir Leybn Eybek! —the title of the song my uncle wrote that I sing as the finale of my play: "We live forever; we will survive." The article turned out to be a review of a concert of Yiddish songs revived by a local German klezmer band, and mentioned the Vilna Ghetto and my uncle's lyrics. This time I didn't hesitate to shout out. "Look at this!" I cried excitedly, waving the newspaper article to everyone at the long table of Germans and Jews dining together. "This is my uncle's song. They're singing his songs, right here in this little town!" What bittersweet irony. There, in Berlin, a city whose citizens were once united by an Austrian painter's iron will, then divided by a brick wall, modern day Germans were reviving the prophetic Yiddish lyrics once written by a Vilna Jew, who was killed according to their former dictator's orders of genocide.

From the hands of a German woman dedicated to preserving articles about Yiddish songs and plucking weeds from ancestral Jewish burial sites of those forced to leave their family homes, I received my message. Uncle Leyb's words will find me wherever I roam: "Remember! We are here. We will survive. No matter if enemies try to smear our faces in dirt or blood, we will survive. We live forever. We shall overcome. *Mir Leybn Eybek*. We still are here!"

The Painter

✦

Danzig and Stutthof, Poland, 1944

When life starts to stink, get out your paintbrush.

"It is important now that I tell you about someone who saved my life," my father says.

If he had known the Latin expression for "It's not so important what you know but who you know!" my father would undoubtedly have shared that nugget of wisdom in his usual pedantic way of offering me Latin quotations as life lessons. Somehow I assimilated that knowledge and passed down my own version of "You never know who you might need to count on or when" to my children, encouraging them not to take lightly any connections with people they might meet.

My father began my training early on, grilling me in primary school about the last names of my school friends. "I'm going to play with Marcia and Hilary," I'd say innocently, only to be countered by the Jewish inquisition delivered in a heavy Polish accent: "Hilary who? What does her father do? Where do they live? What is Marcia's last name?" I hadn't a clue what any of the parents of my seven-year-old friends did or even why it was relevant for my father to know such things. As the last names were revealed to him, he would nod knowingly, pronouncing who was Jewish and who was not. It was unfathomable to my childish brain how he could divine such things as a person's religion from their last name, but still, that skill of his impressed me to no end, reinforcing my belief in my brilliant father's mysterious super powers. When I asked him once how he knew such things, he whispered: "A little bird told me." I trusted him implicitly. I had read about that particular tattletale bird in my fairy-tale books. Even though I couldn't determine exactly how those birds relayed information to my father about my bad behavior or my friends' heritage, I was convinced he had friends of all kinds of feathers in all kinds of high places.

He continues: "You remember? I told you before, that without warning we were taken by those three young SS men from that camp in Port Kunda to Tallinn and put on a big boat headed toward Danzig. The boat was packed solid with inmates from different camps in the area. I was with a group of people from my camp on the upper deck. Rumors were spreading that the war was turning over, the Germans were scared and we, the remaining few Jews were to be shunted from place to place until who knows what. Suddenly, someone I vaguely recognized from Vilna comes up to me. 'Do you know that your father is down on the lower deck?' he tells me. 'What?' I say. 'My father here on this boat?' 'Yes, yes, your father,' he repeats again excitedly. 'Your father, the doctor, he is downstairs on the bottom deck.'"

Immediately, my father headed downstairs, pushing and straining against the throngs of people packed tightly against one another. Weaving through the crowd, he called out his father's name, checking to see if anyone had seen Zacharias Jutan. How could his father be on the same boat as him? Impossible! He began to doubt it was true. What if that man had been bluffing? He started to worry about the food parcel he'd left up on the top deck with his friend, fearing someone would steal it. "That is how we were," my father explains, "always anxious about saving what we had and worrying about what could be taken from us next. People would snatch things away from us at any moment."

At the precise moment he decided that he had been duped, the victim of a cruel joke, he caught sight of his father and shouted out his name. Maneuvering their way toward each other, they met, pressed up close together in the crowd, and caught up on what had happened since the evacuation from Vilna, cramming in as much information in the short time they imagined was left.

When the ship arrived in Danzig, father and son realized they were to be separated once again. "Whatever happens," my father said, "wherever you go, send a message to try to find my group and I will do the same to find yours and get word about me to you." Zacharias nodded and was quickly shoved back into his group and pushed in a different direction. Reorganized into their original groups, the passengers were herded off the boat. He was certain that would be the last time he would see his father. "We waved and blew kisses to each other for as long as we could. Then I just turned away, and didn't look back any more."

From Danzig my father's group was transported on a barge making its way through the swamps and lakes deeper into Poland, until they landed in a place called Stutthof. They had no idea that this was a concentration camp. Up to that point, all through the war, his group had only been in forced-labor camps, not death camps. "We had never heard of anything like that. Everything—all the information—was so secretive. Perhaps, even had we heard of such a machination, we would not have accepted or believed it," my father acknowledges. Arriving at Stutthof, they were shocked at the frightening scenario that greeted them. A hailstorm of screaming commands and orders pelted down on them by SS soldiers herding and beating the prisoners into the camp, their loud, barking attack dogs at their side. "You must run! *Schnell!* Run! Quickly, quickly! All the time they are shouting at you and beating you to move faster, faster. Your clothes must be taken off. You must go to the showers to be disinfected! There must be no lice on you. Make sure you are clean. Continuous shouting and beating. Everything is forced rushing. No time to breathe, to think, to scheme. We are moved quickly, like people without a will, in large groups to where other people wait with small electric shavers to shave off our hair," my father recalls, his voice conveying the hectic pace of the orders.

"Our barbers are fellow Jews. As they begin the punishment of shaving our scalps, they say to us: 'You are lucky you have only come now to Stutthof, and not before. Now the ovens are not working.' I, of course, was confused. 'What are you talking about—what ovens?' I asked them. I remember thinking that perhaps here they had hot food prepared. But why would they say we are lucky then, if the ovens are not working? And they reply to me: 'The ovens where they burn the people, idiot! You don't know?'"

My father didn't believe what his Jewish barbers told him. He could not for the life of him get what they said into his head. How could that be? They were in the heart of Europe, the most civilized continent in the world, a center of culture and thought, of science and technical progress. Ovens to burn people? More likely a folk story, a fable for children, not a reality for grown men. My father was horrified. The men seemed so serious. He wondered what kind of inferno was awaiting them. Was this, he thought, the moment that death came to claim him?

"After an all-over shaving and all the cleaning procedures, a cold shower with a small dishcloth to wipe ourselves, we were issued striped uniforms and 'clothes' from an inventory room. It was at this point that I recalled something my father had said to me. I remembered his words: 'If there is ever a change of clothing, always make sure you have good shoes. Good shoes and warm feet. Because you will surely have to do much standing and walking. Shoes are most important.' In this allotment of clothes, there was no such thing as measuring us for size. Whatever they handed you is yours. Too big, too small? Too bad. You get what you get. Maybe you can swap it later with someone else in your group."

My father was lucky enough to get a uniform that fit him. But the shoes they handed to him pinched his toes. Heeding his father's advice, he began looking around for other shoes, checking other peoples' feet to see who had a better pair. "We were also given half a slice of bread and tea that was like dishwater and a tin container. Then they told us: 'One of you is responsible for the knife. With this knife you will open your tins and then you will keep your tin for the rest of your meals. From this tin you will drink your soup and water. It will be your only cup and your soup bowl. Do not lose it. Do you understand?' Hearing all this did not distract me from my task of acquiring a different pair of shoes. I said to myself: 'I have half a piece of bread. I will cut the bread in half with the knife. Then I will hide the bread. I will keep this quarter slice of bread and try to exchange it for a pair of shoes, more comfortable shoes than I have now.'"

And he did just that. Bartering his portion of bread for another man's shoes, he was most pleased with his exchanged shoes with their leather soles. My father was prepared to go hungry as long as he had comfortable shoes to walk in. In the warehouse he noticed the mounds of thousands of shoes in different styles, colors, and sizes, even boots and shiny lacquered ones that he realized were the leftovers of Jews from previous transports, disposed of with speed. A special commando of inmates had the job of sorting out various pieces of leftover clothing from the transports of Jews that arrived daily. Every item was to be recycled to keep the German war machine going. Learning later that the groups of Jews who came to the camp after his shipment were forced to undress and run straight to the shower rooms to be gassed, my father was extremely grateful for his good fortune of good timing.

The men, assigned to groups, were then rushed to the roll call, where the SS men counted and then separated them, twenty-four here, twenty-four there, sorted by numbers to be sent to the different barracks. The men in my father's group were forced to run quickly to a set of barracks far across the yard. Barefoot they raced, clutching their shoes tied together with a string tightly against their chests. When they arrived at the barracks, they were counted once more in the large field outside.

My father was sent to barracks No. 12, where a German kapo stood waiting for them. "He was the meanest, foulest-looking individual I have ever seen," recalls my father with a grimace. "A face, ugly like a pig. His skin with little holes, you know, like the marks left from chicken pox. And scars down his cheeks. It turned out that this kapo, like Klee, was a criminal who had spent twenty years in a German prison for some terrible crime. He and his fellow inmates were freed by the Nazis to serve as watchdogs of the barracks."

The repugnant kapo lined up his prisoners, then walked up and down staring at them, right up close, from under his bushy eyebrows. He delivered his welcoming speech with a sneer.

"First of all, he told us, he was going to look for the younger boys to help him get to sleep. Secondly, he said, he wanted his barracks spotless. 'Third of all,' he shouted at us, 'I expect quiet at night. Nothing but sleeping at night. The only noise I expect to hear is the sound of you all snoring.' Then he said to us: 'If you behave according to my instructions, you will experience no problems in my barracks. But if you do not obey, I will simply take the offender and kill him. Then some of you will have the pleasure of tossing him out of the door. *Kaput!* To me, killing is not a problem. I have committed murder before, so it is nothing new to me.' All this he said quite proudly."

The irony of the situation was not lost on my father. The innocent Jewish prisoners were being guarded by a convicted felon, a murderer and former prisoner. My father, who had thought Klee to be the epitome of evil, was to witness at Stutthof how the Nazis perfected their depravity.

Prisoners were labeled, sorted, and identified by their particular offensive status to the Nazis. Each new arrival received a number and a colored triangular fabric patch. In my father's case it was a yellow triangle for Jews. For communists, it was red. Jehovah's Witnesses were violet and homosexuals pink. Next to all the Jewish prisoners in No. 12, in Barracks No. 13, protected by the Geneva Convention, was the whole communist government of the Lithuanian Soviet Republic, including the cabinet ministers and the president at the time of the German invasion in June 1941. My father watched them receive parcels and goods from the International Red Cross. Naturally, the neutral Red Cross had no packages for the Jews next door.

Standing behind my father in the assignment line was a man a head taller than him. They were designated the same bunk, where they had to sleep head to toe, pressed together in the small, cramped wooden bunks lined with thin, flat mattress pads stuffed with straw. My father's bunkmate introduced himself, stretching out his big hand for a firm handshake. "Leon Malenker," he said. To my father, Malenker was an impressive fellow, and did not look Jewish in the stereotypical ways suggested by exaggerated Nazi propaganda or in the more subtle ways Jews identified fellow Jews by the indications of face contour, features, and coloring. He was tall, with a strong physique and open, smiling, bright face that inspired confidence.

They exchanged brief histories. "Malenker told me he had been a house painter before the war. I told him I was a journalist. At that moment, looking at each other and shaking hands, we established a camaraderie. It was the basis of the partnership that was to evolve naturally over time, given our mutual fate of being assigned the same sleeping quarters. Well-planned marriages have turned out far worse than the good friendship Malenker and I were lucky enough to share. This tall and intelligent man was to be my guardian angel," my father says. "I did not know then how much my life would depend on him."

Malenker, on the first day of camp, had already scanned the area for familiar faces. He was a master at communicating on the sly, like a ventriloquist, without appearing to talk at all. While on the go, he would mutter something to someone he made contact with and pass on information. With eyes like a hawk, he collected small pieces of bread, sweets, papers, and tiny treasures found in the gritty sand of the camp yard and brought those treats back to the bunk to share with my appreciative father.

Every morning at five o'clock they had to stand outside in the cold air for the roll call while the Nazis counted and sorted their prisoner workers. One particular night, the inmates of the barracks were woken up and ordered to assemble in rows of five for selection. Suddenly, he realized that his father, who had been sent to another barracks, was standing in the row next to him. "We were standing, partly illuminated by the headlights of several trucks, whose motors were running. I took a chance to move nearer to him and kept exchanging places with people one by one, until I had managed to push myself next to my father. Of course, under strict observation, I could not say anything to him, but I reached out my hand to meet his and we squeezed each other's hands."

"Schnell! Schnell! Laufen!" came the orders. The front rows were ordered to run forward. "I heard my father's voice in my ear: 'Those who are good runners will be transferred to labor camps. They will kill the others. Try your best to run fast!' The SS men were yelling, using their sticks to indicate which row was next," my father continues. "When it was our turn, we began to run, my father next to me. I knew I could run fast, so I wanted to be in the same surge as my father to help him. To my surprise, I noticed that he was running faster than I was. He was one of the first of the row to finish, with me close by." Tired and out of breath after the sprint, Zacharias turned to his son and grinned.

As the kapos assembled their own groups, father and son were separated again. Those who fell and died during the roll call were left on the field. The others who could not make the full run of about a hundred meters were taken away and never returned to their barracks. With the selection over, the good runners were put into new groups of about fifty or sometimes a hundred men and taken on foot through the mud, forests and dirt for long stretches of time until they reached their forced labor destination in distant fields. My father was most thankful for his relatively comfortable shoes during those arduous treks.

"My first group was sent to a quarry. We had to carry huge stones from one place to another. Then, after noon, we had to haul them from that place back to the original place. We also had to cut stones and rocks with a heavy hammer in a quarry, work in which one's hands would get bloody and calloused after an hour. This was daylong outdoor work that required chopping and carrying rocks up and down the quarry hill, in the freezing cold with nothing but our thin pajama uniforms to protect us from the weather. People were dropping from exhaustion. Many were kicked and pushed into the ravine for not doing the work fast enough. Others were simply shot. The brutal German guards, ex-convicts put to official use, watched our every move, always yelling at us and striking us with their wooden batons, forcing us to work faster, keep working, don't stop, never stop, not even to wipe your brow," my father says, "because they curse at you and spit at you and push you to work harder till you think your lungs will burst from exhaustion or rage."

My father did the work required, watching his hands get scraped and blistered from the rough rocks, those delicate hands his father had once declared were destined to be surgeon's hands. Blood oozed from open tears in the skin. Surgeon? What a joke. As a young boy he would become weak at the knees from the sight of blood. He felt no different now. Realizing early on in the quarry that he was not cut out for this kind of hard labor, he feared he could not survive this intense outdoor physical work. After about three or four days handling the heavy rocks, straining his body beyond endurance, he appealed to his bunkmate, Malenker, now the elected leader of the barracks, for a solution.

"Malenker," I told him one night, "I just can not take it anymore! I will die in that quarry if I carry on there." Malenker offered to help.

"No!" insisted my father. "You cannot help me. That is impossible. They'll shoot both of us. I just cannot bear this anymore. Look what has become of my hands. This is not work for me to do! I cannot make it out there, with the winter coming. I will perish among the rocks. I must find a way to do something else, anything else, but not this futile work of hauling rocks from one place to another and then back again.

I am not a mule! I am not an animal!" Malenker listened with his natural, stoic compassion. At the end of my father's desperate outburst, he simply said: "Well, I'm not sure what we can do about this. It is our assigned work. The only thing is to think how to get you out of there." My father was insistent: "Look, we must do something that will keep us indoors. Any kind of work, cleaning or scrubbing or something that will keep us from getting sent out there, to face the bad winter and the hard labor."

At that time, Malenker was also being used as a physical therapist and masseur for the Gestapo officers. Returning from one of his sessions, he happened to mention how one of the officers was complaining about his inefficient Latvian servant and the mounting filth in the officer's latrine. My father was reminded of his own disgust of the putrid smell of their latrines. In the front of the barracks was the kapo's room, a small, self-contained room with a little window. On the other side was a longer room my father refers to as the *pissoir*, the place that held their crude toilets which were basically cesspools covered by planks with holes in them. It reeked from the stagnant urine and stinking feces.

"I couldn't breathe, the stench was so overwhelming, even after our first few days. I could certainly commiserate with the officer's complaints," my father said. "Then it hit me. I shouted out to Malenker. 'That's it! The latrines! We can clean the latrines!'

I was very excited with my new idea. I said to him, 'You know these Germans and their *Reinheid* compulsion, their obsession with tidiness and cleanliness. You are the painter. You know how to do this. I can be your assistant, and together we can clean up the latrines to make them smell nice.'" Malenker could not comprehend why his friend would want to spend time in that foul-smelling place, but my father convinced him that it was the perfect way to get out of the work at the quarries. "I need your help," my father kept repeating to his bunkmate. "You must do it with me. You are the painter. You're our leader. You are the man they trust with their bodies for massages. They will listen to you." Persuaded by my father's urgent pleas, Malenker agreed.

The next time he was summoned to give a massage, he suggested to the officer that he and his fellow prisoner be permitted to solve the problem of the stinking latrine. All that was needed were some basic supplies of lime, tar, and brushes, he told the officer. The officer consented. And so it came to pass that my father, by inventing the role of latrine painter, saved himself from the grueling rock-cutting work, which he was convinced would have killed him. Cleaning and painting that latrine meant that he could be indoors and safe once more. His whitewashing idea caught on so rapidly that soon the painting team was in popular demand by other Gestapo officers eager to clean their latrines as well. With the plan working out so well, my father decided to push his luck further. His desire to improve his own surroundings necessitated approaching the dreaded kapo of barracks No. 12.

"Haftling 10052 reporting," my father addressed him. "This was how we had to report to an official, by our prisoner number," my father explains. The convict kapo scowled at my father, who had knocked on his door. "So, what is your complaint today?" he barked at him. "I assured him that I had not come to complain about anything. Then I added, 'I do have something I wish to ask of you.'" Thinking of the rocks and his bleeding hands, he kept his eyes on the ugly face of the kapo and tried to keep down the sick feeling in his stomach, a mixture of nerves and revulsion. "My friend and I wish to volunteer to undertake the cleanup of the toilets of our barrack. I am not sure if you have passed there recently, but the smell is quite bad, sir. It would be a shame if one of the SS were to walk past and be offended and enquire whose barracks these were and why something had not been done about the awful stink. My friend, a professional painter, and I would be willing to undertake such a job of cleaning it properly for you. We have already discussed what is necessary for the work to be done as quickly as possible, and he is convinced that some tar could do the job of getting rid of that awful smell." The hideous kapo glared at my father all through his appeal.

"Yah," he said, "it stinks something terrible. Like all of you. I will see about the tar." Then he dismissed my father.

The next morning at roll call, the kapo came up to my father, pointed his finger at him and said: "You! Stay!" When my father heard that command, he knew immediately what it meant. Wasting no time, he pointed to Malenker, saying, "that man also."

The kapo hesitated a moment, then nodded. He grunted his orders for the two men to report to the kitchen. There, they found a giant barrel of tar waiting for them. Quickly devising some kind of stirring spatula from a piece of wood, my father and Malenker lugged the vat over to the urinal barrack at No. 12.

"You should have seen us!" my father says. "We looked so official. We set up a barricade outside the door and kept that *pissoir* closed for about a half a day while we cleaned that *farshtunkeneh*, stinking place, mopping and pouring tar all over the place. We did not allow anyone to come in to use it while we were working, and let me tell you, those men were furious with us. Oy, you should have heard them shouting, yelling obscenities and curses at us. 'Wait, wait,' I shouted back at them through the walls. 'You curse us now, but you'll thank us later!'"

By the afternoon, their job was completed, and the *pissoir* now smelled heavily, not of urine, but of rich tar that was far more preferable. Only once the tar was totally dry would my father let anyone in. Those who had yelled obscenities before were now mumbling compliments as they relieved themselves. It was a private victory for my father. Not only had he saved his precious hands, he had overcome his loathing of the kapo and momentarily transformed their latrines from a wretched place of retching to a restroom of relief for them all.

At the completion of their job, the kapo called them into his office to offer his gruff compliments. They had done a good job, and he was pleased with their work. The next afternoon, my father was called into the kapo's office again and told he was to be escorted to barracks No. 7 for his next job of tarring. An SS man arrived to accompany Malenker and him to the barracks, since at no time were Jews allowed to wander around without supervision. Malenker believed they had a good business going. With the already prepared tar waiting for them at their next destination, they went back to work. After No. 7 came work on No. 5, then No. 2, and so on. "Malenker was right," my father admitted. "Because the latrines had to be cleaned fortnightly, we were needed now, for the time being."

The kapo summoned them again. "'Now you have done this fine job, I've decided you should be the carriers of the bread. Get two other people to help you and that will be your new job,' he told us," my father says. The bread for the prisoners was transported daily from the kitchen to the yard in front of the barracks. All the bread, just enough to feed the approximately two hundred and twenty people in the barracks, was placed on a large board of flat wood which four people carried from the kitchen. The bread was precut into pieces, so the four people carrying the bread were able to obtain pieces to share and offer others. The German chef, also a former convicted criminal, having heard about the famous toilet tarrer, called my father over to him.

"Hey, you! You the one from the latrines?" My father nodded. If there's one person he wanted to be on good terms with, it was the chef, the provider of paltry daily sustenance in the camp of hourly death. "Well, we have some more tar. You do our latrines now too, yah?" My father quickly replied that he did not have the authority to do anything without his kapo's permission, and suggested he consult first with him. The German criminal-turned-chef replied: "Oh, I know that kapo. This will cost us a good piece of meat!"

The very next day, my father received orders to report to the kitchen, where the bunkmates were rewarded an extra piece of bread for their work. Reporting back to the kapo, my father thanked him for granting permission to let them do the work and then told him about the bonus pieces of bread. "May we keep it?" my father asked the kapo. Malenker, whose instinct had been to swallow the bread right away, thought my father crazy for wanting to disclose their reward with the kapo. But my father insisted that it was important to include the kapo, who had given them the job in the first place, in the deal as part of their 'business' transaction. Begrudgingly, Malenker went along with my father's reasoning. For a moment, standing in front of the glaring, ugly kapo, my father doubted his own decision. The kapo stared at them and then replied: "Yes, you may keep the bread." Pushing his luck even further, my father asked the kapo if they could store the two pieces of bread there, in the kapo's office, on his desk in his safekeeping, until a later time when they could come and retrieve them. He was worried others might discover their prize of extra bread and steal it from them or be jealous and cause a fight. Knowing from bitter experience that when people are starving, politeness and civility disappear, he wished to avoid being the cause of any such trouble. Life was precarious enough without incurring the wrath of fellow sufferers. And so it was arranged with the kapo that their payment would be kept safely in his office, allowing the two toilet painters to enjoy at their own discretion the bread they had truly earned.

Having now established good relations with the kapo, Malenker and my father had the luxury of spending some time in the barracks during the day, on call when needed. Of course, if they heard footsteps outside, they would immediately spring into a pretend display of cleaning activities. One day, the two friends were lying on the bed talking and resting, when the sound of heavy boots hastily clomping up the stairs propelled them into action. Jumping up immediately, they began to sweep the floors.

The door burst open and there stood the kapo, his face flushed from running. My father could sense he was agitated about something.

"Quick," the kapo said in a gruff whisper, "hide yourselves immediately!" The two men stopped their pretend cleaning and stared, stupefied. "Do as I say. Go! Find a place to hide!" he ordered. But Malenker and my father, stunned by the surprise visit, remained frozen. The kapo lurched toward them, pushing them forward, pointing up to the ceiling. "*Schnell!* Upstairs, in the attic! Now!" he hissed. Then he was gone.

"Malenker and I looked at each other for a second, and then we scrambled onto the bunks and up into the attic rafters. Malenker hoisted himself up through the trapdoor, then pulled me up beside him into the attic. Hiding up there in the dust and dark, our mouths dry, our foreheads sweating, we waited for the worst. Suddenly, an announcement came over the loudspeakers for all prisoners to go outside in the yard and stand in formation for counting. It was one of those unexpected *aktions* the Nazis were so famous for. We found out later the SS had arrived to gather about 5,000 people and remove them from the camp. Those who had already left for their work outside the camp were spared. The rest of the prisoners left at the camp were rounded up and removed by trucks to an unknown destination. Gone! Just like that. Cleared out. One, two! We used to call it *chapoones*, from the Yiddish word *chap*, to grab, to snatch," my father explains. "The same as in the ghetto—people grabbed and taken away, never to be seen again."

Lying in the attic, the two men waited until the roars of the engines and the noise of tires grinding against the gravel road grew faint. They waited until the only sound they heard was the beating of their own hearts. Then they climbed back down, wiping off the spiderwebs and dust from that impromptu hiding place in the roof. My father, shaking, almost collapsed on the bunk.

"We just sat there," my father says. "What can you say when your life has been spared by your captor, an ugly criminal? We were saved. For the moment at least, with the knowledge and fear that the next moment can bring another Fate." My father understood all too well that their lives teetered precariously on a split-second decision or a moment's notice.

My father glanced at Malenker. His usual air of good-natured joviality seemed to have vanished along with the SS trucks carrying thousands of their campmates away. Even though they had been treated relatively well because of their latrine-cleaning operation, always in the back of my father's mind were grave concerns about Stutthof. Now he turned to his friend and said: "This is not good, Malenker. I have a bad feeling about this."

"It's only another *aktion*," Malenker replied. "This is the way it happens here. We were lucky. It probably won't happen again. We have solid work here, and the kapo is now our friend. All will be all right, you'll see. We are needed here," he tried to reassure his bunkmate. But my father, always one to trust his own gut feelings, would not be swayed. The gentle optimism of his friend could not allay the ominous feeling at the pit of his stomach. That nagging dread more gnawing than hunger warned him that something bad was about to happen—that they would eventually run out of luck. By now, he was painfully aware of the German strategy to get rid of all Jews by any means available. The Nazis's effective propaganda had degraded Jews to the status of subhuman slaves, a convenient source of labor and collectible goods and, as such, dispensable. They would literally be worked to their death—from cold, starvation, or exhaustion. To the German forces, Jews were just numbers to be counted, added and subtracted, 5,000 at a time.

"Malenker," he implored his friend, "listen to me! Look around you, for God's sake! People are dying here all the time. We are only here to work and be killed. We have to get away from this place. It is one giant trap! Don't you see—we are just a storehouse here. The SS men can just come and grab people any time they want. We must try to go somewhere where we are put to useful work, where we do not have to worry about sudden attacks and changes to our schedule. I don't like it, Malenker. As good as it may seem for us at this moment, it is bad, very bad here, Malenker. I feel it in my bones. We have to get away from here."

Arriving at Stutthof, my father had hoped to be placed with his father in the same barracks. Zacharias was being used as a doctor in the makeshift clinic and had the privilege of walking around relatively unsupervised from barrack to barrack. Able to meet sporadically by the latrine in his barracks, father and son would share some spare bread or soup, in relative privacy, and talk about the events happening around them.

One day, Zacharias informed his son of his imminent departure to a medical unit up in Königsberg and said, "You know, I am an old man already. I'm not sure what will happen to me, but I feel that you will manage. You will survive this thing. Just remember, try to be invisible. Do not make yourself noticeable. Try rather to blend in and remain undetected. Then they will not single you out, because they will not know that you are there. That is the only advice I can give you. The rest you will learn on your own. Good luck, my boy. May God always be with you in whatever you do."

My father was extremely sad. This, he was certain, would be the last time he would see his father alive. Zacharias had an air of resignation about him, his movements slower than ever. They kissed each other on the cheek, hugged, and wished each other well. As Zacharias began walking away, my father called out to him, the affectionate Yiddish word for father springing from his lips:"*Tutteh!* One thing I want to know from you, *Tutteh*. You divorced Mama and married another woman, but somehow in my mind I think that you still loved Mother. Did you, *Tutteh?* Did you still love her?"

His father looked back at him, his eyes moist: "I will love your mother until my dying day." Then Zacharias turned around and began his slow shuffle back to his barracks. My father watched him walk away, his chest aching from the weight of the unutterable last goodbye.

The Welder and Poet

✦

Stutthof and Danzig-Burggraben, Poland, 1944-45

Kindness is food for the starving soul.

Zacharias's departure filled my father with a new vigor and resolve. Just as he had scrubbed away the stench of waste fluids from the latrines, he stoically brushed away his own morose feelings of loss. Hurrying back to Malenker, he told him about his father being sent away to work. "We must do the same," my father urged. "We must leave here."

A couple of days later, while they were standing on the *appell*, a call came for a team of welders and electricians needed to report for duty in the port of Danzig. My father quickly motioned to Malenker that they should offer themselves for this job. "Malenker and I stepped forward out of our lines and volunteered our services. We were, after all, electricians of sorts. My vacation job in 1939 with my electrician father-in-law was qualification enough for me. Malenker, a house painter, was handy at most things. The officials took our names, and within three days we were on a train, in a group of twelve people, guarded by the SS men, bound for Danzig and a new line of work. I felt sure that if we were needed for work, we could get out of death's way … for the time being."

My father's group was taken to a new labor camp called Burggraben, about twelve kilometers outside Danzig, where my father saw for the first time the imposing sight of the huge German tankers, ships, and U-boats, docked in the harbor. A small train and the watchful SS men would transport the workers back and forth from the camp to their workplace, a welding shop at the harbor where nearly 250 Jews worked alongside more than 25,000 other prisoners of war, the majority of whom were Russian.

"Welcome to Germany!" announced an old man of about eighty, greeting his new group of workers sent to repair the damaged U-boats in the dry dock. The tall, stooped, scrawny man wore a perpetual grin under his giant gray moustache, and seemed oblivious to the war or any suffering around him. For him, the world was something to smile at. "Do any of you understand German?" They all nodded. "Well, very good," he beamed.

"Now, before we start, I ask that you all show me your hands. Put them out like this," he instructed them, stretching out his own large, bony hands in front of him. As the prisoners displayed their hands, the old man went around inspecting each of them. When he came to my father, he peered into his face, the deep wrinkles at the corners of his eyes crinkling as he grinned. "You have never been a welder, have you?" he said. Looking down at his betraying hands, my father replied in German: "Please, sir. It was the only way I could think of to escape from the camp. Whatever you will ask me to do, I will do. I give you my word." The old man nodded, gave his kindly smile, and moved on to the next person in line to continue his examination.

The tall old man taught them welding for three weeks, during which time he told them his story. He was a socialist, he explained, and because he worked as a tradesman, he was a member of the union, which required membership in the Nazi party. He assured them that he hated the Nazis and promised that he would teach his group whatever he knew so that they would be able to do their job just well enough to keep them working for as long as possible. The elderly German made a distinct impression on my father. Walking around wearing his little blue army cap from the First World War, he would address them slowly, as if there were all the time in his relaxed world.

"Now remember, boys, when it comes to the welding of our U-boats, you must try and do it very, very thin. Do not do the best job as I trained you to do. No! Let the joints be thin and fragile. Because, when it is time for the boat to be launched in the water, the pressure will be too great for our little repairs, and the boat will be brought back here, where we will once again have some holes to mend. Yah? That is what we want, you and I. In these final months of the war, our young boys should not go out on the boats to their deaths in the ocean."

Repeating his socialist philosophy confidentially to his workers, he would shake his head from side to side, muttering, "Germany is *kaput*! I cannot understand this new Germany, this insanity." He'd stroke his moustache with his long, bony fingers and sigh. "*Kaput,*" he'd mumble to himself, "*altz is kaput.*" To him, the Germany he knew and loved from his youth was over, finished, destroyed.

The old German supervisor seemed especially kind to my father's Jewish group. "Be good socialists and care for each other," he told the twelve men. "I will leave something for you each day in the waste basket, but you must take turns, making sure to share. Each one of you is responsible for the well-being of everyone. You understand?" Each day the old German would bring several pieces of leftover food and leave it in the trash bin so that the guards would not be suspicious. And, like the good socialists their supervisor urged them to be, staving their ravenous hunger, the men would take turns once every twelve days, to quickly dig down into the basket and get the extra piece of food he faithfully left for them. It did not escape my father's attention that the old man wrapped the food in the latest newspaper for them to read and get information about the events on the warfront.

Most of the time Malenker and my father worked side by side on the night shift. One day, feeling rather proud of himself for mastering the craft of welding, my father suddenly felt a sharp pain in his hand. A piece of metal had lodged in his thumb, and the instructor immediately stopped him from working. The next morning his hand had swollen to twice its size. At the clinic, the metal sliver was removed, leaving him with little feeling in his hand. In this strange way, he was saved five days of welding work, but since idleness was rarely tolerated, my father was given some other chores. When he was able to return to work, he was assigned to the day shift, which meant he would no longer be working alongside Malenker. My father sorely missed the company of his best friend. The only positive outcome of the change was that they could both sleep more comfortably now that each had the whole bunk to himself.

A week later, one of the SS guards came to his barracks. Their group had just lain down after their day's work when he roused them from their bunks, stressing he needed four "lazy Jews" to help him with a job. My father was one of four people randomly chosen by the guard to go out on a special nighttime visit to a nearby farm to collect potatoes. The reward, the guard assured them, would be to keep some of the takings for themselves, once they had helped him steal the potatoes.

"It was snowing that night. In the freezing cold he pushed us out of the gates," my father recounts. "For about an hour we had to trudge in the snow to get to a little hill. Then the guard, with his rifle, made us scrape away at the ground with our bare hands till our frozen fingers were bleeding. I managed to gather thirty potatoes from that hill of ice that night. The young guard took twenty-five for himself. We hobbled back to the camp, our bodies freezing from our excursion. I kept reminding myself how lucky I was to have some extra food at least, and looked forward to eating those potatoes the following day. As soon as we reached the camp gates on our return, the other sentry appeared. Suddenly, our guard started shouting at us. 'You thieves, you lousy Jewish scum thieves! You think you can get away with this? You go out at night to steal from our good German farmers, and think we will not find out?'"

The four men were instantly ordered to lie face down on the frozen ground. Goading the other guard to search them thoroughly, the young SS man laughed as the stolen potatoes rolled out from their pockets. Continuing his curses and accusations, he began to beat my father on the back with his rifle, pressing his head into the snow-covered soil with his heavy boots. My father could feel the clumps of frozen soil wedged into the grooves of the SS man's boots digging like daggers into his back. Bloody and bruised from the beatings, the prisoners were locked up in solitary confinement cells as punishment for the crime that the SS guard had instigated. The next morning they were released, the guard smirking and informing them that he had returned the potatoes to the farmer. The men returned to their barracks and, more importantly, to their job of welding the submarines. My father, his back aching with each move he made, was grateful to be seated during his long working hours.

"It was this 'potato beating' and the bayonet attack from when I worked outside the ghetto that crippled my back for life," my father says. In the early days of the Vilna Ghetto, during a work assignment in a nearby German military station, he told me, he was up on a ladder fixing a light bulb in one of their barracks, when a young teenaged German soldier came up to him and began insulting my father for fun. Suddenly, the German youth jabbed the protruding bayonet of his rifle hard into my father's rear. "Filthy Jew!" he yelled. "We shall finish you off soon!" The pointy steel shot like a spear through my father's body, and he fell off the ladder onto the hard, cold cement floor. He was in such pain that he lay there, trying to catch his breath. "I felt so ashamed of myself for crying out in fright and pain as I fell down," he admits. "Of course, a Jew lying on the ground was like a soccer ball to a German soldier. This young boy started to kick me in the back. I struggled to pick myself up as quickly as I could, which was not fast enough and hobbled back to the ghetto to the infirmary. I could hardly walk it was so sore."

My father's back pain was a recurring theme in our house. Whenever it rained or the weather was about to change—a common occurrence in the overcast, rainy winters in Cape Town—my father would suffer from severe backaches. When I was six, he suddenly keeled over, immobile. I was terrified, seeing my father in such incapacitating pain, so pale and weak. Without my strong daddy, who would take care of me? *Sciatica,* was what they called the invisible axe that chopped down my hero. Back in those days my parents tried various remedies. My mother, never a cook, experimented by making lentil soup, following a suggested homeopathic recipe. Little was known about vegetarianism, which at the time seemed rather radical in a country famous for its *biltong* (beef jerky), *braaivleis* (barbeque) and *boerewors* (farmer's pork sausage). I remember the lentil soup distinctly because I'd never heard of lentils before and the funny way my mother pronounced the word made me giggle. But there was nothing funny about my father's illness, especially when he was abruptly removed from our flat and taken to the hospital more than an hour away, leaving me alone with my childlike mother. Since she didn't drive, friends of my parents drove us to visit him there. Down the maze of long, gray linoleum hallways we walked till we reached the white room where my fallen hero lay in a starched white bed, strung up to the ceiling with contraptions made of metal and leather. "Lying in traction," he explained. To the scared young girl staring at her wounded god, it sounded and looked like a torture chamber. Putting on my best, bravest, smiling face for the adults in that hospital room, I hid the panic I felt at the sight of my father lying flat on his back in that sterile place.

As a naturally upbeat and happy-go-lucky young child, I had this one inexplicable dread that I never told anyone about. It had to do with very old, frail, or sick people. I didn't want to be left alone with them. My fear was that they would collapse and die right next to me and I wouldn't know what to do or how to save them or bring them back to life. Seeing my father in the hospital evoked that worrisome fear in me. A strange notion occurs to me now. Could that fear have been transmitted to me through my DNA? After all, how many frail bodies had my parents witnessed dropping dead around them, while they had to stand by, unable to help? What if it were true that we genetically inherit more than just our physical attributes, like the color of our eyes and texture of our hair, but we carry cellular memory of ancestral fears and fortitudes as well?

"Recently," my father continues, "I was reminded of that hard time at the end of the war in Burggraben. I was busy cleaning out the garage in the flat, going through old boxes, looking through old papers, when I came across the poem I wrote after the potato incident. I had been in a good mood before, coming back from a nice walk on the beachfront, happy your sister had come to visit. When I saw the piece of paper with the poem, my happiness disappeared. Reading it again, I was once more in Danzig. Everything came back to me: the tension, anxiety, and fear; the pain of being kicked into the hard, cold ground, the horrors I had seen, the family I had lost, the indignity and injustice of being forced to steal, and on top of that, the jeering and cursing, and jailing for something not even my fault. Even during the bright sunshine of a glorious Sea Point day," my father says, "the nightmares came over me, like a black cloud. That is war, you see? A slow poison. Even when the mind tries to forget, the body remembers. My body is now old and changed. All that took place so long ago. But still, deep in my bones that complain to me on a rainy day, still, are the memories of my punishments. You ask me to tell you about my life during the war. I shared with you my memories. I am happy you want to hear the stories, but still, it pains me that you, my daughter, have to know what I went through."

Several months after my father's sudden death, I was to experience my own incapacitating, excruciating attack of sciatica that crippled me. It coincided with the timing of my protracted divorce. Going through my own kind of traction—the stretched-out, stressed-out, contentious legal separation from the man who had once been my fairy-tale prince, I felt the unrelenting agony of searing pain from my lower back all the way down my right leg. It became so bad I couldn't walk or drive. I could barely sleep. The prescribed painkiller, Percoset, seemed like a mild sedative to someone with a high tolerance for pain, who hardly ever took pills. Attempting a slew of traditional and alternative remedies, excluding the famous lentil soup, I finally, after months of unalleviated suffering, resorted to back surgery for what was diagnosed as a bulging disc problem. I understood the metaphor. Clearly, it was not only the hazel eyes, skinny legs, long flat feet, and history of divorce that been passed down to me from my father. It was his psychic pain, too.

At the time my father told me about this incident in Danzig and his subsequent finding of his poem, I had not thought to ask where the piece of paper was or how he had managed to keep it. In 2006, when Lizzie and her mate Martin came to visit me in New Jersey, I hauled out the big brown cardboard box marked "X.P.," which I had shipped to America after his death. Among its contents of assorted papers my father had collected and saved, were his hand-drawn diagrams of the branches of the Jutan family trees that Martin eventually organized into computerized spreadsheets. The X.P. box, stacked with its treasures of memorabilia, was ready and waiting for my next visitor, Richard Finkelstein, the set designer hired by the New York State Theatre Institute for their production of *Better Don't Talk!*, who came to photograph the original documents for the evocative collage backdrop we had discussed creating. An acclaimed photographer, he wished to make sure all my father's *papierlach*, or little papers, were digitally captured for posterity. It was during that process of closely examining, for the first time, each piece of the over 400 items, including passports, letters, articles, photos, stamped envelopes, and newspaper clippings my father had accumulated over the years, that I found the poem. There it was, hidden in the pile of papers, a flimsy piece of old brown paper, with faded sentences in Polish, a language I don't understand. The handwritten 1945 date and the word Stutthof were the clues that this was the poem my father mentioned in his recollections to me. On another piece of fragile paper, buried deeper in the box, I found my father's translation.

I am here on a foreign soil, brought by force, by a vicious foe.
My home is burnt down, my family all killed,
I sit and my heart cries out, Woe!
Imprisoned, shackled, I last saw my home town
Through the bars of the cattle train speeding far north
I cried out my anguish, and the willow trees answered and the wind cried.
I heard it myself.
Hey! Swallow, you free bird, fly southward and take
My soul on your wings, for my body lies here while my heart is in Vilna.
But my spirit, no enemy can conquer.
I shall always remember the place of my birth,
The years of my youth, my family and friends.
The joy of success, the excitement of study,
I shall never forget the murder and plunder
The Nazis inflicted on us in their barbaric ways.
Allow me, dear Fate, which follows me always
To take my revenge for the innocents' blood.
For the millions of graves, for the villages destroyed,
For my young years so forcefully broken.
And do help me, dear Fate, to have strength in my body
So full now of pain, of disease and of hunger
To be able to carry a gun or a rifle,
That will be my armor in a fight for my freedom.
I am here on foreign soil, brought by force, by a vicious foe
My home is burnt down, my family all killed
But I shall survive to take revenge on my own.

—Israel Ben Zcharya

The Survivor

✦

Danzig, Germany, 1945

When all seems lost, one can find oneself in the heart of another.

On an early, frosty January morning, all the prisoners in Burggraben were called to the roll call held on the open ground. Even Malenker and those on the night shift had to attend the early morning wake-up call. Running out into the large yard in their formations, the prisoners automatically formed themselves into the five lines of long rows, one behind the other. Standing there, they waited, emaciated figures with little tin cups, from which they'd drink the watered down cabbage soup called lunch, dangling from string belts tied around their concave bellies. My father remembers the feel of the icy cold of the metal cup through the paper-thin uniform that was their only clothing, aside from the coarse gray blanket they wore as a winter coat against the frigid Baltic air. "My bones were shivering in the below-zero temperature of that winter morning. But I had to ignore it and keep standing. Just keep on standing," he says soberly.

They were made to stand out there in the bitter cold until every single one of the 30,000 men was accounted for. A head count could easily last for more than an hour. Up on the watchtowers, at each corner of the camp's yard, watching every movement down below, stood armed soldiers on guard, ready to shoot. Sometimes, after standing in one place for hours, people would simply fall to the ground, dead from the cold. It was the toll of four years of hard labor, torture, beatings, lack of food, lack of sleep, sub-zero temperatures and ever present, ever persistent fear. Those standing were forbidden to help those who fell, nor could they look at the fallen. "We had to keep our eyes straight ahead, like in the army," he recalls. "Only at the end of *appel* could the corpses be carried away, always by us Jews who were forced to be the pallbearers. The bodies were taken to fields just outside the camp walls, where they would be tossed into mass graves. "To survive such harsh conditions, one must be impervious, without emotions. At this point, each moment for me was a battle between my mind telling me, 'stay alive' and my body crying, 'No—I give up.'"

This particular *appel* took much longer than usual. Those people who toppled to the frozen ground were left lying where they fell. The SS officer informed everyone that the camp was being evacuated immediately. "We were ordered to take our belongings—a spoon, fork, tin cup, and blanket—with us," my father adds. "There were no trucks to transport us, so, under the direction of the hurrying SS guards, we began the march out of the camp northward. The rumor was, when we reached the shore, we would be dumped into the Baltic Sea. I wasn't sure what to think. I just knew I must concentrate on prolonging my life, on making it through this long stretch of marching through the thick snow, because by now I was very, very weak. We tried to find bits of burnt wood along the way to chew to help control the diarrhea affecting us all. My wooden clogs absorbed a lot of heavy snow and it was difficult to walk with the guards pushing and shouting at us all the time to keep moving faster. *'Schnell! Schnell marchieren!'* Quick, quick march! Always in our ears. But in those moments when I felt faint, my quivering legs starting to give out, I would feel Malenker's hand at my back, pushing me forward."

Malenker, taller and stronger than my father, marched behind him, helping him, propping him up, keeping him in the rhythm of the forced march that had started in the early afternoon and continued till late at night. The men were not allowed to stop until they reached the outskirts of a village. There, the SS men pushed their prisoners into a church at the entrance to the village, hurriedly locking the front doors behind them.

"What a turnaround it was since the beginning of the German occupation," my father says. During the early days of their invasion, the German soldiers, bloated with inflated delusions of superiority, openly derided the Jews with impunity. At the end of the war, however, it was a different story. Now, their orders were to hide all physical evidence of their atrocious crimes. He wondered if the Nazis, losing the war, were feeling the same effects of deprivation and demoralization they had forced on the Jews. Were they now afraid for their own future? Were they now trying to avoid the curious eyes of their own fellow civilian German residents, who might be witness to the results of their evil persecutions—the parade of staggering human skeletons—through their countryside? It certainly seemed so. Those old people left in the small rural villages, my father claims, had been relatively untouched by the Nazi fanaticism that had swept the cities and the youth. Some still demonstrated their compassion and humanity in small ways which he noticed. That night, he saw an elderly woman and a few children sneaking into the back entrance of the church with potatoes, carrots, and bread to hand out quietly to the few prisoners fortunate enough to be sitting near the door.

"We managed to sleep for a few hours, some on the floor, in between the pews, on top of the pews, and near the altar, pressed into every corner of that small, cold church. In the early morning, we were woken up by the guards. We must begin marching again," he continues. "Three people who had died in their sleep were dragged and dumped in the field outside." They marched by moonlight through the early dawn, so as not to be seen. During what was later called the death march, many of the prisoners were either shot by the SS guards or fell down from exhaustion, their bodies discarded on the roadside. When they reached the next village, the remaining prisoners were herded into an empty school. This time there were many faces peering through the windows at the woeful sight of the moving striped skeletons. "The same thing happened there again," my father recalls. "Two very old Germans crept in through the back door and distributed some food to the prisoners."

At midday, some thin soup was dished out, and soon thereafter the marching resumed. The SS men kept forcing them to move faster into a brisk march, shouting that they were too slow, that they must hurry to reach the next village at dawn. Often, the prisoners were directed off to the side of the road to make way for military trucks and cars speeding westward toward Germany. In the distance, they could hear the yak-yak sounds of the Soviet airplanes flying in the same direction.

"We must rush even faster, faster," my father says. "They used their rifles to push us, hitting those who could not keep up the tempo. I remember my lungs feeling about to explode. My body ached and my legs felt numb, but I kept moving, with Malenker assisting me. I could hear his voice behind me, repeating my name in his deep voice, giving me words of encouragement to keep going. 'Go! Go! You can make it. Just a few more steps. Hold on! Hold on! Soon we'll be free, my friend. Soon we'll be free.'" My father was glad he had listened well to his father's previous advice: "Always remember to keep your head and your feet warm, and you'll be all right." Before setting off on the march, he made a special effort to wrap his bare feet with old pieces of newspapers he'd found. Grateful for Zacharias's words at his feet and Malenker's words at his back, he clutched his thin gray blanket tightly over his head and hurtled blindly through nights of forced marches in the heavy snow toward the unknown.

On the fourth night they reached a side road in a forest where they were shoved into a deserted, isolated camp consisting of two barracks, some huts and a kitchen enclosed with barbed wire. Under a pile of snow they found shoes, blankets, and kitchen utensils, some of the belongings of the previous occupiers. "It is simply impossible to describe how cold and exhausted we were," my father tells me, shaking his head. "Many of us simply collapsed onto the bare, cold, cement floor and fell asleep immediately. I found a corner near the window and sat down. Through the window I could see the snow falling outside. My thoughts swirled around like those snowflakes. What was to be our future? Is this some bogus march, fated to end in a mass shooting to wipe us out, the witnesses of Nazi crimes? Or will they desert us here? Are they running from the Russian troops? Is the Red Army close? Will we be rescued in time? My eyes were closing, but I could not sleep. Suddenly I felt a nudge on my arm. It was Malenker. He had found me. He had been outside gathering some snow for us to have as water. He also shared with me a piece of bread. We ate it very slowly. Each morsel must give us strength for a day ahead. We discussed our situation. Was this it, then? The end?"

The following days were spent just sitting in that camp with nothing to do but wait for the next Nazi move. One old man, whom my father remembered as the owner of a Vilna bookshop, was given a special assignment by the SS. With the pair of pliers handed to him, he was told to remove any gold teeth from the fresh corpses that still lay there, before the torsos were tossed out in the snow. Malenker meanwhile took on leadership of the small band of surviving Jews. Somehow he had convinced the guards to let him accompany them on their trip to the nearby village, where they secured a horse that would serve as their meat and soup for the next few days. My father's admiration for his friend kept increasing. After all their trials and hard labor, Malenker remained strong, full of energy, with a will to survive that was inspirational to the other survivors, too.

That same evening, my father began to feel light-headed and dizzy, his body wracked with diarrhea. He began to vomit. Malenker advised him to drink snow to get better. What he didn't tell my father was what he had learned from the SS guard: that the deserted camp they were in was infected with typhus from the previous inmates, all of whom had perished. That night, my father dragged himself over the bodies of sleeping people so he could go outside to relieve himself. In the morning, even though he had no strength to move, his body began convulsing, his arms thrashing wildly about from the typhus fever that now consumed him. Malenker now attended to his sick friend. Placing his blanket carefully under his friend's head, Malenker took the cold compresses of snow he had made and pressed them against my father's temple, gently squeezing the cold water into his mouth. Sitting next to him on the floor, Malenker would patiently restrain him whenever he writhed in spasms or yelled out impulsively. "In my fever, I remember hitting Malenker over and over again, saying I wanted to be left alone, to die, to be put out of my misery," my father admits. "I truly—for the first time—wished death for myself."

From off in the distance came the whining of planes swooping through the sky, and the sounds of bombing. Malenker assumed the Russians were near because the SS men were hastily making preparations to depart. Fearing the Nazis might burn down the camp before running away, as was their practice in other places, Malenker quickly devised an escape plan.

In the middle of the night, Malenker wrapped my delirious father in a blanket, lifted him up, and pushed him through a small back window onto the snow-covered ground outside, near the barbed wire fence. Hoisting himself through the window, he dropped to the frozen ground and began dragging and pushing my father and himself under the hole he had managed to prepare under the fence. With his friend slumped over his shoulder, Malenker ran through the forest until he came to an old farmhouse. Bursting through the door, he ordered the surprised, sleeping old German couple to make a bed for his ailing friend. Under Malenker's commands, they first washed my father with hot water, then put him in a clean bed in a room at the back of the cottage. Asking for a bottle of schnapps, he poured the brandy into my father's mouth, making him swallow it. Then he rubbed the rest of the alcohol onto my father's feverish, skinny body to rid him of the lice that caused the typhoid fever.

"After a few days I awoke to find myself in a warm, soft bed in a strange room" my father recalls, "being fed good food by two old Germans. Three plump feather cushions were behind my head, and a beautiful quilted duvet coverlet was on top of my body. I thought I must be dreaming. After a while, I recognized my friend Malenker and slowly began to talk to him. He smiled, took my hand in his and nodded his head. We made it. We were alive. We were free. Yah!" my father sighs. "It was over."

After a long pause my father shakes his head, looks at me, and says quietly: "You know, out of the Jutan family of about seventy members, my father's brothers, his parents and uncles, aunts, sisters, and their children living in Vilna at that time the Germans invaded Poland, I am the only one to have lived through the camps and death march and survive the Holocaust."

I glance at my father, the sole survivor. What were the odds of my father's chances at survival when well over ninety percent of the Jews of Lithuania of his time were killed? I look at him with new eyes. My former benevolent despot, the dictator who ruled over my formative years, disappears. Instead, I have a vision of a gaunt, shivering, homeless, bewildered young man, clutching a thin gray blanket, standing alone in a field of snow littered by miles of piles of corpses stretching as far as the eye can see.

I am gazing at a miracle. Perhaps what they said about him at his birth was true after all—he was one in a million. My own father had come back from the dead.

PART III

✦

Resurrection

The Daughter: A New Generation

✦

Newton, Massachusetts, 2000

There is evolution in revolution.

If, according to Darwin, the evolution of the species depends on those who are fittest at adapting to their changing environments, then it may turn out that the wandering Jewish descendents of Abraham, like my father, are prime examples of that theory. Deprived of almost everything material, thrust into the harshest of human and natural conditions, my chameleon-like father exemplified the art of adaptation to his ever-shifting wartime circumstances. With agility and intellect, intuition and imagination, flexibility and daring, and a relentless will to survive, my father reinvented and renewed himself at every turn, learning skills to last a lifetime.

I am amazed by the fortitude and resilience of Holocaust survivors in conducting ordinary lives after such extended extraordinarily horrific circumstances. Without the luxury of psychological rehabilitation services, now more readily available for victims of trauma, they were left to their own devices to heal gaping psychological wounds. There was no replacing what had been stolen from them. And yet, they ventured forth into new territories, adjusted to new lands, learned new languages, and created new lives, starting over, from nothing, to achieving in some cases a level of personal success, wealth, and freedom far exceeding what might have been possible in their original countries of birth.

But what of the German Nazis and the SS men who caused the decimation of so many millions of families across Europe, Russia, and America? What hereditary factor caused them to transform themselves so quickly into predators, becoming the fittest of sadistic, willing executioners of their own species? Once upon a more tender time, weren't those cruel Nazis sweet toddlers running crying into their mothers' arms? Did they learn to hate so easily because of their fathers and *their* stories that they heard when their wounded heroes returned home from the First World War, crippled and crushed by derision and defeat? What do little children know but what is pummeled into them from voices screaming from pulpits or pubs or trenches? Could those boys have been the same beguiled little children of Bremen from my fairy-tale books, the ones who came pouring out of their German houses, crossing rivers, valleys, and hills to follow the seductive tune of the psychotic Pied Piper, whose melody cast its spell of redemptive pride, power, and salvation, if only they kept marching to his warped tune?

Vision

Scene: Rolling German hills. A band of boys, flaxen-haired, rosy-cheeked, and naked— except for their big, shiny black boots—are marching. "Our sons! Our sons! Snatched from our bosoms!" screech the German housewives, those buxom *hausfraus* leaning out their shutter-framed windows, arms outstretched, their straw-colored hair coiled tight around their heads in snake-like braids. The little boys keep on marching. They don't hear their mothers. They don't care about their fathers. "Hate,

hate, open the gate," sing the little boys in falsetto, shrinking into their enormous black stomping boots. "Bring back bones, we want bones!" bark the hungry, mangy dogs roaming in packs in the dirty alleyways. A blind old man, hobbling on a wooden leg, steps into the middle of the street: "Our dictator is d-d-demonic, our d-d-despot is d-d-dangerous!" he stutters. But the boys in boots keep on marching, right on top of him, crunching him into the ground till he's no more than a crumpled pile of old clothes and broken bones that yelping, rabid dogs and circling crows swoop down to pick and pounce upon. "One, two, three, four! How we love to go to war," the little boys chant. Row upon row, they march in boots that grow larger and larger. "We're the Brotherhood for the Fatherland!" Hundreds of thousands of stomping boots march left, right, left, right, crashing into churches, crushing green forests, crumbling whole cities into dust and rubble. "Soldiers of war, doing our drill, following orders, sanctioned to kill!" they shout to the amplified sound of their marching boots grown too big for their own country. "Blame to kill! Aim to kill!" the boys cry, their metronome mantra ticking like a bomb. Up in his castle tower built deep in the granite mountain, the Pied Piper, that paranoid predator, stops blowing his pipe to lift his hand to smooth his moustache and salute his own lies. Stepping out of his bunker, one hand pressed to the middle of his back, the other patting the flushed cheeks of innocent boy soldiers, he whispers how brave they are to march to his last call. Stepping back into his bunker, he takes out his revolver, and aims it at his own head. Down in the stone-walled cellar of a beer hall, bands of ignorant, intoxicated little boys, minus their boots, jump and splash in vats of beer that turns to blood that stains their feet forever. The furor is over. But the guilt has just begun.

◆ ◆ ◆

My father's generation emerged from the ravaged ruin of two world wars, already soaked with the bloody sins of their wounded fathers. In their old world, fear and domination were the order of the day, punishment lauded as an effective teaching tool for those in authority. Anything that could inflict pain on flesh—beatings and whippings, the pulling of ears, the twisting of noses, the withholding of food, the spankings by hand, paddle, leather belt, brush or obligatory cane—were all sanctioned methods of instructing minors how to behave and tow the line. Corporal punishment and verbal criticisms were not considered perverse, sadistic, or even counterproductive. Spare the rod and spoil the child? Never. Not in that generation. Children and soldiers, or anything else regarded as one's property or inferior, were to be manipulated and managed, molded into obedient and obliging servants. If nothing else, they had to be whipped into controlled submission.

My generation arose in revolution.

Tasting the bitter poison fed to us, we, the children born after the Holocaust, determined to find the antidote. Unlike our fathers, we refused to simply follow orders. Looking forward to the new millennium, we strove to break the chains of what came before, challenging and defying the so-called establishment, rebelling against stifling restrictions, fighting for our own freedom. While some young women burned their bras and other young men grew their hair long, all of us danced to the new music made to rock and shock our world out of its old ways. Transcendence and transformation were our new guides to the galaxy. Singing about the "Age of Aquarius," we stuck flowers in our freeflowing hair and slogan-filled placards in our clenched fists. "Make love, not war!" we shouted, mixing sex with liberation. Those were the signs of our times.

With our newly created symbol for peace, my rock-and-roll generation marched in droves to the sound of visionaries proposing a new world of tolerance and freedom, ringing out in the voices of Pete Seeger, Joan Baez, Bob Dylan, Robert Kennedy, and Martin Luther King Jr. We congregated in groups, holding candlelit vigils and sit-ins for peace. We broke through barriers, launching ourselves into outer space and bringing down the Kremlin and the Berlin Wall and the Apartheid regime. We impeached a president of the free world with the power of the free press. Like John Lennon and Yoko Ono, we brought together East and West, in politics and in medicine, in bed and business, too. My baby-boomer generation began to bend the rules of the gender game, giving permission for men to grow domestic and women to go corporate. "A good hiding" was renamed "physical abuse" as new laws were created to safeguard children. No longer willing to tolerate or keep silent about violations of human rights, we dared take to task the venerated sanctity of the church for violating young bodies under the pretext of saving their souls. Playing with our new tinker toys of technology, we shrunk the world to fit onto our laptops and hold in our palms, letting continents communicate with the tapping of our fingertips.

Tumbling from the tarot tower of outdated institutions and outmoded traditions, spitting out the smoke and dust of toxic waste, we envision our world with new thoughts, committing ourselves to cleaning up the environment and making our new earth virtuous and verdant again. But what about the long and toxic afterlife of wars, fought and lost—the contaminated rubble of families ruined, children damaged, and lives corrupted? How do we absolve and resolve all that?

The last of those little boy soldiers of World War II are dying now. But their soft-spoken adult daughters have spent their girlhood crying themselves to sleep for want of knowing who their fathers were and what crimes they committed in the name of duty or love of country. The Holocaust is the story of their fathers, too.

Helga Mueller is one of those daughters. Searching to know the truth about her father's past in the face of family resistance, Helga dug up the incriminating evidence on her own. The man the rest of the family touted as a hero, she discovered, was a Gestapo mass murderer responsible for the execution of 40,000 people in Russia. The cold-blooded murderer was also the one who had molested her as a child. Finally, with the help of therapy, Helga understood why as a young girl she had developed the strange habit of pulling out chunks of her own blond hair. As a grown woman, the sad-faced Helga disowned her family. "I feel his guilt on me—I've carried this burden ever since. I have sensed genocide victims walking through my bedroom," she confessed. Grappling with her Nazi legacy, she found comfort in an international organization called One By One, devoted to German-Jewish reconciliation. There, she found affinity with Jews who became friends she now views as family. I am one of those.

Ostensibly daughters of enemies, the perpetrator and the victim, we share a common heritage: We are both innocent heirs to the degradation, pain, and shame that is the legacy of the wars of our fathers.

The Friend

✦

Lauenberg, Germany, 1945

Victory is leaving the past, loving the present, and living the future.

April 1945. The German army had been defeated by the Russians on the Eastern Front. Once my father was strong enough to walk again, his friend Malenker arranged for a horse and carriage to take them to Lauenberg, the nearest town. On their way, they met a group of former camp inmates from Vilna who decided to team up with them. My father remembered two of them as the Blumenthal brothers, oil and petrol suppliers from one of Vilna's outlying suburbs. They told my father and Malenker what had happened at the deserted camp from which they had been liberated. How on March 8, the Red Army soldiers entered the camp, and when some of those who were barely alive reached out to their liberators from among the mass of dead bodies, claiming they were Jews, one of the Russian officers expressed disappointment that they were still alive. His army, he boasted, could have done a better job than the Nazis of finishing them all off.

The group of survivors arrived in Lauenberg, which would change its name to the Polish *Lembork* after the war. There they found a deserted, spacious, three-storey house and moved in. Still very weak from the typhus, my father spent most days lying in bed to get his strength back. His new friends went out scouting for food, finding it readily obtainable from the German farmers living nearby, who were now visibly afraid of everyone. Whether out of pity for the emaciated Jewish survivors or fear of their retribution, the farmers willingly parted with their food.

When the news broke about Germany's ultimate defeat by the armies from the West, the boys from Vilna were too weak to celebrate. While the Allied troops celebrated their military victory, my father and his newfound friends, still slowly recovering from the effects of malnutrition and typhus, quietly contemplated their own triumph: the miracle of being alive and free, of having endured the long years of imprisonment, torture and slavery, and surviving the death marches. They also knew that the war's end did not mean that Jews were out of danger. They still had good reason to fear for their lives. The liberating Russian army, advancing toward Berlin, had demonstrated its own threatening ways. The battle-scarred, war-weary Soviet soldiers, drunk on vodka and victory, were celebrating with rampages of rape. Ten-year-old girls and seventy-year-old grandmothers were equally at risk to the so-called liberators.

"One day," my father continues, "when I was already on my feet, but still very weak, the boys returned from one of their outings with news about a group of Vilna girls who had been released from a nearby camp. We immediately got hold of a horse and cart and went to visit them. They hardly resembled the healthy, robust girls I remembered from Vilna or anticipated seeing from my memory. Their short hair was matted, and they were skin and bones. I was not a pretty picture myself, of course. We were all very thin. But for some reason, a woman looking like that is more dreadful to me," my father admits.

"I recognized one of the young girls. She was Chayela, the young singer who had been chosen to represent Vilna in the Federal Festival of

Folklore Song in Moscow in the summer of 1941. I told her how much I had appreciated her performances in the ghetto theatre and mentioned the article I had once written about her. She smiled and introduced me to her sister, Mary, and a friend of theirs. I quickly suggested they stay with us in our three-storey house, assuring her that we boys would protect them from harm, from those Russian soldiers, already infamous for their escapades of rapes. The thought of these women suffering any more than they already had disturbed me greatly. So they agreed to stay with us on the first floor of our temporary home."

Soon, the small band of survivors, recovering together under one roof, began to operate as a makeshift family. Sitting at night and during the day, sometimes two at a time, sometimes as a group, they shared their reminiscences, their sufferings, ordeals, and losses. They took turns recounting their personal experiences of who they knew had died, which camps they had been in, what they had seen, what hard labor they had done and how they were rescued, recalling incidents they felt compelled to unburden. "It was a way for us to connect, to recover, through our stories," says my father. "And so we talked and kept talking, feeling safe in our small company."

Chayela told them that when the Vilna Ghetto was liquidated, the women were transported to Riga where they had worked in the Kaiserwald labor camp, cleaning and washing the uniforms, shirts and underpants of dead German soldiers. Because of her celebrity status as the Vilna songbird and reputation from her stage appearances in the ghetto, she was often asked by her fellow prisoners to sing popular Yiddish songs, including those her brother wrote. She would perform special concerts at night, singing Leyb's songs to provide moments of rare pleasure. In return, she was given gifts of extra food or easier tasks from the overseers or the inmates. "She cried when she told us how some of the girls would steal extra pieces of food to give to her, so she should have the strength to sing. Her singing meant that much to them," recounts my father. From Kaiserwald, she was sent to Stutthof in transit to Germany. At the end of war, she was part of the women's death march to the Baltic Sea. It was rumored that they would be loaded onto barges and bombed to erase the last witnesses of the atrocities. The reality was that when they reached the shore of the Baltic, near Lauenberg, the women were ordered to keep marching into the sea. Pressed forward by the bayonets of the soldiers pushing them further and further into the water, many of the women were shot while many drowned. When the liberating Russian troops arrived, the German soldiers scattered and ran away, leaving the remaining women behind on the beach. Chayela and her sister were among those left alive.

In the chaotic aftermath of the war, this small band of new friends tried to create the semblances of a normal life, doing chores around the house. My father recalls one particular incident when Chayela volunteered to cook a chicken one of the boys had brought back from a nearby farm. "The girls helped young Chayela to pluck this chicken the way they remembered it being done in their homes by their mothers," my father recounts. "All of us in the house were looking forward to having a good home-cooked meal. But when it came time to eat the cooked chicken, the taste was awful. The chicken was completely bitter! We spat the pieces onto our plates. After some investigation, we realized that Chayela had forgotten to take out the gall bladder and the giblets from inside the chicken. We all had a good laugh, except for Chayela, who blushed and started to cry. A *bitterer gelechter*—a bitter laugh for a bitter chicken! She was embarrassed that her debut in the kitchen was a failure. A marvelous singer she might have been, but a terrible cook. You must understand, she was just a high school student when the war broke out, focused on academics and singing, not cooking."

One day, my father came back to their house to find out that Malenker had disappeared. "The Russian military police, the NKVD, arrested him when I was not at home. I heard that somebody from the last camp had denounced him as a kapo, the overseer of the prisoners. I was outraged. As soon as I heard about this, I rushed over to the administration building to talk to one of the Russian army officers. I wanted to see if I could do anything to get him released. The officer warned me not to interfere." Later, my father learned that the Russians had secretly employed Malenker, who was originally from Kaunas and spoke both Russian and Lithuanian, to help track down Lithuanian Nazis. "After he was gone," my father admits, "I missed him a great deal. He was like my right hand by that time. Luckily, my attentions and feelings were directed toward sweet, charming Chayela, which helped to take away my sadness over losing my best friend, Malenker."

It was only much later, when he had the time and distance to reflect on all that had happened to him, that he realized how much he had depended on this kind, caring, and devoted friend.

"You must understand," he says, his eyes misting over, "we had been together in the worst of situations, when we were so young and vulnerable. It was only natural we grew close to each other." There were many occasions during those dark days, he discloses, that his feelings for his friend seemed to be more than just friendship for a bunkmate. "There were times when I longed to hold him close like a brother, or perhaps, even, it seems strange to say it, I must admit, even wishing to hold him as I would a beloved. Nothing like that ever happened, of course. We were both of us married men. We would never speak about such things like that. But if I am honest, like you requested, then these are the feelings I must relate when I speak about Malenker," my father says. "The truth is, he saved my life. And this, he must have done out of some feeling for me as well, that was love and caring. In that time of war, we were there for each other, partners in survival, together, enduring the worst days of our lives." My father clearly had a deep love, admiration, and respect for the man who was both his friend and rescuer. He told me how grateful he was that the popular Malenker chose to stay at his side, when he could so easily have left at any time to be with the others. To me, it seems they had a perfect partnership: my father with his intuition, intellect, and enterprising schemes and Malenker with his physical strength, affability, leadership, and know-how. They trusted and relied on each other, forming a bond, friendship, and understanding that they would be there for each other, no matter what, whatever it took. "If that is not love, then I don't know," he adds wistfully.

All through the war, Malenker had kept reaffirming to my father his strong belief that his wife was alive, and that after the war he was going to find her. Despite all the terrible stories about the death camps, despite all they saw around them, he was confident they would be together again. Years after the war, my father learned that Malenker had indeed found his wife alive, that they had reunited after the war and emigrated to Israel where they lived a simple, unassuming life. Tracing his whereabouts, my father made a special trip to the village outside Tel Aviv to visit Malenker there. "I went to see him in his modest house. I told him how much he had meant to me at that time. But it made my heart sore to see that things between him and his wife were not so good. The war badly affected their relationship. Each one confided in me separately about the mistrust, accusations, and arguments they had over what each believed the other had done during the war. Very unpleasant. Very sad. It was very upsetting to see him like that with the woman whose memory he cherished so fondly during the time I knew him. When I left, we hugged and I thanked him again for everything he had done for me," my father says. After that one visit, he never saw Malenker again.

The Caretaker

✦

Lembork, Poland, 1946

In sickness and in health, the body speaks its truth.

Steadily, slowly, the little band of Vilna survivors began their recovery. One afternoon my father, sitting in the living room, heard a heavy pounding on the door accompanied by loud shouting. Two rowdy, drunken Russians had stumbled up to their house and were busy banging their fists on the door. "Open up in there!" they yelled. "We know you have women inside there. Let us in!" Alarmed, my father, quickly responded in Russian, "There are no girls here, only a group of boys!" Remembering the reports of the Red Army soldiers raping women, he knew instinctively that the drunk and dangerous men outside his door meant business. The Russians eventually pushed open the door and staggered inside, their revolvers drawn, ready to shoot their way to getting what they wanted. While doing his best to stall the soldiers, he shouted to one of his housemates in Yiddish to quickly run out the door and fetch an army official. "Who do you have upstairs?"

they asked, pushing my father aside as they headed toward the stairs. "Wait, wait!" he told them. "My friend will come back with some girls for you. There is no one up there!" he insisted.

Just then, his friend arrived back with an officer from the Red army and my father explained how these two soldiers had invaded their private house, demanding women. The Russian officer promptly disarmed the soldiers, ordering them back to the barracks for some appropriate cooling off. Looking my father squarely in the eye, he announced, "I am one of you." My father was confused. What did he mean? The officer took him aside and explained that he was a doctor in the army and a Jew. My father threw his arms around the man, telling him about his own mother's Russian background. Soon they were conversing like old friends, the Jewish officer offering assurances that he would try to secure them better food and check on their safety periodically. My father understood he now had an important ally plus a helpful new friend.

Several days later, Chayela began to complain of an upset stomach and dizziness. Within hours, she had developed a high fever. My father recognized the familiar unfortunate symptoms of typhoid fever. Gathering her in his arms, he took her upstairs to her bedroom, insisting she stay there and that the room be isolated. Considering himself immune to the disease from which he had himself recovered, he took it upon himself to be her nursing caretaker. "I carefully took off her clothes and cleaned her body thoroughly, washing her with the alcohol from the good bottle of vodka our Russian officer friend had managed to get us, at my request. He was happy to donate it for medicinal purposes. What Malenker had done for me in that small German farmhouse, nursing me back to health, I would do for Chayela. I would bring her back to good health."

My mother, in brief moments of lucidity in between feverish, ranting outbursts, begged him not to shave her head, which was a common procedure in the cure of typhus. Her hair, shaved in the work camps, had begun growing back, and she cherished the thought of having her once beautiful, thick, black hair long again. In consideration of her wishes, my father washed her hair, he told me, not once or twice, but over and over, maybe five or six times, just to please her. Wrapping her shivering, naked body in a sheet and blanket, he tenderly placed her, like a newborn baby, in the bed to rest and sat devotedly at her side while she slipped in and out of consciousness. Under my father's dedicated personal care and attention, my mother's fever abated and her health improved. Once she showed signs of full recovery, he knew what the next step would be. He would tell her that he wished to take care of her forever. This time, he knew for sure: This special girl from his home town of Vilna, this very one, whose shining spirit and radiant smile had begun to heal his own heart, was the one whose body he wished to hold and protect in the years to come. He was now ready and willing to be a husband, and if his friend Fate were to continue to bless him, in the not too distant future, a father too.

The Refugee

✦

Lauenberg, Poland, 1945
Vilnius, Lithuania, 2003

In someone else's words one can find one's voice.

On May 5, 1945, the citizens of Lauenberg celebrated Victory Day with a big parade in their town. Instead of joining the rowdy crowds in the streets, the small group of Vilna refugees sat on the steps of their borrowed house not far from the Baltic Sea and quietly let the sun warm their thin, tired bodies, as they discussed the significance of Victory Day.

Having been liberated two months previously by units of the Red Army advancing on Berlin, they felt extremely blessed, if not amazed, to have survived the Nazis' planned agenda to exterminate the entire Jewish race in Europe. Their thoughts turned to the future. They wondered if the defeated Germany would be punished for the horrendous atrocities its army committed against Jews and other nations. Would the declared peace bring change to their world, making it a better place to help them forget their terrible experiences of the past years? Or would they always be running for their lives? Which countries would be the best to offer them new lives, good lives, free from prejudice and hatred against the Jews? For my recuperating twenty-five-year-old father and his fellow survivors who for so long had focused primarily on staying alive, the challenges and practicalities of how and where to make new lives now faced them head on.

Some of them wanted to go back to Vilna, which was once again under Russian Communist rule. Even though none in the group were communists, they still longed to see what they remembered as home, hoping to find some members of their original families alive. Others, already informed of the tragic fate that had befallen their kin, expressed hopes of starting anew in Palestine where they had some relatives.

My father tried to remember the names and locations of relatives in England and the U.S. he could contact. He had ascertained at this point that his own father had died in the Panemunde camp near Königsberg, but he had not heard from his mother in Paris since the last postcard he received from her in 1940. He often thought of her, hoping for contact as soon as possible, sending letters to the Red Cross enquiring if anyone in France knew what happened to her.

"Let's celebrate! *Na zdarovye!*" smiled their Russian officer friend, dropping by to visit and bringing a gift parcel of food and drinks. He was going home, he announced, back to Minsk, to his wife and family. "While we were happy for him," my father says, "we knew that for us, there was no home to return to. No going back anywhere. Only forward somewhere. Where, exactly, we still didn't know."

The recovering refugees enjoyed the impromptu party with the boxed lunch specially prepared for the V-Day celebrations. They drank the sweet lemonade and the Crimean wine the officer had brought as substitute for the traditional vodka, which was still too strong for their diseased stomachs. Through the window, they watched the inebriated, victorious soldiers marching in formation past the house, shooting off their guns into the sky. Their loud shouts of "*Za pabyedu*"—"For

Victory!—ricocheted into the charged crowds enthusiastically cheering with appreciation for the war's end.

Inside, the subdued group grew hushed when Chayela stood up and began to sing. Her song was not one of celebration. It was the plaintive cry of nostalgia, "I Long for Home," the song her brother had written in the ghetto that she had sung from the stage, bringing tears to her Jewish audiences as well as to the homesick German soldiers. *"Ich vil noch eynmol zen mine heym*—I want to see my home again, just as it used to be back then. I never thought to stop and stare, I left my childhood over there, I long for home," she sang to composer Misha Veksler's pure and haunting melody, her soprano voice clear and true in contrast to the boisterous noises of triumphant festivities blaring outside. The small band of survivors sat around her, crying softly. Even the Jewish Russian officer, joyfully anticipating his return home to his family in Minsk, stood there with his drink in his hand, tears in his eyes.

When my father told me that Victory Day story toward the end of the twentieth century, I did not know what fate would have in store for me in the new millennium— that I would find myself singing that very song in that same language on the same stage on which my mother had performed during the war.

The Vilnius performance of my play took place in the same auditorium in the large building in Rudnicka Street that had once housed the ghetto administration offices, where my father had heard Jacob Gens passionately declare, "We shall outlive them all!" and where he had first listened to my mother's heartfelt renditions of her brother's soulful songs. As Chayela Rosenthal's daughter, I was treated like a VIP, escorted into the offices of the Vilnius archives to view the original ghetto posters advertising the performances of plays, jazz concerts, and musicals which listed the names of my mother and her brother. The day after my performance, a special tea party in honor of my mother was held at the small Holocaust Museum, the Green House, to which I had brought the schoolchildren I met in the park. Entering the upstairs room of the green painted wooden house was like stepping back in time. It could have been a movie set straight out of the 1940s. Tiny, ornate porcelain teacups in decorated saucers sat perched next to doilied plates of homemade cookies on a lacy embroidered tablecloth. The assorted, aging Holocaust survivors, several of whom had flown in from around the world for the international commemoration of the 1943 liquidation of the ghetto, sat squeezed around the table in an animated exchange of wartime recollections. When the friendly Yiddish discussion escalated into a clash of opinions and memories, a stern-faced woman who was now a librarian and had once been a resistance fighter in the forest stopped the rowdy conversation with her hand in the air. "*Shah!*" she ordered. Turning toward me, she asked in a resolute voice, if I would please sing my uncle's song, *"Ich Benk Aheym,"*—"I Long for Home"—once again. Unprepared for an impromptu *a cappella* performance in such close quarters, I hesitated. But the dour woman, who'd seen her fair share of hardship, repeated her firm request: "Please. We would very much like to hear that song again."

Everyone's eyes were on me. How could I let them down? After all, I had come halfway across the globe to the birthplace of my parents and death place of my mother's parents to pay tribute to their heritage. I had felt hugely relieved that I had pulled off the previous night's performance entirely in Yiddish, something I had never done before, and hadn't planned on doing again. I knew it was to be a unique occasion. But now, the request to sing the whole song in Yiddish once more, no brightly lit stage to separate me from them. My nerves kicked in. Could I pull it off again? At that moment I had an epiphany: *I* was the one in Vilnius now, not my mother. In her absence, these old, resilient people who remembered the youthful Chayela with adoration were looking to me, the next generation, now more than double the age of my mother back then, to bring back their treasured songs. I choked up with emotion. Could I make it through the whole song without crying? Would I remember all the words? Please, I prayed, let me have my mother's will and my uncle's determination to keep going, to hit the right notes, to sing the right words and not falter. Please, let my voice be strong and unwavering, for them, for this special moment.

Taking a deep breath, I began to sing my uncle's Yiddish song into the tiny, hushed room. As I sang, I was overcome with an overwhelming sense of spiritual connectedness. My mother's strength and my uncle's yearning filled my lungs and flooded the air. I felt the pride of being their descendent. Singing in the language my mother knew so well, and my Russian grandmother did not, I repeated Uncle Leyb's words of carefree childhoods in warm beds, of night winds moaning like a mother's sigh, of simple, precious homes stolen away, never to be returned. "I long to see my home again, just as it used to be back then," I sang in the precious language of those who were there and those who were not. Singing into the silence, I felt my heart break open, wider than the gaping, cavernous pits of Ponar that today stand empty, yet filled. I knew the souls of the dead were listening, right there in that room. I was present to it all: the gift of my mother's voice, the healing of my uncle's poetry, the persistence of my father's memory, the timelessness of suffering, the transience of beauty, the constancy of love, the past clinging to the present, the dead breathing life into the living, and the living holding on tightly, afraid to let go.

When the song ended, I glanced at the librarian, sitting stiffly, who had requested the song. Tears stained her face. The other survivors who had heard my mother sing in the ghetto in that town more than sixty years ago, whose opinion, comparison, and critical judgment I had been so concerned about, sat quietly, their eyes glistening. We had shared a sacred moment.

But as all special moments do, it came and went without a second glance. Soon, it was back to the old Yiddish ways of noisy interruptions and crisscross arguments about who had gone where and done what during the liquidation of the ghetto and afterwards. My elderly audience may have thought I had brought my mother back to them. In truth, it was those hardy Holocaust survivors, those few of the last remaining witnesses, with their shared remembrances and their very physical presence in the Vilnius of today with its walls of swastikas, Stars of David, and graffiti advocating self-expression, who had brought my mother's eternal essence back home to me.

The News Reporter

✦

Bydgoszcz, Poland, 1945

The wandering keep on wondering:
Who is chosen for what and why?

Once my father's good health was restored, his new friend, the Red Army officer, recommended him to the new Polish administration of Lauenberg. He was promptly hired to help with the registration of refugees and incoming Poles looking to settle in houses deserted by German families fleeing to the West. "I was able to give false papers to many Vilna and Lithuanian Jews, saying that their birthplace was in middle Poland, not Vilna or Lithuania so they could avoid being taken into the Russian army, which was still mobilizing people to reconstruct the destroyed towns and villages. Several of them wanted to be able to return to Vilna to find out what had happened there and if any of their family were still alive," he recalls.

Unfortunately, his fortuitous employment incurred the envy and gossip of some of the refugees who came into contact with my father in the office. Suspicious about how he secured a job so fast, such a nice house so easily, and food that was better than what they had, they gossiped and made pointed remarks about his excellent position near the top of the administration. My father was well aware of the undercurrents of envy. "It's true, I was lucky," he says, pensively. "When I thought about everything that happened to me, the only thing that made sense of my survival was luck. How else to explain it? Yes, I schemed to put myself in positions to be indoors where I knew I had a better chance of surviving, to be safe. But it did not have to work out that way. My luck was to have Malenker at my side in those last days of the camps and the death march. My luck was also to meet the right people who could help me later, like the Russian officer. You see," asserts my father, "this is my conclusion: Luck has nothing to do with goodness, religion, or righteousness. Many people of high moral standing and learning, men of prayer and charity, good, loving mothers, and over a million innocent children were killed in cruel, unjust ways. So many talented people, artists, doctors, scientists, murdered in cold blood. Those of us left alive, how are we to make sense of why we were the ones to be spared? You understand? How many people keep saying how the best were killed in the Holocaust? How does that leave us, who survived, to feel about ourselves? But it does not matter what people think. This I learned too, the hard way. It only matters what *you* think and what you do with *your* life. What makes one person lucky and another person not, I simply cannot tell you," concludes my father. "I just know I was one of the lucky ones."

In asking other survivors what they attribute as the reason for their remaining alive when others did not, the same answer keeps popping up. Shrugging and shaking their heads, many say the same thing: Luck. Blind, random Luck. The Hebrew word for luck is also used to indicate astrological signs. *Mazal.* Could Luck then be just another word for Fate? Did the ancient Hebrews link chance or luck to the stars of destiny? If we dare to believe in Destiny, in the *bashert,* in what some call karma, are we prepared to consider that perhaps everything is already preordained, written in the stars or even inscribed in the big Yom Kippur Book of Life? What if there's more to the whole story behind survival? Of course, there's no denying that being at the right place at the right time, with the right person helped, too. But wasn't that part of destiny too?

And what about the theory that character determines fortune? Even though many of my father's actions seemed motivated by his inclination to avoid pain, it appears that the qualities of being resourceful, decisive, pragmatic, and self-directed helped him navigate his way through hard times. Most important, I think, was his knack of listening. My father knew how to heed the good advice of others and also, maybe even more importantly, to trust his own intuition and follow his own hunches or instincts. Whatever higher intelligence, divine providence, or transcendent system guides our lives by whatever name we wish to call it, it seems clear to me that my father was blessed with a direct link to it. Like those transistor radios he loved so much, Mr. Piat was plugged into the universe. Attuned to the airwaves, he received signals, guidance, and directions from other realms that he somehow knew how to translate, heed and apply in his life in a timely fashion. Call it sixth sense, hunches, gut instinct or as I refer to them, the "little voices," my father could hear what the shifting tides were saying even without the aid of giant seashells pressed to his ear.

When I asked him once, as a child, what exactly did he do for a living, his eyes twinkled. "Ha! I am a *luftmensch!*—an 'air person,'" he replied. "I take ideas from the air and sell them to others." Although that definition didn't help clarify his promotions business to his curious but confused daughter, I liked the sound of the foreign label he gave himself. Now, I see the validity of his explanation. The sensitive, creative, open-minded Mr. Piat was more of a sky walker than even he himself understood.

"Yes, I have to admit," he continues, "I was lucky. I met good people who helped me. But as fortunate as I felt about my current job situation after the war, I also felt the malevolence of envy directed at me. Of course, it was to be understood, how some refugees could get enraged seeing me in a position of power and influence. But too often, I saw how some others turned their own misery into excuses for nastiness against those around them. I didn't need more ugliness directed toward me, especially from my own people."

Worried about the escalating jealousy over his postwar official administrative position, he put in a request for two weeks' leave. He wished to accompany Chayela, now his romantic partner, on a trip to Lodz, where a Jewish theatre was being formed. His request was granted. Everywhere, the train stations were swarming with the destitute and displaced, mostly refugees desperate to catch trains leaving Germany. The train they hoped to catch, scheduled for Lodz, was full, every seat and standing place occupied. People hung from the doorsteps and squeezed out the windows of the train compartments. Undaunted, my father went straight to the Polish train driver and persuaded him to grant him and his wife the special favor of letting them ride up front with him in the engine. For the resolute Mr. Piat, there was always a way to have his way.

They arrived at Bydgoszcz, an old Polish town, where a Jewish committee of survivors had recently been formed to help resettle the swell of refugees. Hearing a radio announcement calling for artists, actors, and singers to audition for an entertainment group, my father immediately told Chayela to register. Her audition of songs went off so well at the radio station that she was asked to return the following day. That night, along with hundreds of others, they slept on mattresses on the floor of the community centre. While Chayela was busy at the radio station the next day, my father decided to take a walk in a nearby park. It felt good to stroll in freedom, savoring the sights of the brightly colored grass and flowers in the sunshine. Nature seems entirely impartial to man's inhumanity, he noted to himself.

Suddenly, he saw a face he recognized. Walking toward him was a man in a Red Army uniform, with insignia denoting high rank. Uncertain where he recognized the man from, my father was determined to find out. "I stop him and say, 'Excuse me, but you look very familiar to me. Do we know each other, perhaps?' He stares at me, surprised. I tell him I was from Vilna, a survivor from the concentration camps. 'Ah, Vilna' he says, nodding his head. 'Yes, well it is certainly possible then. I was the editor of the local newspaper, the *Vilna Truth*.'

"When he says that, I immediately remember who he is. With great excitement I shout out loud, 'Citizen Malinowski!' He stares back at me again and then says slowly: 'Is it—are you—wait! I think I remember you. Didn't you write our youth column, some sports, and theatre reviews?' I am shaking with relief at being recognized," recalls my father. "My eyes are already full with tears, and I can barely speak. And now it's his turn to shout out: 'Piontka! Yes, now I remember, Ksavery Piontka!' He shakes my hand. Looking me up and down carefully, he says to me: 'Piontka, I hardly recognized you. What on earth have they done to you?'"

On that fateful day, my father tells me, from a walk in the park on a sunny afternoon with the spring flowers in bloom, he was given a new lease on life. By a chance meeting, he was given back his name, his identity, a job, papers of registration, and a new sense of dignity that had been denied him for too many torturous years. After hearing my father's story of hardship and imprisonment and how badly he needed documentation for identification, Major Malinowski said to him, "I will give you a uniform, I will give you rank, whatever you need. I will help you, because I can use you and I know you from the old times in Vilna." The willing major went to the office of records and provided him with the documents bearing his photograph, signature, and rank. He also testified that my father was a journalist employed by the daily newspaper. "Yes, indeed, I was lucky," my father repeats. "I was given a job as a roving reporter for a newspaper called *Wolna Polska* (*A Free Poland*), published and freely distributed by the Red Army. And this is how I adopted my new identity—from a name I invented when I was a teenager."

The identification papers listed his name as Ksawery Piatka, spelled Piontka, with his town of birth conveniently listed as Warsaw. After granting Poland their so-called independence, the Soviet authorities were demanding that people, not originally from Poland, return to their home countries to become citizens of the Soviet Union. Having documents saying that he was born in Warsaw meant that my father could avoid being sent back to Vilna.

Working for a Communist newspaper, my father was well informed about the continuing outbursts of anti-Semitic violence in Poland. He read about the tragic event carried out by a group of xenophobic Poles from the underground nationalist movement in the town of Kielce. Using the pretext of a missing Polish toddler to accuse some Jewish survivors in their town of abducting and murdering the boy, they staged a murderous rampage or *pogrom* against the Jewish war refugees still reeling from their ordeal under the Nazis. According to my father, the Poles who despised their Russians occupiers vented their anger at the influx of foreigners coming to work for the Russians by lashing out against the Jews. It did not matter to the Poles that the missing boy was later found safe with his relatives, or that the killers of the Jews were never sought to bring to justice. In the postwar upheaval, justice, like wandering toddlers, often went missing.

The bloodletting was not yet over. My father knew that even though the Jews of Eastern Europe had survived the horrors of a German-planned genocide, they still faced spontaneous and unbridled racial attacks from their former neighbors in Poland. Having documents identifying my father with a Polish name helped not only for his job but for his life. There were definite advantages in being identified as Ksawery Piatka rather than the obviously Jewish Israel Jutan. From then on, all the subsequent identification documents, including a passport and his marriage registration to Chayela Rosenthal were based on that first journalist union card he was given, thanks to his chance encounter in the park.

My father recalls another chance meeting from that time period. "You remember I told you about Dora, my mother's good friend, the youngest of her faithful band of friends, the three Mooskateers?" he asks. "Back home in Vilna, Dora was dating a very handsome German man from Leipzig by the name of Walter, who visited our town as representative of a textile factory. Her Jewish parents knew about this gentile, this *goy* who wanted to marry their daughter. Of course, they would never give their consent. When the war with Germany broke out, Walter arranged for Dora to be placed with his German friends in safe custody. Even though he was mobilized, he always managed to see Dora during the war years. When the war ended, they were free to marry, which they did. Now, during my short stay in Bydgoszcz," my father continues, "I was walking to my new job at the newspaper, when I see a beautiful woman walking toward me. She reminded me exactly of my mother's good friend who had spent so much time at our home, and who used to give me little gifts whenever she visited. I stop her to tell her she resembles someone I knew in Vilna named Dora. Imagine my surprise when she says it's her. We walked together down the street and spoke about the past. She promised to get in touch with me to give me her new address, but she never did."

Many years later, during his visit to London, he met up with Raya, his mother's other Mooksateer friend, who had moved there. She told him about Dora's mental illness. Raya speculated that it may have been caused by the birth of her daughter, or the annihilation of her entire family by the Germans, or most likely, she reckoned, by the guilt she bore being married to a German. Raya gave him Dora's address and phone number in Krakow. "When I called the number," my father says, "her daughter answered and told me that her mother had died. I was deeply saddened. It was Dora's daughter who sent me the photo of my mother and Dora smiling together, the two women I loved so deeply as a child."

The Editor

✦

Jelenia Góra, Poland, 1945

A helping hand can get one's foot in the door.

Soon after working as a news reporter, my father received an assignment to go to Wroclaw, a Polish territory near Breslau in Lower Silesia, where he was to run the editorial office of the newspaper. Many Jewish refugees from Russia, as well as survivors of concentration camps, had gathered in that area. In the autumn of 1945, he was transferred to Hirschberg, now known as Jelenia Góra, a beautiful holiday resort nestled against the large Snieszka Mountain. Just fifteen minutes away by train there was a health sanatorium, or *kurort,* as he calls it, named Cieplice, where my father was treated for the first time to a massage and hot mud baths, and received physiotherapy for his sore back, a constant reminder of the painful beatings he had endured under the Nazis.

At 26 he became editor of the newspaper in Jelenia Góra and manager of the Office of Information. When one of his staff, an elderly reporter, got drunk and let loose a volley of anti-Jewish slurs, my father was glad to be in a position of authority to fire him. The Communist party, he explains, did not tolerate such behavior from government employees. Even though my father was employed by the new regime, he deliberately avoided signing on as an official member of the People's Workers' Party, despite several official requests. Intentionally stalling, he persuaded his bosses that it was better for his role as editor and information chief for the region that the Polish people view him as a neutral, nonparty official. As always, he was keen to keep his options open, his vision of his own future being broader than the immediate politics of the time.

"As editor, I became the proud owner of a beautiful apartment, and a car that drank up a combination of water and gas and left oil deposits on the roads as it chugged along," my father adds. "I also had the benefits of a maid, a German woman who lived with her daughter in the attic of our same building. Because I oversaw the local edition of the paper called *Trybuna Dolnoslaska,* I had under my command the local office for the promotion and propaganda of national information. This was a very influential position."

The organizational experience from his teenage leadership roles in the Jewish youth movement served him well in dealing with local authorities. Local administrators such as the country governor and the town mayor would come to him for advice, often requesting his help in improving and rewriting their speeches and public announcements. They appreciated and applied his helpful tips on governing the region. He also made sure he established good connections with the police and the Bezpieka, the security police, of the Polish People's Republic, an important government investigation agency.

Chayela, meanwhile, after her successful May public concert of her brother's songs in Lodz, had joined the newly formed State Jewish Theatre troupe, which provided entertainment for the recovering Jewish refugees. Composed of several prominent Yiddish actors and directors, like Ida Kaminsky, who had fled to Russia during the war and then returned to Poland, the troupe presented plays, revues, and satirical skits in the new territories, mostly in the Lower Silesia region. Working as an ensemble, they performed the better-known plays by Chekhov, Pinsker, and Moliere in Yiddish for their appreciative, culturally deprived audiences. "You see, masses of Jews, deported from Russia by the Soviets, had been settled temporarily in houses left by the expelled German population," my father tells me. "For these Jews, hungry for Yiddish theatre, the popular troupe brought back a piece of their old way of life with the Jewish classical repertoire full of songs of hope and humor in the language of their mother and their home."

By now, my father and mother were married in a simple ceremony in a judge's chambers. Spending days of quiet recovery together in the pretty little mountain town near the health resorts, they would sometimes go hiking in the knee-high deep snow of the Snieszka Mountain in the winter, and during the summer months, spend time in the Olympic-size pool near their apartment.

"We were both busy with our separate work that often kept us apart—me in my domain of newspapers and civil servants and Chayela in her theatre world filled with unpredictable but amusing actors, bohemian singers and musicians who, when they visited us, brought fun and drama into our home. But the times we spent together, just the two of us, were times of quiet happiness and contentment," my father remembers.

Sometime later, Chayela's older sister, Mary, who had married the Vilna born director of the acting troupe, realized she was pregnant. Anxious, distraught and beset with bouts of crying, she kept repeating that she could not bring a baby into such a cruel world, nor was she ready for that kind of responsibility. Her circumstances, she moaned, were not conducive to raising a child, and she begged my father to use his personal contacts to arrange for a *skrobanke*, an abortion. My father adamantly refused.

"I felt very strongly about this," he says. "This new life should not be destroyed. For me, this was our sweet revenge—to live, have children, and carry on. To experience the joy of life, no matter what they have tried to do to us. That is our victory. This was how we could laugh in the faces of the Nazis to say, 'You see, despite your cruelties and evil intention to kill our nation, to wipe the Jews out of Europe and history, we have survived, and we shall bring forth new life to replace those you took from us. Whenever another Jewish baby is born, it will be the sound of our triumph, not yours.'"

My father is no longer telling me a story. He is making a speech, his voice resounding with the bass vibrato of compressed rage and redemptive passion. Mr. Piat, the authoritative sounding, commanding speaker, had the kind of presence and gift of delivery that could silence any crowd. At my son's *bar mitzvah*, I remember how everyone in the hotel ballroom, including the fidgety adolescent boys and chatty girls, even the waiters peering into the room, grew quiet when he began to speak. Called forward by my son to light the ceremonial candle on the customary cake as the most honored guest who'd flown in from the greatest distance, he strode proudly across the room towards his only grandson. Standing beside my father, I felt him tremble with emotion. After a moment of silence, he held up the silver *kiddish* wine goblet, a gift from his Cape Town Holocaust survivors' group in honor of his American-born grandchild, and launched into his solemn speech. Everyone could sense that we were in the presence of one of the few remaining witnesses of humanity's monstrous crime of the twentieth century. The elegant, somber Mr. Piat, with his Polish accented English, was the living, breathing symbol of a decimated culture. His speaking revealed the unspeakable. His voice echoed the suffering of millions. In his tone, was the defiance of man's indifference. In his pauses, the tragedy of war and loss. Choking back his tears, Mr. Piat told us how proud he felt, after all he had been through, to be there, at that moment, in America, with his beloved family at the *bar mitzvah* of his only grandson, who bore the middle name of Zachary in honor of his own father who had perished in the Holocaust. Slowly, ceremoniously, he lit the candle in tribute to the memory of my mother and all those who were no longer with us. Watching my father, the victim-turned-victor, light the candle, it became clear to me that the triumph over evil lies not in revenge but in the continuation of the generations, the communal celebration of cultural traditions, and the perpetuation of memory.

For my father, the revival of family was extremely important. Back in Jelenia Góra, he was unequivocal in asserting his convictions over the objections of his nervous, pregnant sister-in-law. His will prevailed. In July 1946, a little girl was born into their family, and they celebrated with joy, drinking some wine, and toasting: "*Am Yisroil Chai!* Long live the nation of Israel! Another Jewish baby. To life!" She was given the name Fama, in memory of her maternal grandmother, Fruma, the one who had pushed my mother to the right, to the side of life, before being taken away and killed by the Nazis.

"Mary's little baby girl became all of ours. She was the symbol of life reborn from the ashes," he says. My father relished the sounds of the gurgling baby girl. Fama, with her beautiful dark eyes and black wisps of hair resembled less her own fair-haired mother than her young aunt, Chayela, who took great pleasure in parading her around the streets in a pram and collecting compliments. In the grand scheme of things, it seems only natural that Fama, who grew up in Israel and served in its army, would eventually spend most of her adult life working in the field of Holocaust education, as an archivist and curator at the Simon Wiesenthal Center in Los Angeles.

For many of the Jewish refugees in Poland during that period of post-war resettlement, the focus was on heading west. Every time Chayela returned to Jelenia Góra from her performance tours at the various displaced persons' camps in Poland, she would recount her meetings with former friends, who were concerned about the increasing anti-Semitic outbursts by the ultra-nationalistic Polish groups, and were making plans to leave for Palestine, England, America, and Canada. Various Zionist groups, eager to reach Palestine by any means possible, even if it meant illegal *aliyah* or immigration, would assemble and leave from Jelenia Góra, situated close to the Czechoslovakian frontier. Stuffed into trucks, the hidden Jews would be driven across the border to Prague, from where they'd make their way to Palestine aided by clandestine operations funded by the American Joint Distribution Committee and other charitable American organizations. Through his contacts with the local authorities, my father was able to help several people with their departure, including a future member of the Israeli Parliament.

"So we lived," my father says, "one foot where we were, one eye on the rest of the world."

They discussed at length the possibility of joining those groups headed for Palestine but were afraid to take the risk of leaving illegally and possibly ending up in a displaced persons' camp somewhere in Germany or Austria or Italy. "We had already been fortunate enough to taste the comfort of normality, of sleeping in a soft bed with warm comforters, of having a car at our disposal," my father admits, "and we were not yet desperate enough to give up what we had acquired to potentially endure more hardships and deprivation in those transitory camps that reminded us of the harsh conditions of the Nazi camps." The vivid images of the refugee camps were still fresh in his mind. During his first year in Jelenia Góra, he had made friends with some neighboring Czech journalists who had invited him to visit them in Prague. Considering it a good opportunity to investigate the situation of those Jews arriving in the Czech capital, he hired a driver with an old Mercedes who drove him, Chayela, and her sister, Mary. With the necessary official papers stating he was a guest of the Czech National Radio, my father and his companions were taken on a tour to visit Hradczany Palace, a museum, and Wenceslas Square. Along the way his friend was able to sneak the three of them into the hotel-turned-refugee camp for the displaced Jews.

"I never expected such a picture of distress," my father says. "Before me was a hall full of people shuffling around, waiting for food rations. The sleeping arrangements were primitive—mats on the floor, cots lined up in rows. People were standing in lines, queuing for ablution and toilet facilities. It had the same grim atmosphere of a labor camp, but at least these residents had a glimmer of hope in front of them—the promise of getting a visa, a permit to get out. Meantime, it was a long, grueling waiting game for all. No one knew how long it would take for their paperwork to arrive. It could be days, months, waiting in squalid conditions, sitting and sleeping, coughing, spitting, one on top of the other. That same night we returned to our apartment in Obroncow Avenue in Jelenia Góra and fell happily into our soft, comfortable beds. We were very, very grateful indeed for our good fortune."

Their ticket to the West, away from Poland, came about in an unexpected way.

Soon after their depressing visit to Prague, Chayela left for Wroclaw to star as the young ingénue in Priestley's play, *The Inspector Calls*. On opening night, my father proudly drove his car to the theatre in the old opera house, which had remained intact between the many destroyed buildings. At the cast party, the actors, their partners, and associated friends mingled, ate snacks, and discussed the future success of the Jewish State Theatre. Chayela's acting partner and close friend disagreed with the positive outlook most of them were expressing. Voicing his concerns about Poland, he called Europe a dangerous place for Jews, announcing that he was planning his departure for the United States. Once again, the topic of leaving became the focal point of their thinking.

Opportunity literally came knocking on her door at their next premiere, a few months later, when Chayela was playing the lead in a Yiddish play, *Grineh Felder*—or *The Green Fields*—by Peretz Hirschbein. Waiting backstage to congratulate my mother on her outstanding performance was the famous Yiddish American comedic actress Molly Picon, who had starred in the same play in New York. Visiting Poland on a tour of the refugee camps, Ms. Picon took a special interest in the young, talented actress who had survived the Holocaust. "You must get out of Poland. It is a cemetery for the Jews," she urged Chayela. My mother replied that it was not so easy to leave, given the extensive bureaucracy of the Communist regime. Molly Picon promised to do her best to use her contacts in America to aid the young refugee star leave Poland.

Two weeks or so after that meeting with Molly Picon my father received an unexpected visit from his Jewish friend with the security police. "I understand that you are looking for your mother in Paris," he said. "I suggest you go there and find her." My father looked at him quizzically, asking how he knew about his mother in Paris. "Oh! We keep files on everyone," said his visitor. My father's file, he told him, was full of information about his life, the people he knew, his Zionist youth activities, his father's role as Vilna councilman, his mother's residence in Paris, and the suspicious fact that even though he had a politically important position, he was still not yet a member of the Communist party. All this meant that sooner or later—probably sooner, intimated his acquaintance—there would likely be a full investigation into his past. He was bound to be accused of some mistake and then dismissed from his post. "Do you want that for yourself?" asked the fellow, who let it slip that he was considering retiring from his own investigation duties. He encouraged my father to leave officially on business as soon as possible. "I got the hint," my father says.

Within a week, his friendly Bezpieka visitor had vanished from Jelenia Góra. My father took immediate action. Getting in touch with some newspaper-related friends in Warsaw, he explained that he needed to search for his mother in France and that a perfect opportunity to serve the Polish Press Agency would be to report on the forthcoming UNESCO conference in Paris. Once again, my father put his creative *luftmensch* mind to work to solve an anticipated problem. Having a friend in the right place at the right time helped immensely. He was issued an official passport to leave Poland for a period of two weeks.

Thanks to Molly Picon, my mother obtained her passport too.

She had kept her promise to the petite actress, so similar to herself in size, comedic style, and expressive vitality. Apparently her husband, Jacob Kalich, had written a lengthy article in New York's Jewish daily newspaper, *The Forward,* about their visit to Poland, mentioning the acting abilities of the "wonder child of the Vilna Ghetto," singer Chayela Rosenthal. They solicited their friend Sol Hurok, the entertainment impresario, originally from Russia himself, to see whether he could get Chayela out of Communist Poland to perform for the international Jewish communities. Fortuitously, Mr. Hurok was scheduled to visit bombed-out Warsaw on his mission to help restore the Opera Company and bring culture back to the devastated city, which lay in ruins.

When a telegram arrived from the famed Mr. Hurok inviting Chayela to audition for him while he was in Warsaw, my parents were thrilled. They had heard of Mr. Hurok, the influential American impresario. His introduction and promotion of his native Russian icons of culture and dance, like Pavlova to his adopted country, played a huge part in popularizing the role of ballet in the United States of America. The problem was: How to get from Jelenia Góra to Warsaw at such short notice, that very week?

"To travel by train in those days would have taken us two days," my father recalls, "and Mr. Hurok had only a few days free in Poland. We had to get there as fast as possible not to miss him." My father sprang into action. Using his official connections with the local authorities, he managed to arrange a ride on an army transport plane leaving for Warsaw from a nearby Silesian army base. "We were the only passengers in this plane, squeezed in between boxes of ammunition at the back. It was our first flight and we were, of course, nervous, not only for the flying part, but for our future that was riding on the audition."

My father recalls their fateful meeting in the Bristol Hotel with the illustrious Mr. Hurok. "He was a jovial, large man, wearing a Fedora, speaking English with a heavy Russian accent, and looking at us through big, black-rimmed glasses. He joked that for such a small woman Chayela made a big impression on his friend Molly Picon, who urged him not to leave Chayela behind in Europe." Hurok treated them to a lavish dinner that night and took them to see the opera, *La Boheme*. He was most interested to hear their stories about their experiences and listened with compassion. The next morning, while

Chayela rehearsed with an accompanist, the multilingual Mr. Piat served as interpreter for Mr. Hurok and his small entourage on their tour of the remains of the opera buildings given by the directors of the Polish Opera Company.

In the city almost entirely demolished by German bomb attacks, an unusual venue was found for the audition—an old cathedral, half in ruins. The audience was made up of Sol Hurok, his secretary, my father, the American consul, his aide, and a representative of the American Joint Distribution Committee, along with his Polish aides. They all sat together in the broken pews. A chipped statue of Christ, the sacrificed Jew, lay askew on a mound of rubble, lit by a stream of sunlight filtering through the half-cracked stained-glass windows. What a perfect symbolic setting for the petite Jewish singer who had been spared death a thousand different ways. As the sounds of the organ began, she stood in the ruins of the cathedral and sang her brother's heartfelt Yiddish songs. When she was finished, the visibly moved Mr. Hurok took out his crisp, white handkerchief from his coat pocket and wiped his eyes. The next day, my parents were on the train back to Jelenia Góra.

"After our meeting with Hurok, my thoughts were now completely directed to leaving Poland," my father continues. "I had the impression he liked Chayela's singing, so I knew we must be well prepared to leave when the chance came. Since the liberation, I had acquired everything we needed to live comfortably in our three-roomed apartment in Jelenia Góra. We had a piano for Chayela, an Encyclopedia Britannica for myself, and other expensive items like a radio, electric heaters, and kitchen mixer. Upon our return from Warsaw, I made a notarial document, leaving all our belongings to Chayela's sister, Mary, who was moving to Wroclaw to be with her husband who ran the theatre company there."

The second telegram from Mr. Hurok arrived with the news they had been eagerly awaiting: Chayela had been engaged for cabaret concerts in Paris, to be conducted through the Office Artistique

Continental with one of Hurok's agents, a Jewish-Russian impresario named Leonidoff. The train ticket and visa were on their way. My father made arrangements for his press assignment to Paris to coincide with the dates of Chayela's trip, so they could travel to France together.

"We were ready now," my father nods. "I had taken care of the apartment and its things. Now, our safe exit from the county depended on being able to leave without anybody finding out that we were not coming back. We did not want to arouse any suspicions with the authorities that we were emigrating, so only one light suitcase each—a change of clothing to look as if we were going on vacation, should they check, and of course, my typewriter. We had survived the war with very little, and we were to leave Poland with little."

Chayela bought some miniature porcelain Limoges dolls, thinking they could possibly sell them later, if money was needed. Gently wrapping the tiny fragile, dancing figurines in old newspaper, she placed them carefully among her clothes in the single suitcase that would accompany her permanent passage from Poland. She folded the banknote my father gave her and tucked it into her thick hair. Before leaving their apartment, she insisted on carrying out the traditional superstitious ritual they had always done in her mother's home in Vilna. First, she spat three times over her left shoulder against the evil eye. Then, telling my father to sit down, they both sat for a moment and repeated: "*Zol zine mit mazel!*" It should be with good luck! Only once the whole routine was done, could they stand up and walk out the door, making sure to take the first step with the right foot. Always the right foot first—for good luck, of course. *Ptu, ptu, ptu!* That old Vilna procedure of sit first, then blessing, then off on the right foot would accompany them on every auspicious journey of theirs and be passed down to my sister and me. "Always with the right foot," my mother would say, "and once you start walking, you don't go back, no matter what you leave behind."

For my parents there was certainly no going back. "*Vos iz geven iz geven, is nisht daw!*" my mother used to sing the once popular Yiddish song to me. What used to be used to be and is no longer here. Leaving Poland, they closed the door to what used to be firmly behind them.

The tiny Restoration-period porcelain dancing dolls my mother bought traveled with her from Poland to France to England to South Africa. They were never sold. After her death, they came across the Atlantic wrapped in newspaper in a wooden crate to come live with me in the United States. Broken, chipped, and glued back together, one missing the fingertips of her tiny outstretched hand, they remind me that fragile things, no matter how well protected, may get fractured along the way, but still, no matter the damage, they stretch out their arms and keep on dancing.

"One more stamp encounter I have for you," my father says. After the war, during his stay in Jelenia Góra, he resumed his stamp-collecting hobby, obtaining several good collections from Germans leaving that part of the region lost by Germany to Poland under the post-war resettlement order. In that one suitcase accompanying him on his transcontinental trip to Paris, he packed an album containing Polish stamps with issues from the 1920s up until 1944, enhanced with descriptive pages written in German. He believed it would be a valuable asset for their future. Traveling on a train bound for France, they stopped overnight in Katowice where they met other Jews also en route west, some bound for Canada and some heading to Australia. During a discussion about his album, they informed him that under Polish law, stamps were considered "national treasures" and warned him that if he were caught smuggling stamps out of the country it would be viewed as a crime. Chayela, anxious that they could be turned back at the borders if the authorities found the collection, urged him to leave the album behind. Early the next morning, he scouted several stores to try and sell his stamps, but found the shops glutted with discarded albums. On a whim, he stopped in at the store of a watchmaker who, he was told, collected stamps. "I was getting desperate at that point, so I reluctantly bartered my valuable collection for a Schaffhausen Continental watch and rushed back to make it in time to board the train. Imagine my surprise," he continues, "when the ticket collector comes to our compartment to check our passports and I recognized him as an old school mate of mine! He expressed such happiness to see me alive and insisted I let him know in advance the date of my return. He wanted to make sure he could be there to help me bring through whatever merchandise I wanted to smuggle in. As long, he said, as I give him ten percent of the total value, of course," my father smiles.

"I couldn't believe it. What luck! I had spent so much time worrying, full of fear about getting caught and losing my precious collection. In the end, it turned out I did not have to worry after all. That incident taught me a good lesson. While our train passed through Germany, I gave myself a good pep talk about the need to become bolder in my actions, not to panic at rumors, and to be brave within good reason," he says. "Many a time later on, when I regretted the sad loss of that beautiful stamp album, I would remind myself: 'Take chances! Be bold!' That lesson helped me all through my life."

The Tour Guide

✦

Paris, France, 1948–50

There is a divine order to everything, even chaos.

Sol Hurok's associate, Mr. Leonidoff, met Ms. Rosenthal and her husband, Mr. Piat at the Paris station and drove them to a hotel in Clichy, the entertainment center of town near the Moulin Rouge and Pigalle. The next day, my father took the metro and headed straight for the Polish embassy. Having landed in Paris with only ten dollars, the banknote that Chayela had carefully hidden in her hair during their journey, his first priority was to get money to support themselves. Presenting his card from the Polish Press Association along with the papers indicating his assignment to attend the UNESCO conference in Paris, he asked to see the purser at the embassy. He was told all fiscal matters were handled by the embassy secretary.

"You won't believe what comes next," my father says. "I am ushered into the secretary's office, and who is sitting there in front of me? My old school friend, Pavel Krubitsch. He had left Vilna to join the

International Brigade to fight the fascist General Franco in Spain in the 1937 uprising. He told me all about his war injuries and his life afterward in Moscow where he helped to establish the Polish Peoples' Army. Later on, he went to Warsaw, joined the diplomatic service and married a French girl. Now here he is in Paris. *Voila!*"

My father was extremely happy. Happy to be in the West. Happy to meet with an old friend and happier still that Pavel was perfectly positioned in the Polish Peoples' Embassy in Paris to help him at a time when he needed it. My father turns toward me, leaning forward. "Are you wondering," he asks, "how I, the Zionist activist, could have been so friendly with what others would refer to as the enemy?"

"'No,'" I reply, smiling. "'Not at all.'"

I know my father. For Mr. Piat, past friendship superseded current ideology or political affiliation. Everyone was his friend until they proved otherwise.

After hearing the details of his wartime stories, not much astonishes me about my father. Other than his outmoded, autocratic child-raising philosophies stemming from his own strict Eastern European background, my father had always exhibited an unusually broadminded, progressive attitude about life, people, and ideas. Granted, I grew up in a relatively secluded, provincial town in racist South Africa, where the common way of looking at things was, pun intended, black-and-white. In that class-structured, segregated society, my unconventional, worldly-wise father broke the rules. Moving effortlessly in all social circles, he kept company with white businessmen, black street peddlers, "Colored," (the official term for mixed-race) tradesmen, right-wing Afrikaner bank managers, left-wing English journalists, Chinese restaurant owners, Communist Russian ship captains, rich, poor, old, young, and any breed of dog. While my friends moved in tightly defined groups of the same race, ethnicity, and religion, my cosmopolitan father introduced me to people with all kinds of accents, colors, religious backgrounds, and professions. There was the Jewish diamond dealer; the Afrikaans theatre impresario; the blue-eyed Italian chicken farmer, the Muslim press photographer; the theatre producer who in the conservative 1950s daringly staged concerts of indigenous African tribal dancers, apparently giving Miriam Makeba her break into show business; the Polish sailors from the ships that docked in Cape Town harbor, who brought him fresh kielbasa to eat and old Polish newspapers to read; the slew of big name stars who came out to South Africa to perform and whose autographs I collected in my little red leather autograph book; and even the blonde German and Belgium "lady friends," who beat out the rest of his bevy of eager female companions, accompanying him to the movies and theatre and other dark places after my mother's death.

An independent thinker, secure unto himself, a man who had lived through hell on earth and walked among the dead, Mr. Piat did not judge people by their cause *du jour* but by their character, moral fiber, and capacity for caring. Marching to his own drum, dressed in his eclectic style, for example, his favorite lightweight, red-and-white-striped seersucker suit, maroon shirt, bright yellow tie, and white Italian leather shoes, he marched right past the raised eyebrows and wagging tongues of members of his own small-town Jewish community. Mr. Piat lived by his own rules, following his own calling in his own inimitable way.

To me, what was most remarkable about my father was how he differed from most other Holocaust survivors and Jews of his time in his philosophy toward the German people. He didn't only speak it, but, most especially in his later years, he lived his mantra, "Forgive, but don't forget." Advocating education instead of retribution, compassionate understanding rather than conflict, he wished to liberate himself from the shackles of hate, judgment, and anger that he knew would only continue to add bitterness and resentment—and ill health—to his life. From him, I learned to seek greater understanding for everyone's situation before summarily dismissing those with opposing ideas. His own life had shown him the infinite varieties and vicissitudes of history, of people's shifting beliefs and allegiances. Mr. Piat knew firsthand about the damaging divisiveness of political parties and the uprisings and downfalls of political regimes. In the process of sharing his stories, he did not shy away from examining some of his own misguided mistakes, made in the arrogance of youth or the heat of the moment. Strip away all externals and what truly mattered was a person's morality, integrity, and good intentions. What counted was their willingness to help a fellow human being in need.

My father's philosophy was rather pragmatic: Find the friend beneath the foe.

The Communist official who sat in the consulate in Paris had been my father's childhood schoolmate. Back in Vilna, the boys had shared a mutual passion: the movies. Pavel would invite my father to watch the latest films shown at the two cinemas run by his mother, the prestigious Helios in Wilenska Street and the smaller Kino Lux on Mickiewicz Avenue. Up in the balcony in Helios, the two friends would sit together, staring at the big screen that brought stories alive. When the teenaged Pavel joined the Communist party, he turned to his Jewish friend to help hide his banned political literature and leaflets. My father obliged by stashing the papers between the cabbages and potatoes in the basement of his father's apartment. Now, it appeared, fate had traveled across Europe to return a favor.

Pavel provided my father with money for the duration of his UNESCO correspondent engagement. After those two weeks were up, Pavel offered him a job in Paris, working for a government-sponsored Polish daily read by about half a million Polish immigrants in France. My father was grateful for the opportunity to be working again as a reporter, this time for *Gazeta Polska*, printed in a print shop that happened to be owned by a Jewish immigrant from Lodz. Once more, he was writing reviews about art, theatre, and cinema, covering special sporting events, particularly soccer, a favorite Polish sport. When Pavel was later transferred to a higher position in Warsaw, the two friends who had helped each other in their times of need eventually lost touch.

Chayela in the meantime was busy making a name for herself in the local Jewish cabaret and theatre scene, and when her former acting partner from Poland came to Paris on his way to the U.S., they left together for an engagement in Germany to perform in the Jewish Displaced Persons' camps. My father decided to occupy his lonely nights by becoming an English-speaking guide for tourists. It was an easy and fun job, he recalls, meeting elderly Americans looking for excitement in Paris. Ever the natural networker, he made it his business to get to know the hotel porters and concierges, asking them to recommend his services to tourists. "In turn, they would receive a nice gift from me, you see? A referral fee. I learned through my war years that a favor requires a reward in return. And so, I created a side business as a tour guide that was both enjoyable and lucrative," my father says, smiling.

As much as he attributed his survival to fate or luck, it occurred to me as I listened to him, that much of it was also due to his natural ease with people and his *luftmensch* abilities to offer people services he could convince them they needed. I admired his creativity and *chutzpah*. A foreigner himself, he boldly took on a new venture of giving tours to other foreigners—in English, no less, translating his passion for Paris, the city of love, the city his mother had chosen to make her home, into fascinating stories to be shared with strangers.

My father smiles as he sips his tea and slowly, methodically munches away at his favorite chocolate-hazelnut wafer. In his house in Sea Point, he always had a good supply of European cookies to enjoy with the customary English tea. On his visits to his daughter's *dacha,* he made it clear that he expected me to have a steady supply of his special cookies or what he still referred to by their English name, biscuits. On our frequent father-daughter grocery shopping sprees to the supermarket to stock my pantry and satisfy his taste buds, he would stride down the baked goods aisle making his selections with his pointed finger and the royal nod. Thanks to my father, I am now addicted to the delectable combination of chocolate and hazelnut.

"Ah," he sighs, taking another slurp of tea. "Delicious! You remember, of course Maurice Chevalier with his white straw hat and his famous song in English, 'Thank Heaven for Little Girls'? my father asks as he begins to croon like the congenial old white-haired French singer. Of course I remember the song from my childhood.

I was so grateful that someone famous on the radio was grateful for me, a little girl, who my father had wished to be a boy. "Wizout zem what would leetle boys doooo?" my father sings, raising the teacup into the air, as if making a toast. I'd like to think he's singing in honor of me, but I suspect in his humming reverie he's reminiscing about his good times in Paris, or the many women to whom he owed thanks in his past.

Just as suddenly as his good mood had brought song into our conversation, his face clouds over and he turns somber. Where had he suddenly gone in his mind, in his soul? Was it the French words that triggered something? Like a drunken hobo in a tattered coat darting out in a dark alley, his sudden moroseness bumps up against me. I have no protective shield when it comes to my father. His emotions too easily infiltrate mine. My father's moods remind me of the joke people make about the New England climate. "If you don't like the weather, just wait a minute." I can vouch for the accuracy of that saying. One April day, standing in my living room, I saw bright sunshine beaming through the front bay window, and out the back kitchen window a passing shower of rain. With Mr. Piat, you had to watch out. There was always the threat of thunder.

"You know, it was more than forty years later," he says, "after the war ended, after that time with your mother performing in Place Pigalle and me as reporter at Palais Chaillot and tour guide for the other foreigners, that I would return to Paris. I made a promise to myself in 1949, that one day I would return, not as a refugee tour guide, but as a tourist myself." My father's eyes are misty. "I kept that promise." He tries to fight back tears, and his voice begins to quiver. "I returned to the same places I had been during my vacation at Mother's before the war. I stood in front of that same building where she lived, 19 Rue de Couer, staring at the fourth-floor windows. I could remember her so clearly, Mother looking out the window to the sky, trying to predict the weather, always telling me to put on a sweater or a raincoat before going out."

He takes a moment to collect himself. I wait in silence. Like the undertow of an ocean, my father's nostalgia tugs at my soul, pulling me deeper into the swirl of his unresolved longing for his mother. He resumes his story: "Even though I walked the same streets from my old times in Paris, everything felt completely different." This time, he had new information regarding the famed city of love he had first discovered with his mother, and then later, shown others how to discover.

Forty years of constant inquiries regarding his mother's fate had finally produced the facts. In 1985 he received a letter from the Klarsfeld Foundation revealing the results of their research on his behalf: Vasa Sor, born February 28, 1897, in Kronstadt, was deported from France on convoy sixty-nine on March 7, 1944. The convoy of 689 women, 812 men, and 178 children was sent to Auschwitz. One hundred and ten men and about eighty women were selected for work. The rest were gassed on arrival. Only fourteen women survived at the end of the war, but their names were not listed.

My grandmother, the outcast: First cut off from her family in Russia, then cast out from her first husband's family in Vilna, and finally cast out of her adopted Paris and into the poison gas chambers of Auschwitz. She was forty-seven years old.

In 2003, eighteen years after that letter was sent to my father, I came face to face with the legendary Nazi hunters, Beate and Serge Klarsfeld, founders of the Klarsfeld Foundation, who happened to be staying in the same hotel as I was in Vilnius. The erudite Beate was being interviewed for an Israeli TV documentary chronicling the contribution of Jews in the different countries of the world. Approaching Serge Klarsfeld at breakfast, I introduced myself with my old password phrase "Hello. I'm Mr. Piat's daughter," I said. "Your organization brought closure to my father. On his behalf, I want to thank you for the work you do in documenting the Holocaust and pursuing justice." He told me that my thanks really belonged to Beate, his fearlessly outspoken non-

Jewish wife, whose relentless commitment to rooting out injustice and confronting Germany's criminal past inspired him to create the foundation.

Rereading that original Klarsfeld letter recently, I was struck by the synchronicity of the date it was written: July 25. It was the same date my father was found dead.

The Corpse

✦

Newton, Massachusetts, 1998

We move blindly, walking in the invisible footsteps of the dead who show us the way.

Saturday morning, July 25, 1998. My designated day of triage. My father was back in Boston again for the summer, this time recovering from the brain surgery he had undergone several months ago in Cape Town to remove a tumor, the cause of a minor stroke. He had managed to endure the long flight. Rather than walk out from the airport with his usual brisk, confident stride, he was escorted off the plane and through the airport in a wheelchair. Moving and talking significantly slower, Mr. Piat was nevertheless in reasonable spirits, determined to regain the full use of his now limp right hand as well as his former stamina. I marveled at his physical resilience. He had bounced back from an emergency operation for a ruptured, bleeding gastric ulcer a couple of years back and from bypass heart surgery before that. Now, he was determined to make a comeback from the stroke and the brain surgery.

The man who once considered himself a weakling had certainly proved otherwise, with a body that seemed to have a mind of its own. In a matter of months, his slurring speech was almost back to normal. He would not let this frustrating physical impairment get the better of him. Not the invincible Mr. Piat.

"Look!" he'd call out to me, from his favorite place on the sofa in the den. "It's getting better. Watch me!" With a fierce focus, he would practice raising his shaking right arm into the air, higher and higher, following the required daily physical-therapy exercises. Up and down he'd lift his arm, over and over, like a personal "heil" salute. The irony was not lost on me. "Look how high, look how high!" he shouted in his new slurry voice. "Great, Dad," I muttered in response, busying myself in the kitchen. Even though I admired his optimism and grim determination, inwardly I was cringing, loath to watch him strain so hard to lift his incapacitated, floppy hand. This wasn't the strong, vigorous Dad I knew, who used to hold his grandchildren on one arm and swirl them around his waist in the swimming pool. This was a man who wasn't able to swim anymore himself. This was a sick, fragile, aging man who needed nursing. Secretly, I was terrified.

Just two weeks ago, my sister and I and the three grandchildren had celebrated Dad's seventy-ninth birthday at our favorite Chinese restaurant. With his usual flair, Mr. Piat flirted with the waitress and complimented the manager, giving them his signature regal nod and thumbs-up, only this time, just with his left hand. We had wished our patriarch and benefactor good health, raising our cups of Chinese tea to recite the simple Hebrew *Sh'Hechiyahnu*, one of the few prayers we all knew by heart, praising the Almighty for sustaining, maintaining and bringing us together to arrive at this particular moment in time. Tears had welled up in my father's eyes and he blew his nose noisily into his handkerchief. The man knew how to use a hanky, having perfected his nose-blowing to a fine art. It was all about efficiency of resources. No wastage allowed. All available sides of the handkerchief, every square inch, must be used. When I was a child, my father had given me a stern half-hour practical demonstration on how to use one precious piece of tissue for at least four or five blows. Anything less was sacrilegious. Over the trumpeting *shofar* sounds of his nose-blowing, we, his progeny, celebrated the date of his birth, toasting with our Yiddish blessing: "*Biz Hoonderd un Tzvuntzik!*"—may you live till a hundred and twenty!

Two hours ago, I had left my father standing by the edge of the pool. "I will not go in the water," he had said, in his distinctive way of turning ordinary statements into declarations. Standing at the side of the pool on that hot July day, staring blankly into the water, he repeated what the neurosurgeon had told him: "No swimming!"

"It's very hot out there! Don't stay out in the sun too long," I had warned him, more like mother to son than daughter to father. "I'm off to the post office. Got a quick errand to run. I'll be back soon to make you lunch. Okay? Wait for me. See you later," I chirped, kissing him hastily on the cheek. I was on the run again. Desperate to escape my father's frightening vulnerability, I had created the perfect excuse to get me out of the house. The errand I was running was really running me—another thing to do for Dad, to keep him happy. It was my knee-jerk response to his angry words lashed out at me several days before.

"What about the book?" he had reprimanded me in his sharp, accusatory tone that stung like a slap across the face. "The book. What is happening with it? You promised me it would be done. I want to see it published before I go." His voice had quivered with the simmering of betrayal and blame. Go where? I thought. You're here for the whole summer. "Dad, you know what's been going on here, with me," I had replied as kindly as I could, aware of the tone of impatient annoyance in my voice. "This whole divorce thing, Dad, and my job at night because of the money situation, not to mention having to look after the three kids and the house. It's a lot to handle, you know. I haven't had the time or the energy." There I was, defending myself yet again. But the truth was, I was avoiding the book. His life and our relationship: two heavy subjects. And something else, something I was keeping to myself—my secret premonition—that the book I truly wished to write about his life could only surface after he was dead. But how could I tell him that? As close and open as we were with each other, I couldn't bring myself to tell him what I knew deep down. Some things were better left unspoken. That much I had learned from my deceased mother.

When I had started the process of recording my father's memoirs, back in 1991, intending to have it published, I had been buoyed with anticipation and enthusiasm, imbued with a sense of purpose. Spellbound, I sat and listened to my former god who had for so long governed my life. Somehow, with each passing year, the mission to complete the book turned into a duty. The duty turned into a burden. Heavier and heavier it weighed, pressing down like a rock. In the process of learning about his previous life, his original family, his former choices, I began to wonder about mine. Patterns emerged. Questions arose: What was love? What was duty? Where was freedom? How does one live a fulfilled, authentic and meaningful life? Why was I born to these particular parents? Was there something connected to their unique heritage that I was destined to do? I began to examine my marriage, my career, my past, and my present. Even my future. My midlife madness made me sanely question everything.

As my father's stories brought to life the people who were missing—my grandparents, my mother and uncle—I began to wonder: What if it were me, the real me, who was missing? Missing out. Missing them. Missing the true essence of me. Discovering more about the women I didn't really know—my independent grandmother and my creative mother—spurred me to explore more deeply into myself. Something was stirring in my soul. Was Chayela returning, through my father's words, to put me back onto the stage? Was I given my particular mix of inherited talents so I could express myself in the theatre? And what of my role as mother and wife? New insights revealed how I had trapped myself in old-fashioned roles. I'd been obedient for so long: the good girl, the good daughter, the good wife, the good mother, the good volunteer, trying so hard to please and take care of everyone around me at the expense of my own unique creative expression.

My own evolution seemed to be bringing me to a point where I could no longer ignore my uneasy restlessness of being trapped in a stifling marriage that appeared to have run its course. I began to feel the stirrings of separation from the two dominant men in my life. At the same time my troubled marriage was dying, my artistic life was beginning to blossom. I threw myself into the new roles of writer and performer and went to places I'd always wanted to go: places out in the world and spiritual places within. The music I began composing, the songs I was singing, the plays I was writing, the actors I was directing, all allowed me to express myself with a passion I had not allowed myself before. Working in the theatre made me feel delightfully alive and at home.

Up till now, I thought that my father's encouraging support of my play about my mother meant he didn't feel slighted about his book being abandoned. A few months back, in February, my recovering father had been able to summon the strength to attend the premiere of my show in Cape Town, an event he helped arrange. Taking my bows from the stage, I called out his name and asked that he too stand up and receive his deserved applause from the audience. Without his stories, there would be no play, I announced proudly. He stood up slowly and waved his shaking hand.

Like Job, I thought I could escape my ever watchful, sometimes wrathful god. I was wrong. There was no avoiding that old familiar summons of my father's emotional command. This summer, his angry comments let me know of his displeasure, impatience, and irritation with me that I had not completed the book about his life. Like the shrill ring of the servants' bell we used to have in our old kitchen back in Sea Point, the hurt and disappointment in my father's voice rang in my ears, demanding a response. Quick, hop to it! Take action to make amends! My plan was to take a rough-draft chapter and send it off to a literary agent I had met. A little bandage for a huge gash. A conciliatory gesture. Hopefully, my quick-fix errand to the post office would serve to assuage him. My idea was to surprise Mr. Piat by reporting back, "Guess what, Daddy! I sent off the manuscript. I got an agent for the book. It's going to be published. Happy now? All better?" Good girl! Honor thy father! Guilt is such a wonderful motivator.

Was the sun shining too brightly for me to see the ominous shadow stretch its way across the lawn? Was I too preoccupied with my agenda of crossing off one more thing from my "To Do For Dad" list? Whatever it was, I dismissed my father's frail presence beside me at the pool or his comment that he had stumbled while out on his morning walk. I missed any warning signs that this seemingly ordinary July day could become one I would never forget. Like a wild animal in the scorching savannah air, sniffing fear in the wind, mine, his, or both of ours, I had taken flight to protect myself from my aging, needy father and my own dread of the inevitable. Running away was my default.

"*Vu leiftz du?"* my mother would call out to me in my college years, her Yiddish refrain chasing after me as I bounded out the door to my car, waiting at the curb ready to whisk me away from the house of bondage where I still lived. An automobile is a teenager's best friend. "*Vu leitz du?"* Where are you running to? At that time I didn't have an answer. All I knew was the freedom of constant movement. But this time I knew the answer to "*Vu leiftz du?"* Away from my father's frailty and my own guilt.

Long after my mother's haunting Yiddish question remains a distant memory from a faraway place, my getaway vehicle is larger and sturdier, more appropriate for a midlife mother of three. "The Silver Bullet" is what I call my spacious van, wisely selected for its practicality for a suburban family life. It's taken our family of five, sometimes six counting my father, to the beach and the movies, shlepped carpools of kids and their gear to dance rehearsals, sports games and summer camps, hauled my large canvas paintings to my art shows, stacked used furniture salvaged from sidewalk yard sales, conveyed nurseries of potted plants and evergreens from discount hardware stores, transported overflowing garbage bags of used garments to Goodwill and driven my father and his suitcases back and forth to airports every summer for years.

It's in my trusty Silver Bullet that I unsuspectingly turn the corner of my dead-end street on this sunny day, speeding back from the post office where I had accomplished my most important mission for the day. Driving up the broad, tree-lined street, so nicely designed for people who can afford comfort and security, I catch sight of something that rips a hole through my stomach. Wedged at odd angles outside my house and in my driveway, like shiny toy cars tossed by a screaming, hysterical two-year-old in the midst of a temper tantrum, are a police car, fire engine, and ambulance. My heart turns to stone. With that sick, sinking feeling of "Oh God! Too late!" I rev up the road. *Vu leiftz du?* Where are you running to? As if speeding now would make a difference when time itself has stopped. In a flash of panic, I have a premonition that everything I've been running away from all my life, is what I'm about to face when I walk through my front door.

"Don't let it be what I think it is, please God, don't let it be," I plead with the silent jury in my head. But I know. With numbing certainty, I know what is waiting for me in my home. I know it in my bones, the same bones that carry traces of my father's DNA. I know it in my soul that has already begun its painful separation from his.

"We tried everything, but he was already gone," one of the paramedics says, trying her best to explain the situation as I rush inside the house and introduce myself to the uniformed strangers who occupy my home. The policeman in my kitchen tells me what he knows. "Apparently your daughter found him," he says. "He was lying at the bottom of the pool, in the deep end. She called 911. She was very calm and gave us all the necessary information." He asks me how old my daughter is. The doorbell rings. In a stupor, I turn back to see who it is. A local news reporter has appeared, wanting to know details. Would I mind speaking to him, he asks with urgency. Would I mind? I want to yell at him to get the hell out of my house. The burning hole in my gut has now etched a crater in my chest. Ambulance chaser! Those people actually exist? Instead, I shake my head and apologize, polite as ever. "Sorry, don't know anything yet. Just arrived home myself." (How was I to know that the so-called journalist would report his version of events to the local newspaper anyway, and a tiny item would appear the next day about an unidentified man found drowned in a swimming pool? "Ugh, shame!" Yet another travesty of justice for the far-from-anonymous Mr. Piat.)

"Twelve," I reply. Apparently, some part of my brain is still functioning. "My daughter is twelve this year," I inform the policeman whose last name on his silver nametag reveals that he is Jewish. A Jewish policeman. What are the odds of that? Probably the only Jewish cop in the precinct, and he happens to be on duty today, sent to take care of matters dealing with a Holocaust survivor. Of course, how perfect! Even in death, the indefatigable Mr. Piat can still work his magic.

"It's her *bat mitzvah* year," I tell the officer, figuring he'll understand the significance. My youngest daughter had just recently begun preparing for the Jewish celebration marking the rite of passage from child to adult. Before driving away on my "urgent" assignment to the post office, I had suggested she keep her grandfather company at the side of the pool, leaving her alone in the house, by her computer. What had happened? Had the invisible mother-daughter primal bond of contagious fear kept her away from my father, too? Was the act of discovering her grandfather dead at the bottom of the pool to be her initiation into adulthood? In my view, her composed handling of the whole traumatic incident including the emergency crew was enough of a rite of passage into adulthood, sans any religious ceremony.

"We need to ask you some questions," the ambulance attendant apologizes.

"And we'll need an autopsy." An autopsy? "The circumstances, you know," she continues, "with no one being around at the time he drowned. It's just routine. We need to rule out any foul play, you know, just for the record."

In the drama of guilt and confusion, my mind begins arguing with itself. White noise for the black hole. I can't believe what I am hearing. My life is turning into a soap opera. Mr. Piat always had an affinity for high drama. He married an actress, after all. But this, this was too much. This resembled one of those schlock, B-rated, sci-fi whodunit crime movies he loved to watch on TV, sitting on the den sofa, way past midnight. The macabre fascinated him. How could it not? He had lived through the real thing, the thing that could never be accurately portrayed in total on any screen. But what's unfolding in my nicely landscaped suburban house on its safe dead-end road is not drama. It's reality. My grim reality. No running away from this one, orphan girl! A funeral needs to be arranged. People need to be notified … on both continents. It will be up to me to organize it all. "Sure," I say to the attendant. "Whatever you need to do."

◆ ◆ ◆

Vision

Scene: Courtroom. I am in the defendant's box, defending myself, as usual.

A chorus of bearded old men draped in gray sackcloth tunics is chanting: "Autopsy!" They are the jury, a bunch of Greek-Jewish looking shaggy elders from a vintage Woody Allen movie, pounding their walking sticks onto the jury box like it's a giant xylophone. The judge, a Cheshire cat, keeps appearing then disappearing, meowing: "Autopsy! Aw, topsy-turvy!"

The prosecutor paces back and forth, pointing his crooked finger at me: "FOUL PLAY!" he yells. I know that look. I've done wrong yet again. I had deserted my father when he needed me most.

"Foul play?" I retort. "Objection! You don't know the half of it. He assured me he'd be fine. He specifically said that he would not go swimming. I knew he really wanted to. But he said he wouldn't. He was going to lie down on the chaise by the pool and wait till I came back to make him lunch."

The jury continues to beat their sticks, faces blank beneath gray hoods. Those three deaf, dumb and blind stone monkeys from the statues of my childhood appear, cavorting animatedly around, shrieking out their names: Shame, Guilt and Regret! Here to pay their disrespects, they jump around the jury with high-pitched squeals. Guilt, playing peek-a-boo, reprimands me in its nasty, nasal, teasing voice: "Why did you leave him all alone, stupid girl? You should have known something was wrong. He was still recovering, but you didn't care, did you?" Regret chimes in: "Left your young daughter alone, too. Left her to find such an awful sight: the dead body at the bottom of the pool. Ugh Shame! What kind of mother are you?" Shame joins in: "What kind of daughter are you? Why did you run away? *VOOO leifts DOOOOO!?*"

"You don't understand," I shout back into the din. "My father was invincible. He had survived everything: the war, the beatings, the abuse, the starvation, the devastating losses, the death march, the typhus, the stabbings, the heart attacks, the bleeding ulcer, the stroke, the brain surgery, the long plane rides, all of it. He wasn't going to die, not now. Going to live till a hundred and twenty. Leaving South Africa for good. Coming to stay in America to be near his grandchildren, near his daughters. Moving in with my sister. How is it *my* fault he ended up at the bottom of the pool?" The drumming gets louder. The monkeys are screeching. "Foul play!" the prosecutor howls, pointing his finger in my face. "You laugh now, soon you will be crying!"

"There was no foul play," I scream back. "No play at all. Everything always so serious, so formal with him. Okay, I'll concede neglect. Okay, I'll throw in rejection, too. I told him I could no longer have him stay at my house for months on end."

Sudden silence. A communal sharp gasp from the jury. The monkeys stop jumping.

"Please try to understand," I plea. "My husband had just moved out a couple months ago. My oldest was off to college. I was working nights with my new sales job, traveling around. I was preparing for a *bat mitzvah* and a divorce! That's a bit much, don't you think? Even for me, Ms. I-can-do-it-all-myself super-tough-mom. This was the summer my father was moving in with my sister, just around the corner, down the road. She needed equal time with him too, right? Besides, I needed some breathing space. What's wrong with that? What's wrong with me wanting time for myself for a change? Huh? Is that a crime for a woman in her mid-forties, I ask you? Is wanting a little bit of freedom foul play? Let me tell you about foul play. The foul play began long before I was born. You hear me? It began in Europe. In Poland. In Germany. Why don't you do an autopsy on the crime of all crimes, the foul play of the Holocaust? Isn't that the real cause of his death? I rest my case."

◆ ◆ ◆

Opening the sliding glass door that leads from the den to the backyard, I step onto the back lawn and into a perfect, peaceful summer's day. The aqua blue water of the swimming pool sparkles in the noonday sun against the emerald backdrop of shimmering trees. The purple potted flowers I bought especially in honor of my father (it's his favorite color) are in full bloom. Everything shines in brilliant colors taking on an almost surreal intensity. With a quiet horror, I see my father's pale, lifeless white body stretched out on the bright green grass by the side of the pool.

I cannot believe he is dead. The man I had left alive, staring at the water, less than a couple hours ago is no more. The last time I saw him, he was standing right there, by the edge of the pool. "Put him back there!" I cry out silently to the crystal-clear day.

My god, my master. Gone.
My rock, my mountain. No more.
My Daddy. Dead.
Final and forever.
Sorry, sorry, sorry!

No more, the familiar pronounced footsteps and imperialistic commands. No more, the distinctive bass voice with its heavy Polish accent, announcing "Telefon!" in sing-song cadence every single time the phone rang. No more special preparations of his favorite dishes of grated carrot salad with orange juice and raisins, saltless turkey slices on toasted seedless rye bread, the drier the better, and ketchup. Plenty of ketchup. Stock up on the ketchup! The man loved his ketchup … on everything. No more trips to the airport to greet him and then send him off with a smile on my face and a lump in my throat. Is this what liberation feels like? Empty?

I call my sister. This was the day of his expected move to her house. She was coming over later to pack his clothes and set him up in the room she had built specially to accommodate his stay. Ground-floor room, handrails in the shower, TV on its moveable stand, all prepared in advance for his comfortable recovery. Everything perfect for Mr. Piat. Affectionate and attentive, my sister was a much better nursemaid than I was, catering to his needs ever so cheerfully, patiently, and considerately. Respectfully, she hid any disappointment she might have felt that he seemed to prefer spending time in my company by the swimming pool, tanning and reading his favorite *New Yorker* magazines that he'd haul back in plastic shopping bags from the "help yourself" bin at the public library.

"Sorry," I utter into the phone. "It's Dad. Come quick." We spoke in shorthand, my sister and I. We're that close. She could tell immediately by my voice what there was to know. This is the call she's been anticipating with dread all her life. She was the one to break the news to me from South Africa of our mother's death, all those years ago. Now it was my turn to call her with the terrible news. Foul play—the unexpected "Sorry to tell you this, but Mom/Dad is dead!"—phone call. Secondhand farewells. Undignified leave-taking. The missed chances to say what needs to be said before it's too late. Our legacy of loss. The curse of no goodbyes—our family tradition.

Goodbyes made my father uncomfortable. In the days before his departures at the end of his summer visits, he would invariably grow irritable, snapping and sniping at the slightest provocation. At the airport, he would get out of the car, give me a quick hug and a tight-lipped nod, then promptly pick up his bags, turn his back, and briskly march away. I would stay and watch him disappear through the glass doors of the departure terminal. Lingering goodbyes were not for him. That was my domain. I'm queen of the long, back-and-forth, drawn-out goodbyes: kisses and hugs and more hugs and waves. Trying to say everything there is to say in one moment: "Take care. I love you. Write! Call! Thanks for coming. Thanks for everything. Be in touch. Drink water! Don't forget the sunscreen! Enjoy! Have a good time! Do you have your sweater? Did I say I love you already?" Air kisses. Waves. Hand gestures. More waves, followed by the obligatory stares from tear-filled eyes till the loved one fades into a little blurry dot. But for my already emotionally saturated father, goodbyes were to be avoided. Make it short, concise, then walk away.

My father now lies dead on my lawn. I sit down next to him. His skinny legs hug the grass, his flat, pale feet with the yellowing, brittle toenails splaying outward. He is wearing his Speedo. Suddenly I feel embarrassed. Strangers had seen him like this. Almost naked. The familiar flood of "Ugh, Shame!" The bare body of the foreigner. I'm about eight-years-old. We're at the beach, Broken Baths. My father is doing his usual thing, changing his swimsuit on the beach, for the whole world to see. With one hand, he holds his wrapped towel around his waist. I watch and wait as he wriggles and squirms his body out of his wet bathing suit. At last, the offending, damp suit drops from under the towel to dangle around his skinny ankles. Balancing on one foot, he kicks it off into the soft, white sand. Then he proceeds to dry himself thoroughly with the towel, particularly vigorously in the crotch area. People are staring. I think they're snickering. I look away. I don't belong to that man. Him oblivious. Me mortified. Him foreigner. Me little slave. It's his hand I will have to hold tightly when we eventually leave the beach.

I hold his limp hand now in mine. What must it have been like for Mr. Piat these past few years? The stroke. The loss of use of his right hand. The brain surgery. The slow recovery. He prided himself on his toned physique, exercising at the gym regularly, swimming, and taking long walks along the beachfront. With his right hand rendered useless, how did he cope, having to become dependent on others to help him with the simplest tasks? And what about the loss of his right-hand man, his son-in-law? In treating my father as my confidante, confiding to him unrelentingly all my frustrations, furies and disappointments about the man I had married and the marriage I was ending, I had made him unwilling witness to the demise of a dream. As he heard the news of his golden boy's increasing business debts and depletion of our savings, he was forced to reluctantly let go of his idealized version of the man he loved as the son he never had. The hefty business loan my father had given him did not look like it would be repaid as promised. For my frugal, responsible, patriarchal father, son of Zacharias the generous, the one who thought it important to take good financial care of one's descendents, it must have been insult to injury. The picture-perfect family he loved to boast about, torn apart. Yet another fractured family. A repetition of painful history.

And what of my own distancing dismissal of him? In my middle-age attempt to claim my own independence and spread my wings, I had inadvertently flapped them too hard, knocking my father off his pedestal. The time we had spent together, capturing his stories, had seen us go beyond the mere roles of father and daughter—Mr. Piat, the enchanting raconteur and his devoted listener and scribe, a modified *Scheherazade*. We had become creative partners. By abandoning the book we had begun together, I had deserted my present father for my absent mother. In telling him he could no longer spend summers with me in my house, I had rejected him, casting him out of his home away from home. In breaking the chains of what I regarded as bondage, had I also carelessly broken my father's heart?

Helpless, I sit at his side on the damp grass, stroking his limp right hand. I wanted a different ending for him. Not this ignoble death. Not this semi-naked, embarrassing, enigmatic solitary slipping away in a mystery death. I stare at his wrinkled face that seems so sallow beneath the tan. Something is different, I notice. His jaw is no longer clenched. The creases of deeply furrowed frown lines seem to have softened. He looks surprisingly relaxed, strangely at peace. Could it be that my father traveled all the way from Vilna to Paris to Cape Town to Boston to find his final resting place here, near me, Vavka's *duch*, in my backyard by the pool in the sun?

"Sorry, Daddy," I whisper to the lifeless body. "I'm so sorry."

I kiss the soft, wrinkled skin of his forehead for the last time. A sudden urge to lift him up and cradle him like a baby comes over me, but my sense of propriety prevails. There are strangers in uniforms waiting to take him away. If they weren't there, I swear, I would pick him up in my arms and hold him tight and kiss his cheeks and his closed eyes and tell him how much I had truly loved him all these years. I would tell him how grateful I was for his fierce, protective love, for being my champion, my caretaker, my teacher about life, my mentor, my sponsor, my provider, my guide, my one and only. Last touch, Daddy! I stroke his face. I kiss the hand that smacked me. I feel the crinkled skin of his fingers. I scan every inch of his physical form to imprint in my brain, lest I forget in this lifetime, the physical form of the one who guided my life.

Questions rush in to fill the void of the unanswerable emptiness of death. Why, Daddy? Why the drowning? When a man is rendered useless, is that when he drowns? I stare at the gleaming pool. The water appears undisturbed, sunlight forming glittering warped diamonds on the surface through which strangers had pulled my father's pale blue torso as my youngest daughter looked on. "Death by drowning." That is what the death certificate will eventually record. But there's always more to the story, I imagine my father would say. Another piece of the mystery. Another question remaining unanswered. Why, for his passing from life to death, had my father's friend Fate chosen the swimming pool in my backyard, the one that had provided so many happy family memories during his summer visits, and by which we had also sat discussing traumatic and horrific events in Europe? What was the meaning of his watery tomb? Was it water to cleanse a troubled soul? Water to rinse away the ashes? Water over rock over scissors over paper?

Of course! All those stones and rocks buried under the pool in the clay soil. The weight of all those gallons of water in the pool. The water itself. It's tears. Millions of tears. The man who'd defied death innumerable ways, the father with the heavy heart, limp right hand and tired, pained body, had sunk to the bottom of the pool of the countless tears never wept for the countless goodbyes never uttered.

On that bright Saturday morning of July 25, the expiration date written on his bottle of pills that I still keep in the bottom drawer of my bathroom cabinet, my father had found his final peace and comfort—in the clear and heavy memory of water.

The Immigrant

✦

Paris, London, and Cape Town, 1949–55

The language of love needs no translation.

In 1949 my father was thirty and a war refugee living in Paris, writing newspaper articles for ex-patriot Poles, and guiding international tourists up and down the steps of Sacre Coeur and along the banks of the River Seine. He had no idea where destiny would lead him. Chayela had returned from her successful tour of the displaced persons' camps in Germany and he was pleased to have her back at his side.

Xavier basked in the glow of his attractive young wife's achievements. During her stay in Paris, Chayela continued to receive excellent reviews for her appearances at the Entrepot Theatre and was invited to sing her Yiddish songs at the New Year's Eve Gala Variety Show in Palais Chaillot. That show led to a contract at the Jewish nightclub Habibi in Montmartre, where she performed her cabaret show of French, Hebrew, and Yiddish songs and comedy routines. Art Buchwald, the American journalist writing for the Paris edition of *The New York Herald Tribune*, came to see her perform and praised her comedy act. Danny Kaye, the famous American film comedian, also appeared at the club and became an acquaintance of theirs. She even made cameo performances on TV with Edith Piaf, Yves Montand, and other French cabaret singing stars, and recorded some of her brother's songs.

It was while Chayela was performing at the nightclub that she caught the attention of a Jewish theatrical producer from South Africa, who was visiting Paris on a recruiting mission to find Jewish actors to perform a season of Yiddish Theatre in Cape Town and Johannesburg. The gregarious, smiling, freckle-faced Sarah Sylvia, her perennial gray bun planted on top of her head, was immediately enchanted by Chayela, and invited her to join her ensemble of actors. Sarah's offer meant more steady work and income and the chance to explore a new country described as warm and welcoming to Jews. With her husband's blessing, Chayela left with Sarah Sylvia and her troupe for South Africa.

Once again, my father was left on his own. More and more, he became acutely aware of his status as a refugee, officially labeled a "displaced person" without a permanent home. The idea of settling somewhere and putting down roots was always on his mind. Within a month he received a very enthusiastic letter from his wife describing South Africa as a beautiful place with the perfect climate, exceptional living conditions, and wonderful, friendly people. It was a country in which the Jews in particular were a close-knit, thriving community, predominantly of Lithuanian origin from before the war. Many of them remembered Vilna with great affection, spoke the same dialect of Yiddish as my mother, and treated her like a star.

"With the beaches, mountains, warm weather, and the generosity of her Jewish audiences who reached out to her with open arms, showering her with adoration, gifts, and dinners in their lavish homes," my father says, "she made it sound like paradise."

There was nothing to keep my father in Paris. Many of his Jewish friends had left for overseas. The Korean War was starting, and he was deeply worried about a possible Communist takeover of Europe. Reading Chayela's letters, he became more and more intrigued by the idea of far-away, exotic South Africa. In Cape Town, she wrote, even the former mayor's family took special care of her, promising to help if they wished to settle there. For Mr. Piat it became clear. A wonderful opportunity was presenting itself before him. He decided to take a chance and make South Africa their new home.

Louis Gradner, once the mayor of Cape Town and an influential community leader, arranged a job for my father as linotype operator with *The Cape Times*, the local daily. "Apparently, linotype operators were in demand. So that is what I would become," my father says, explaining the restrictions of the strict immigration laws and quotas that only granted work visas to people with skills deemed needed at that time. He had learned from his experiences that he could be anything he set his mind to be: soccer goalie, journalist, translator, welder, latrine painter, editor, tour guide, and, yes, linotype operator. If it meant a way in or a way out, Mr. Piat would find a way to do it—and do it his way. His Jewish friends at the print shop of the Polish newspaper helped train him in the trade, letting him practice on the paper, even recommending him to the printers' union, which he paid to get his union card. Now prepared, he was able to apply for the necessary visa to enter the new country as an immigrant.

When Chayela returned to Paris with her fellow actors from her South African tour, she and my father immediately began preparations to leave Europe. As soon as he knew they'd be leaving for Africa by boat from Southampton, England, my father sent letters off to his cousins in London informing them of his upcoming trip. He tells me how he came to obtain the addresses of the offspring of his grandfather's brother who had settled in England. Immediately after the war, when all the survivors were attempting to locate family and distant relatives any and every way they could, he wrote to the Red Cross offices in Geneva and New York trying to find relatives. Even in Paris, my father says, he was always searching, making enquiries. Nothing turned up.

"When Chayela was performing in Germany in the Displaced Persons' Camp a woman came rushing backstage to her dressing room, shouting 'Chayela, Chayela, our ghetto singer!' hugging and kissing her, crying all the time. Who was she? Remember Anushka, my father's cousin and also one of Mother's 'three Mooskateers?' Well, it was her. She had been hiding in Russia. When she discovered that the famous Chayela from Vilna was married to me, her relative, and that I was alive, she gave Chayela her address, insisting I write to her, which of course I did. Anushka then gave me the address of some distant cousins in New York, who still remembered my late father when he was their guest in 1929. Through corresponding with those American relatives, I was given the address of cousins in London."

When he left Poland in 1948, my father had written to those British cousins to inform them of his arrival in Paris. For his first visit to London, the British Utins rented a hall in Stamford Hill, and organized a gathering of their descendents to celebrate my father's emergence from the Holocaust. Over sixty of the Utin clan assembled in London to listen to the unforgettable Mr. Piat tell his stories of survival.

"All these descendents of my Grandfather Reuven's brother who had settled in England came to see me, from the very wealthy who lived a distance outside London, to the rather poor, elderly cousins who lived in London proper," my father recalls. He was particularly touched by the generosity of a small, energetic woman in her eighties. Jane Krysanty had married for the first time in her fifties and had no children. My father was amazed by how nimbly she could climb the many stairs of her tenement building at her advanced age, while he struggled to catch his breath at each landing. It was Jane who gave him the big Jutan family portrait taken in the 1920s in Vilna that his father, Zacharias, had sent to her. My father treasured that rare photo of his family, which showed him at age four posing with all his cousins and aunts and grandparents. It was the photo in which his mother Vava, the scorned outsider, was not included.

Writing to his English cousins again, he told them about his impending immigration, and asked if they could meet once again in London on his way to Southampton, where he and his wife would be boarding the cruise ship heading for South Africa. Several members of the Utin family came specially to see him off at Victoria Station and to meet his wife Chayela for the first time. It was the snapshot of that train station meeting that would eventually lead my British relative, Lizzie, to me.

"On this second visit to London," continues my father, "Jane, once again, pulled me aside. "Unrolling her stocking, she removed a five-pound note and tried to shove it in my hand. 'It's your inheritance,' she says to me. I gently refused. In later years, when she was placed in an old-age home, I corresponded with her from South Africa and sent her some care packages and gifts from my own meager wages. When I heard she'd died, I felt enormous grief. She was so sweet, gentle, kind. Always with a smile. Her gift of the family portrait meant the world to me. I made postcards of that photograph and sent them to the remaining members of our large pre-war family who were now in Israel and the U.S. and Australia."

My parents crossed the Atlantic on their first cruise ship, the newly built ocean liner Bloemfontein Castle from the Union Castle Line, the first cruise company to offer a one-class-fare cruise to make overseas travel more affordable. On a misty morning in May 1951, the liner pulled into the stunning seaport of Cape Town, which lay spread out beneath the uniquely shaped, majestic flat-topped Table Mountain, with its tablecloth of cascading clouds. This was the Cape of Good Hope, they were told. How fitting, thought my father, that they should sail into that perfectly named magnificent place to begin their new life.

At the immigration center, they were greeted with a heartfelt reception from a woman who embraced the two of them, loudly proclaiming: "I'm the one who got you here!" Mrs. Rae Gradner, the former mayor of Cape Town, was bubbling with enthusiasm as she kissed and hugged my mother and father. A heartfelt humanitarian, she had a passion for helping the needy, especially refugees from Europe. "From the moment we arrived, we were welcomed and treated with tremendously warm hospitality from the generous Jewish community," says my father. "I could tell we would be happy here."

The Promoter

✦

Cape Town, 1950–98

In finding our words we find our way.

My father's first night with his wife in his brand new country was spent at a beachside hotel in Mouille Point, near Sea Point, where the owner's Polish born wife greeted them in their native tongue. The next morning, they awoke to the smell of salty ocean air, the sounds of squawking seagulls and the low moan of the foghorn from the small white-and-red diagonally striped lighthouse perched on a giant rock near the hotel. For breakfast, they were treated to the delicious tastes of ripe mango, papaya, and cling peaches—exotic fruits, the likes of which my father had never seen before. Strolling outside on the beach promenade, he could hardly believe the breathtaking panorama surrounding him. The wide blue ocean spread out in front of him as far as he could see. Behind him, the flat top of Table Mountain appeared over the arch of a sloping brown hill that rose, like a stretching animal, to crest at a round, rocky peak appropriately named Lion's Head.

Stretching alongside the beach was a long row of manicured green lawns, interspersed with rock gardens of lush, tropical flowers and strange creature-like succulent plants. Palm trees like giant pineapples stood in rows along the beachfront boulevard. Strolling along the promenade, watching the ocean waves swell and crash on the rocks sending a spray of sea mist into the air, he sighed with gratitude. "It was truly paradise. To imagine I could make this my home," says my father. "Yah, it was our reward … after all we had gone through."

On the third day after their arrival my father suddenly became so sick that he required the urgent attention of a doctor. "The sciatica pain, my back, and the stiffness of my joints, due perhaps to the sea mist or the long days of standing on the ship, hit me bad," he recalls. He was treated with heat and injections and taken further inland to a different suburb, Belleville, where they were put up at the Boston Hotel for a few days and where, according to my father, I was conceived.

"I was destined for a life in Boston," is my quick retort.

"Yah!" he replies. "And me with the Germans … spending time on Niemiecka Street—or German Street—in Vilna."

"And then in Cape Town, you moved to the little house in Vredehoek, when I was just a baby, right Dad?" I comment. "Vredehoek. Freedom corner. How symbolic!" I say, expecting my father to continue our verbal game. Instead, his eyes brim with tears, and he takes a sharp breath in. I am all too familiar with that sound of his. It is the prelude to a gush of emotion.

"Nochum Glezer," he says, "I will never forget the enormous kindness of that quiet, unassuming man." The familiar childhood name takes me right back to the noisy, overflowing Passover table. Mr. Glezer was the soft-spoken, humble man, originally from Vilna, who had befriended my refugee parents in the early days of their immigration and included us every year in his family's celebration of Passover. Every Friday night, my father tells me, Mr. Glezer would make a special trip to pick them up from Belleville, drive them thirty minutes to his home in Vredehoek, the suburb resting on the slope of Table Mountain to share the Sabbath meal with his family. Then, he'd drive them all the way back to their rented apartment again and return home.

"When I got my new job as a journalist, he found a three-room apartment for us to rent near to his house, in Jamieson Road in Vredehoek. That was the house in which you were born. This gentle man, doing charity in this way, restored my belief in humanity. And so, slowly, slowly," my father adds, "the years went by and we put our lives together."

Mr. Piat, the new immigrant, worked long and hard to make his way up in his new world. At night, till one in the morning, he did his job as a linotype operator at the local newspaper. During the days, he worked as a salesman for a printing shop, bookkeeper for a butcher shop, and sometime tour guide for the Russian whalers docking in port. Within a few months he had gone from typesetting to journalist, receiving the prize of five pounds and a feature article spot for his first story written in English, about the festivities of Bastille Day.

My mother found her own way to settle into the new country, by doing what she did best—entertain her fans. Chayela Rosenthal presented her own variety shows, performing regularly during the summer holiday months at the seaside resort of Muizenberg, where Jews from all over South Africa would congregate for their annual vacation by the warm Indian Ocean, on the eastern side of the Cape Peninsula. At first, her concerts were exclusively in Yiddish, catering to loyal audiences eager to laugh and cry at the sounds of Yiddish, the *mamaloshen*, the mother tongue from the old country of the Lithuania of their ancestors. Once her confidence rose in her ability to speak English, she reached out to a wider audience with her witty cabaret shows of songs and jokes that contrasted the old world with the new. Mr. Piat, her biggest fan, promoted his wife with his usual flair and professional expertise, always standing at the back of the audience, initiating the applause with his loud clapping after each song.

In August of 1955, a decade after his liberation, my father anonymously submitted an article under the pseudonym of "Alien," as part of a competition run by the English evening newspaper. The theme was: "What have you done with ten years of peace?" Chronicling his refugee years of feeling like an unwanted alien in Europe and his thrill of finally being accepted in South Africa, his new home, Mr. Piat won first prize of five guineas cash and a prominent leader page placement of his heartwarming article. "In South Africa," he wrote, "we found a place to live and to enjoy life again, a fresh start for a new generation."

But the country that had been such a welcoming refuge for my parents became for me, the next generation, a land of restless revolution. The ruling government had transformed what was once a European immigrant's dream of paradise into a torturous nightmare for its indigenous African natives. By the time I was a teenager, the forced racial separation system of apartheid had become a position of pride and power for the Afrikaner nationalist party, an inexorable, intolerable prison for the majority of the population—the blacks, and a source of guilt and shame for those of us privileged, liberal-minded minority "whites" like myself, plagued by a social conscience. Prejudice, racial tension, and fear slowly took its psychic toll on the entire nation. The tropical haven my parents had been lucky to find was not a place I was proud to call home. For me, and others of my generation, South Africa, with its legally sanctioned violations of basic human rights, was a place to run away from. It must have been written in the stars that my destiny was to become an immigrant like my parents. I too would leave the country of my birth and find a new home, thankfully under vastly different circumstances to those of my parents.

In 1950, the country my parents settled in was still a colony under the rule of the British monarchy, requiring its citizens to stand up at public events and sing "God Save the Queen!" But that was about to change as the continent of Africa began shrugging off its imperial shackles, and African nations, one after the other, fought to claim their independence. My father's need to stay connected to a larger world beyond the renamed Republic of South Africa, and his wish to stimulate interest abroad in his newly adopted country, prompted him to create the Africa Friendship Club, a worldwide pen-pal organization, of which he was president. In an era when letter writing was the accepted, most affordable way of corresponding, Mr. Piat provided an international forum for people to exchange information via mail about their countries, cultures, values, hobbies and lives. He firmly believed that communication and the interchange of personal stories and ideas was the way to promote cultural awareness and understanding. In his weekly newsletter, he made the credo of his club clear: to foster mutual understanding and tolerance for the goal of international peace.

The Afrika Friendship Club was a great success. Children wrote to other children in different parts of the world telling them about their different religions and families, hopes and dreams. They even exchanged stamps and sent gifts to each other. Adults formed long-distance relationships based on common interests, while some even found love. Mr. Piat's pen-pal club helped bring together strangers, set apart by continents, to discover how much they had in common.

No doubt, his mother's history of truncated, banned correspondence with her own family played a role in my father's avid dedication to letter writing. His last contact with Vava was a postcard from Paris, dated February 1940, enquiring about his well-being, saying that she was happy about the newspaper reports indicating Poland was now under Soviet rule and there was no imminent war. She gave no details about her own life in Paris, presumably to avoid possible government censorship. Vava ended the postcard with her hopes for peace.

My father knew firsthand how precious a few carefully chosen words on paper could be to someone far away. A letter was something tangible in a world full of transitions, where family could be erased and strangers could be your rescuers. Relationships, even the most casual and unexpected, could mean the difference between life and death. Mr. Piat made it a practice to maintain good relations, through regular communication, with almost everyone he met.

The result of his correspondence with Danny Kaye, the American film star he'd met in Paris where Chayela was performing, was an exclusive press interview when the popular entertainer came to South

Africa to perform for the African Consolidated Theatres. At that press conference, he met the head manager of all the local theatres, and turned him into his first client by promoting a few of his creative marketing ideas for upcoming feature films. With a stack of business cards showing his face next to the title, Piat Promotions, and a small rented office in the center of town near the hustle and bustle of Adderley Street, Mr. Piat, the *luftmensch,* set himself up in the business of promoting other people's business.

Just as important to my father as having a business of his own was having a home of his own. Acting on the investment advice of an immigrant friend, he attended his first real estate auction when I was about eleven. It seemed like a smart financial move to put his savings into purchasing a home rather than paying rent to someone else. The little house with the red-tiled roof being auctioned off was set midway up the steep incline of Lion's Head, in a section of Sea Point where tall, tufted palm trees graced the mid sections of avenues with fancy French names. The compact three-bedroom house came with a tiny patch of lawn sprouting one solitary lemon tree, a glimpse of the ocean, and a tight-fitting garage, behind which was tucked the common closet-like maid's room. For my father, having a house on the hill with a view of the ocean meant that he had made it, that he was a success. Standing on the tiny porch of the old-fashioned house, peering past the neighbors' loquat trees, he saw a ship gliding by on the Atlantic. What a wonderful sight! It was my father's view of the future.

Sold! With beginner's luck my father won with his first bid and bought his first home at his first auction. His family of four, now including my little sister would be moving from the rented flat on the busy Main Road to the house on the prestigious hill. Mr. Piat was finally putting down roots. In the tradition of the owners of South African homes, especially those with seaside properties, he gave the house a name. In black lettering, slanting to the right across the white stucco wall on the left of the wooden front door was one word: *Utanvilla.*

It was the house from which both my sister and I went to high school and won top honors and awards, bringing great pride and pleasure to our parents. It was the same house, considerably renovated by that time to enlarge the living-room windows for a more extensive ocean view, from which both of Mr. Piat's daughters got married. It was also the house from which he went in a large funeral procession to the Pinelands Cemetery to bury his wife, Chayela, just weeks after she took her final bows as the quintessential Golda to standing ovations in *Fiddler on the Roof.* Utanvilla was where Mr. Piat continued to live alone, for several years, long after the beloved women in his life had left him for other worlds.

My father stares at me. He has stopped talking. I'm not sure what he wants from me. Another glass of water? Something from the kitchen? I await my orders.

After a long pause, he says, "You know, in talking to you about all that happened to me, and recalling these events from my youthful years, I realize that my young days in Vilna were days of wonder. I see now what I did not see so clearly before. Yah! My life is a cause for celebration and rejoicing."

I switch off the tape recorder. What more can be said after such a revelation? If this telling of stories was a healing journey for both of us, then this last statement of his has brought us to our final destination. The sun is beginning its descent in the sky. I can feel that subtle shift in the air when afternoon turns to dusk and the shadows dissolve. It's probably time to go inside and get dinner ready for the family. There's still time for one more quick swim, though, before the sun dips behind the tall tree I planted as a sapling at the side of the house a decade ago, never dreaming it would grow so large as to block out the evening sun and shed so many leaves during the Fall. As if reading my mind, my father stands up from his chaise, walks over to the edge of the pool and dives in, swimming underwater toward the shallow end. "Hoooh! Haah! What a treat! A *mechiah!*" he splutters, jumping up from under the water to stand and soak in the last rays of the day's sun that still come filtering through the leaves of the tree. He runs his hands through his thinning, gray hair that he used to dye black for a while until he decided to just let it grow natural and long enough to tie in a small ponytail.

"You remember what your mother used to say?" my father shouts at me from the shallow end of the pool. "'Ksuvver,' she'd say, '*leb zich ine a tog!*' Even in the hospital, on her deathbed, your mother, in between all those jokes with the nurses and the doctors, teasing me how she'd be watching me closely from above to see who I marry next, even when she was so sick, yah, she would tell me again her favorite saying. 'Live life to the full, Ksuvver!'" The last light of the setting sun shines on the blue, swirling water.

"Yah! 'Live it up each day!' she'd say to me. 'Each day, live it up, like it's your last!'"

The Daughter: A New View

✦

Cliffside Park, New Jersey, 2008

When there is nothing more to say, then will you hear the sound of peace.

2008. The year I finish this book, my journey with my father. My two parents, their two spheres and vertical infinity. 2 + 8 = 10. One and zero. The one left with the empty circle, at one with the silence.

T'shuvah. Returning to this book after so many years, I stumble like a dazed stranger meandering into a once familiar town, retracing my steps to find my bearings. The woman completing the book is different from the one who began many summers ago to collect and record my father's spontaneous memories. I am not even the same person as the one who later spent hours tediously transcribing my father's narrative from the many cassette tapes of his stories. Alone in my own house up on a hill, in a different geographic state, and a different psychological one too, I look out my window at the ships gliding by on the Hudson River, past the skyscrapers of Manhattan, and think how much my father would have loved this view. It has taken me a long circuitous path to find my way back to new meanings in old stories.

Time, that silent, neutral observer, has watched me go through my own losses, toppling like dominoes, one after the other. The demise of my marriage, for so long my platform of security, identity, and social status, left me doubtful and distrusting. The death of my father, my prime source of motivation and inspiration for achievement, left me floundering. Divorce gave me a crash course in pain, patience, compassion and forgiveness. The emptying of my family nest, as the last of my three children went off to college, taught me about releasing emotional ties and rendered me a "free bird." Claiming my independence, like those African nations, did not come without some turmoil and messy sacrifices.

Relinquishing my sprawling, suburban family home, associated with comfort and ease, I altered my lifestyle to learn to fly solo, released from obligations to others. Now, I was afforded the luxury of being able to travel alone, make important decisions alone, prepare food for one, and have only myself to blame for things that didn't quite go the way I wished. In a matter of a few compressed years, I, former wife, hostess, and soccer mom, had became an orphan, a divorced single woman, an empty-nester, a traveling actress, and a graduate of many personal-transformation workshops, all of which gave me a much needed, broader perspective on myself, my relationships in particular, and life in general.

I moved, of course. Left my old life and the burial place of my father back in Boston. In the ulpan in Israel, I had learned an idiom: *M'shaneh makom, m'shaneh mazal,* meaning change your place, change your luck. Relocating forced me to make some radical choices about what I could live with and without. The jobs of packing and moving from my big house in Massachusetts to a small apartment in Manhattan, and then to my townhouse in New Jersey, forced me to practice, but not always master, the art of discarding, downsizing, and letting go. It turned out to be an interesting and challenging exercise for this daughter of Mr. Piat, the consummate collector and hoarder. Following me faithfully everywhere I went were two heavy cardboard boxes shipped from South Africa after my father's death, one marked "X.P." and the other "CHAYELA" in black permanent marker—my treasure troves of assorted papers, notebooks, sheet music, photographs, scrapbooks, reel-to-reel cassette tapes, and vinyl, long-playing records, all pertaining to a past not even mine.

In the big X.P. box are the many drafts of what began as a series of conversations that turned into a labor of love. Hard labor. And much longer than any of those that propelled my three children into this world. Maybe I can view this book as my fifth child, coming after my three children and my play. Pointka: Five. But, this one, somehow, is the hardest to release. Every time I think I am done with it, something new seems to want to be said or corrected or added. It's as if in completing the book I will be saying a final farewell to my father. In doing so, I want to make sure I have included everything both of us wished to say, to be faithful to his memory, to do him justice. I must get it right, whatever that means. My father, his family, and their history deserve that much. Perhaps it's my affliction, as a writer and an artist, and certainly a child of Holocaust survivors to be obsessed with perfection, with the ideal of making things better, getting things right, of producing my best. I have this compulsive idea that every word counts. Who knows what tiny, random piece of information will make a difference to an unknown reader waiting for the right word to right their world? Perhaps a well phrased insight will help children see their parents in a gentler light, or parents treat their children in a kinder way. Maybe a sentence might help someone discard their disappointments in favor of acceptance, or inspire someone to reach out to find a lost cousin or a missed friend, perhaps even locate that best part of themselves that got left behind in a town far away. What if a certain paragraph helped a person forgive an assumed enemy, or, better yet, themselves? From my own experience with my British cousins, I know that one seemingly insignificant detail can transform a family, one anecdote can alter a life.

My father knew it, too. It was why he loved reading literature and writing letters.

Now, in the end, I still see holes where I could have—should have—asked him for more details. Too late now. *Vos iz geven iz geven.* What was was and is no more, my mother's voice sings again in my head. I must cherish what I do have, not despair over what I don't. Say *ciao* to regret! Farewell, guilt, ol' pal! *Adios* and *sayonara* to shame. *Tot siens* to ugh, shame! Let bygones be gone by. Bye-bye!

Wanting to make sure I left no stone or paper unturned and checking to see that I didn't miss anything, I went back to sort and resort the papers stuffed in the X.P. box. In returning, I found something I didn't notice before. Slipped between the large-print book drafts I had printed out for my father to read more than a decade ago, hidden beneath the collected documents and newspaper clippings of his, was a single page letter in my father's familiar handwriting. Dated "end of 1997," it was written a matter of months before his unexpected death in 1998. The page was marked, fittingly, with the numeral 1. The second page, sadly, is missing. Trust me, I've looked for it everywhere in the piles and piles of papers. The letter was meant for me, that much is clear. How perfect that I should find this letter all these years later, when I needed the reminder and am ready, finally ready, to complete the task I had promised I would do.

I have decided to end with that letter, and leave it as is. This is, after all, how we live: repeating the same things over and over until they make sense, till we feel we've been heard in our attempts to get our message across to those who don't seem to listen, or to ourselves, who forget. I have come to accept that the second page is missing. Another mystery. Maybe the page is missing on purpose—to teach me that whatever it is I am seeking so anxiously to find is what I will eventually have to let go of. Or just maybe, after all is said and done, and written, the point of it all is to be at peace with what seems to be missing.

The Hebrew word *shalom* says it all: *hello, goodbye,* and *peace,* all wrapped in one two-syllable word. As my mother used to joke: "Us

Jews, we say *shalom*, because we never know whether we're coming or going." The first part of the word, "*Shah!*" is Yiddish for "Quiet! Hush!" She used that word often to quiet things down, and to wipe away my childish worries as she stroked my head. The final part of the word is "om," the sound chanted in yoga to invoke the wholeness of the universe. I get the message: Go quietly in the world. With peace. With faith. It's the silence that connects us all.

In the center of the word, *shalom*, I am delighted to discover the word "halo." Within peace, we find the divine.

So, in the spirit of all things lost and then found again, in the understanding that the dead are still with us, and that ultimately there is nothing missing, I share Page 1 of my father's letter, in the hope that you might be inspired to share your life story with someone you love, and maybe even write your own Page 2.

◆ ◆ ◆

The Polish writer Czeslav Milosz wrote "Love of life, passion for life." Perhaps I felt that in my youth, but differently and in different words. Now, one must liberate oneself, at least to some extent from complexities, from taking one's fate too much to heart, before being able to rejoice simply because one is alive and among the living. In my case, the revelation of being alive, soon after the miraculous end of our incarceration, was coupled with the realization that left alone, one must start a new life. Luck or Fate provided me with a partner who gave me supportive strength to go ahead. The course of adulthood depended on a variety of decisions, like leaving Poland for France and then South Africa, when it could have just as likely been Australia or Israel.

The true joy began with your birth and then the birth of your sister. It was worthwhile to be alive and to give life. Your mother and I were determined to have children, and perhaps you don't know, but your mother needed to have medical assistance to conceive. The Holocaust survivors needed it. With perseverance, a new branch was added to the tree of our families.

It was not of our making that some of our suffering passed to your mind and body. I wish that it should not have been the case. Yet as we came out of the concentration camps, our experience touched you too. I am proud that you have inner strength and affirmative insight to bear in a responsible way the name of a survivor's child. You have proven it to me and others in many occasions and I am thankful for it.

You have asked me questions about the "inhuman years." And I have tried to talk about and bring out from the past memories of events, which are hard to describe in words acceptable to enable one to visualize what happened. The truth is only those who themselves lived and were pained during those times can possibly fully understand and transform their experiences into knowledge. Others can never do so. But I trust you to impart these poor words into a picture so that others may see through your eyes what they should never see through their own.

◆ ◆ ◆

The End

or

A New Beginning

CPSIA information can be obtained
at www.ICGtesting.com
Printed in the USA
LVOW12s2326130616
492458LV00001B/57/P